Second Edition

PEACE, POWER, RIGHTEOUSNESS

An Indigenous Manifesto

Taiaiake Alfred

OXFORD
UNIVERSITY PRESS

OXFORD
UNIVERSITY PRESS

70 Wynford Drive, Don Mills, Ontario M3C 1J9
www.oupcanada.com

Oxford University Press is a department of the University of Oxford.
It furthers the University's objective of excellence in research, scholarship,
and education by publishing worldwide in

Oxford   New York
Auckland   Cape Town   Dar es Salaam   Hong Kong   Karachi
Kuala Lumpur   Madrid   Melbourne   Mexico City   Nairobi
New Delhi   Shanghai   Taipei   Toronto

With offices in
Argentina   Austria   Brazil   Chile   Czech Republic   France   Greece
Guatemala   Hungary   Italy   Japan   Poland   Portugal   Singapore
South Korea   Switzerland   Thailand   Turkey   Ukraine   Vietnam

Oxford is a trade mark of Oxford University Press in the UK and in certain other countries

Published in Canada by Oxford University Press

Copyright © Oxford University Press Canada 2009

The moral rights of the author have been asserted

Database right Oxford University Press (maker)

First Published 2009

Library and Archives Canada Cataloguing in Publication

Alfred, Taiaiake
Peace, power, righteousness : an indigenous manifesto / Taiaiake Alfred.
— 2nd ed.

Includes bibliographical references and index.
ISBN 978-0-19-543051-6

1. Native peoples—Canada—Politics and government. 2. Indians of North America—Politics and
government. 3. Self-determination, National—Canada. 4. Self-determination, National—United States.
5. Native peoples—Canada—Government relations. 6. Indians of North America—Government relations.
I. Title.

E98.T77A43 2008   323.1197   C2008-903958-0

Cover image: Cornhusk Dolls by Lindsay Delaronde

17 18 19 — 19 18 17

Printed and bound in Canada.

In memory of Ron Lafrance and Vine Deloria, Jr, true warriors.
Brothers, may you find peace, power, and righteousness
on the other side of the sky.

Today
I suddenly became aware of
your voices sounding across
the forest.
Approaching, moving across,
barriers
you saw, in coming,
traces of them,
our ancestors.
As if just barely,
it is becoming ominous,
for smoke should still be rising
at the place,
the place where they used to smoke
and where, formerly, we gained wisdom.
There, as you came, you saw
numerous signs
of our ancestors.

—from the *Kaienerekowa*

Contents

Thanksgiving 1
Preface to the Second Edition 3
First Words 8
A Note on Terminology 23

PEACE 25
Native American Political Traditions 25
Native Political Elites 54

POWER 65
The Abuse of Power 68
Re-empowerment 70
Sovereignty: An Inappropriate Concept 79
Colonial Mentalities 94
Co-optation 97
Self-Conscious Traditionalism 104
Leadership 113
Responsibility 115

RIGHTEOUSNESS 121
Money 138
Modern Treaties: A Path to Assimilation? 144
For the Youth: Toward a New Native Leadership ... 154

Notes 182
Bibliography 190
Index 198

Thanksgiving

Watkwanoneraton tsi ionwentsateh, tohnon ne rononkwe rohnatahskwaronnion, tsi kanientarehnion, watnehkokwanionkwa, ne onensteh tahnon kahihsonha, onhnonkwasonha tahnon tsi iokwiroton, tahnon ne iokwirowanens iehtiniaheshas, tahnon ne kario onkwatennatsera ihken tahnon ionkiiawis ahtakwehnia, ne kewerowanens tahnon ne kennikawehrasas, ratiwehras, tsitehwatshiha tiokehneka orakwa, iehtisota ennitha ahsontenneh iorahtokeh, tahnon ne Sonkwaiatison rahonahtserahokon, tahnon ohni ne rahonha Sonkwaiatison, ne tehsonkwawis nahoten tehwaniaheshas, tahnon nihtehwetha nahotan iontionniosta tahnon tsi tsionneh.

We address and offer thanks to the earth where human beings dwell, to the streams, the pools, and the lakes, the corn and fruits, the medicines and trees, to the forests for their usefulness, and to the animals that are food and give their pelts for clothing, to the great winds, and the lesser ones, to the thunder; to the Sun, the mighty warrior, to the moon; to the messengers of the Creator who reveal his wishes and to the Creator who dwells in the heavens above who gives all the things useful to humans, and who is the source and the ruler of health and life.

I have a deep appreciation and profound gratitude for those who have shared their wisdom and taught me what it means to know peace, power, and righteousness. If there is truth in my words it is only a reflection of their generosity and genius. I have visited many nations, and been warmly welcomed by indigenous people everywhere. And I have seen that, in spite of it all, there is still honour among our people. On Turtle Island and beyond, I am fiercely proud to be recognized as a brother.

I remain grateful to all those people whose generosity in sharing their knowledge and experiences allowed me to write the original version of this book. I thank, as well, Brock Pitawanakwat, Vanessa Watts, Adam Barker, and Ashley Joe, students of mine at the University of Victoria, for their insights and assistance in completing this second edition.

I could not do without the gift of love I take every day from my beauti-
ful wife, Rose, the inspiration of my sons, Skanekohraksen, Tiòrhonko, and
Aronhiènte, and the support of my whole family, both Kanienkehaka and
Wetsuweten. Niawen'kowa akwekon.

Preface to the Second Edition

It took a long time for me to understand colonialism and how deeply it affects people. It is impossible to understand the impact of the powerful forces of disconnection that define the colonial experience until you begin to try to make change in a Native community or organization. When I wrote this book in the late 1990s, I was articulating an anti-colonial vision founded on ten years of scholarship and of lived experience in Native politics. My experience up to that point led me to base my notion of decolonization on the issue of leadership and on the political choices leaders make in the course of their engagement with white power. The book is an expression of frustration, impatience, and even anger directed at elites within Native communities for their ethical and political failures as a class, for their inability and unwillingness as people to hold a strong indigenous line in the face of assimilative pressures and incentives to surrender land, rights, and culture. I still believe in the validity and relevancy of the analysis and critique presented in this book. But with twenty years of experience and learning behind me, I know now that the problem of colonialism is much deeper and more complex than I thought it was in 1998.

In my first book, *Heeding the Voices of Our Ancestors*, I wrote that the problem was essentially a lack of any real self-government by indigenous communities. Back in the early 1990s, that was how the problem of colonization was defined: the fact that Native people did not control their own institutions of government. Social and cultural issues were subsumed in the drive to reassume political powers that had been taken away from our people by the state; the central decolonizing imperative was a form of nationalism. Indeed, the subtitle to my first book, was *Kahnawake Mohawk Politics and the Rise of Native Nationalism*. In fact, this is still the dominant discourse in Native political circles today. In time, through experience, I came to learn and appreciate the views of those Native people who looked critically at what was being achieved through "Aboriginal self-government" or "tribal sovereignty" and saw the movement as vacuous and devoid of indigenous culture or any spiritual connection to ancestral teachings. In this view, Natives gaining control of governing structures is not enough to allow us to decolonize. In fact, without a cultural grounding, self-government becomes a kind of Trojan horse for capitalism, consumerism, and selfish individualism.

By the time I came to this realization myself, I had, ironically, worked my way up to the position of senior advisor on land and governance in my own home community's band council government. It was a position of responsibility in a large and politically influential Native organization. But when you come to the realization that you are on the wrong path, you have a choice to make: Do I change my course and go in the direction I know to be the right one, compromising the status and power I have built for myself, or do I stay on this mistaken pathway, compromising what I know to be truly indigenous? Anyone who knows their language, who understands ceremonies, who has heard traditional elders talk about what it is to be a Native person knows that there are clear teachings about their responsibilities, their roles, their relationship to the land, and their relationship to one another. Those lessons are so profound and so clear when you hear them. And they are taught to us over and over again. So, when you find yourself at the decision point, without question, you give up your position, your salary, and your consulting fees. You have to imagine what the ancestors would have wanted you to do. When I found myself *reinterpreting* rather than *heeding* the "voices of our ancestors," I figured it was time to get out of the self-government business.

I was very fortunate that, because of my education, I was not dependent on the Indian Act system and my job in the band council to support myself financially. I was able to follow my conscience by taking advantage of the freedom my job as a university professor afforded me. This led me to write *Peace, Power, Righteousness*. The book was, for me at that time, an exploration of what it meant to be a Native leader. I took my task seriously, saying to myself, "If I listen to all the teachings, if I talk to people for hours and hours, if I read as much as I can, and if I put into it as much intellectual energy as I have and try to understand what it is to be a chief, I will come to know what it is to be, as they say in our language, a *royaner*: "a good man." That was my quest.

As I moved along this path, I gained some understanding of the Rotinohshonni condolence ceremony used when a chief or a clan mother dies and a new one is raised up. There are actually a whole cycle of ceremonies in the condolence ritual where different elements of leadership are brought to this person, this new leader, and it is all done through songs, teachings, and speeches. Framing my thinking on leadership in this way led to a whole series of insights that crystallized as the text of this book. The core lesson for me was this one: It isn't enough just to regain political space; we need to fill it up with indigenous content if it is going to mean anything to our people.

Basically, self-government on its own is meaningless if it's not conducted in an indigenous way. The true answer to the problem of colonization then became clear: We need to revive our traditional forms of government. We need to raise up the longhouse again, so to speak; we need to raise up those chiefs, those clan mothers; we need to rebuild the longhouse that is our nation living our own culture according to our own traditional laws in our own lands. Traditional government is the antidote to the colonial disease and its corruptions and abuses of power, and to the disempowerment of our people and communities. This is the view I held in the late 1990s, and I believe it is still the core message of *Peace, Power, Righteousness*.

But, just as I recognized problems with the Native nationalist approach, I have come to see that there is a fundamental problem with this tradition-alist approach as well. The problem with traditionalism is that our people are not the same as they were two hundred years ago, when our ancestral systems were functioning at their full capacity. I don't think anybody would disagree that our people, collectively, have been weakened by colonization: our language, our culture, our understanding of history, our sense of trust, our wholeness, our relationships, the power that we possess as individuals and as family, the ability to work together, the unity that we had that is the foundation of everything for our people, our understanding of our relation-ship to nature, our communication with the spirit world … in all these ways, we have lost so much. Yet the systems of government that we tradi-tionalists seek to bring forward and raise up again depend on the very things we lack today: cultured people and strong families.

So, it is just not enough to call for the restoration of traditional govern-ments. As indigenous nations, we've been disconnected from who we are as people, from the sources of our strength and our very survival: our land, culture, community. Those things have been broken, or nearly so, by col-onization. Understanding the effects of the deculturing of the people is where this book leaves off, and where I started in my third book, *Wasáse: Indigenous Pathways of Action and Freedom*. As I see things today, discon-nection is the root of the problem. Colonization is a process of disconnect-ing us from our responsibilities to one another and our respect for one another, our responsibilities and our respect for the land, and our respon-sibilities and respect for the culture. It's that simple and that profound, but it took me twenty years to work it through. I needed to go through the full spectrum of the educational system and through political involvements at all levels to learn this truth.

Some people might say that I should have just opened my ears and listened when the elders told me what was what a long time ago. But I was 24 years old when I started writing my first book and 32 when I wrote this one. I had to learn from experience and go down those other pathways to figure out for myself what the problem was. I think this creates another valuable aspect to *Peace, Power, Righteousness* because it stands as a record of the unravelling of a colonized Indian identity and a guide to the recovering of oneself as a true Native in and through the ancestral languages, ceremonies, and knowledge. As you are reading the book, think about its author and where he comes from: Indian reserve upbringing, altar boy, Catholic school, United States Marines, Ivy League university, band council, university professor.... What is it that intervened to make him go against this destiny of assimilation? The answer is the beauty and power of *Onkwehonweneha*, the indigenous way.

For me, as a writer, *Peace, Power, Righteousness* stands as part of a trilogy of very personal work and learning on indigenous politics. It is a reflection of my understanding of the problems I encountered on my own journey to indigenous authenticity. Upon writing the first edition, I was consumed by politics and was searching for an answer to the immense and disturbing problems of corruption and cultural ignorance at the foundation of First Nations and tribal politics in the United States and Canada. I still believe my analysis cuts to the core of the problem facing our communities, and it has great utility for people seeking to understand the fundamental dynamics of First Nations and tribal politics as practised today and the contrasting ideals of indigenous leadership drawn from traditional teachings and ceremonies. Focusing as it does on politics and leadership, I now recognize that the book projects only a partial view and analysis of the situation facing our peoples, yet the lasting value of *Peace, Power, Righteousness* as a political statement, in my estimation, is that it is unique as a passionate argument for integrity and courageous political leadership that is inspired by, and accountable to, the spirit and example of our ancestors' struggle to remain truly indigenous in the face of physical and cultural genocide. It is quite apparent that people still need to hear what it has to say.

The ideas in this book resonate, I am told time after time, with Native people who still hold fast to the notion that they are the original people of this continent and the true owners of the land. They resonate as well with anyone, Native or newcomer, who understands the falsity and senses the injustice of the states that now possess and control our continent, our homeland. This book and *Wasáse* articulate the thoughts of those whose eyes and hearts are open to the truth about the world that was created by the colonization of North America, and the world this crime created. These kinds of people experience the exposing of the roots of their own dissatisfaction and disgust with the way things are—in Native communities and in politics in general. To these people, *Peace, Power, Righteousness* provides a vision of alternative political possibilities, one that is cultured and rooted in ancestral wisdom but at the same time secular and politically focused on the here and now and what needs to be done about the problems facing our communities.

I wrote this book to cut through the politics of pity and distraction. It stands against the "Aboriginal" and "Indian" intellectualism prevalent in academic and political circles today, which is so accepting of degraded notions of what it is to be indigenous, so enamoured with the assumption of white supremacy, and so engrossed with finalizing the dissolution of our nationhood. I am proud that its appeal is enduring. I know that this is not a testament to my genius, but to the powerful indigenous intelligence, the simple honesty of the indigenous voice, the courageous love of the land, and the uncompromising indigeneity that have been conveyed to the reader in these pages.

First Words

The ritual of condolence is an ancient and sacred custom among my people, the Rotinohshonni. In its structure, words, and deep meaning, this ceremony is an expression of the transformative power inherent in many healing traditions. For this reason, I have chosen condolence as the metaphorical framework for my own thoughts on the state of Native America and the crucial role of indigenous traditions in alleviating the grief and discontent that permeate our existence.

Indigenous people today are seeking to transcend the history of pain and loss that began with the coming of Europeans into our world. In the past five hundred years, our people have suffered murderous onslaughts of greed and disease. Even as history's shadow lengthens to mark the passing of that brutal age, the Western compulsion to control remains strong. To preserve what is left of our cultures and lands is a constant fight. Some indigenous people believe the statements of regret and promises of reconciliation spoken by our oppressors. Some have come to trust and accept the world that has been created through the colonization of America. But those who find sincerity and comfort in the oppressor, who bind themselves to recent promises, must yield to the assimilationist demands of the mainstream and abandon any meaningful attachment to an indigenous cultural and political reality. And, in so doing, they are lost to the rest of us. Thankfully, those who accept the colonization of their nations form a small minority. Most people continue to participate in, or at least support, the struggle to gain recognition and respect for their right to exist as peoples, unencumbered by the demands, controls, and false identities imposed on them by others.

The collective struggle for indigenous self-determination is truly a fight for freedom and justice. Yet the nobility of the cause does not make life any easier. Amid the seemingly perpetual conflict that comes with defending our ideals, there is confusion, division, and sometimes despair. Sometimes it seems we have lost our way, and then the confusion, division, and despair threaten to overwhelm us again. Distracted from our goal, we wander through a forest of frustration living inauthentic lives that make us easy prey for those who would enslave us. Such times constitute crises, and we are in the midst of one today.

The present crisis reflects our frustration over cultural loss, anger at the mainstream's lack of respect for our rights, and disappointment in those of our own people who have turned their backs on tradition. And I believe it is heightened because the choices we make today will determine whether or not we survive as indigenous peoples beyond the next generation. No one can deny that our cultures have been eroded and our languages lost, that most of our communities subsist in a state of abject economic dependency, that our governments are weak, and that white encroachment on our lands continues. We can, of course, choose to ignore these realities and simply accede to the dissolution of our cultures and nations. Or we can commit ourselves to a different path, one that honours the memory of those who have sacrificed, fought, and died to preserve the integrity of our nations. This path, the opposite of the one we are on now, leads to a renewed political and social life based on our traditional values.

If we are to emerge from this crisis with our nations intact, we must turn away from the values of mainstream North American society and begin to act as self-determining peoples. We cannot preserve our nations unless we take action to restore pride in our traditions, achieve economic self-sufficiency, develop independence of mind, and display courage in defence of our lands and rights. Only by committing ourselves to these goals can we hope to look into the future and see ourselves re-emerging as peoples ready to take our rightful places in the world. The path to self-determination is uphill and strewn with obstacles, but we must take it; the threat to our existence as indigenous people is so immediate that we cannot afford to delay. The only way we can survive is to recover our strength, our wisdom, and our solidarity by honouring and revitalizing the core of our traditional teachings. Only by heeding the voices of our ancestors can we restore our nations and put peace, power, and righteousness back into the hearts and minds of our people.

The condolence ritual pacifies the minds and emboldens the hearts of mourners by transforming loss into strength. In Rotinohshonni culture, it is the essential means of recovering the wisdom seemingly lost with the passing of a respected leader. Condolence is the mourning of a family's loss by those who remain strong and clear-minded. It is a gift promising comfort, recovery of balance, and revival of spirit to those who are suffering.

By strengthening family ties, sharing knowledge, and celebrating the power of traditional teachings, the condolence ritual heals. It fends off destruction of the soul and restores hearts and minds. It revives the spirit of the people and brings forward new leaders embodying ancient wisdom and new hope. This book embodies the same hope.

In the past two generations, indigenous people around the world have broken the rusty cage of colonial oppression and exposed the injustices imposed on them. Brave and powerful leaders have challenged the European's self-proclaimed right to rule and ruin our nations. Our people have achieved a victory of the mind: the attitudes that sustained our subjugation can no longer be defended. Confronted with the moral and intellectual defeat of its empire in Indian country, the former oppressor has presented a more compassionate face.

Newcomer governments claim to be forging historic new relationships with indigenous nations, relationships based on mutual respect, sharing, sovereignty, and our inherent rights. Economic development, modern treaties, self-government, compacts, revenue sharing, and co-management have become the watchwords of the "post-colonial" age. But beyond the words, is the promise holding?

There have been some improvements. But our reserves are still poor, our governments are still divided and powerless, and our people still suffer. The post-colonial promises cannot ease this pain. The state has shown great skill in shedding the most onerous responsibilities of its rule while holding fast to the lands and authorities that are the foundations of its power. Redefining without reforming, it is letting go of the costly and cumbersome minor features of the colonial relationship and further entrenching in law and practice the real bases of its control. It is ensuring continued access to indigenous lands and resources by insidiously promoting a form of neo-colonial self-government in our communities and forcing our integration into the legal mainstream. Real control remains in the hands of white society because it is still its rules that define our life—not through obviously racist laws, but through endless references to the "market," "fiscal reality," "Aboriginal rights," and "public will." And it is still white society's needs that are met. The Canadian government's attempt to retrench its control over First Nations consistently failed in the face of strong opposition from people at the grassroots level, yet Canada has recruited champions of its agenda from among chiefs and indigenous academics willing to co-operate with its plans—going so far as to establish a training institute, the Centre for First Nations Governance, which sponsors academic research and university courses across the country—and is effectively pushing through its plan to remake First Nations governments and reform the First Nations land tenure system based on a municipal model in piecemeal fashion while consulting only band council chiefs.

In this supposedly post-colonial world, what does it matter if the reserve is run by Indians, so long as they think like businessmen, behave like bureaucrats, and are paid to carry out the same old policies? Redefined and reworded, the "new" relationship still abuses indigenous people, albeit more subtly. In this "new" relationship, indigenous people are still bound to another power's order. The rusty cage may be broken, but a new chain has been strung around the indigenous neck; the chain offers more room to move, but it still ties our people to a white society that pulls on the strong end.

This book is about recovering what will make self-determination real. It is concerned not with the process through which self-government is negotiated, but with the end goals and the nature of indigenous governments, once decolonization has been achieved. The machinery of indigenous governments may simply replicate European systems. But even if such governments resemble traditional indigenous systems on the surface, without strong and healthy leaders committed to traditional values and the preservation of our nationhood, they are going to fail. Our grandchildren will judge them to have failed because a government that is not based on the traditional principles of respect and harmonious coexistence will inevitably tend to reflect the cold, calculating, and coercive ways of the modern state. The whole of the decolonization process will have been for nothing if indigenous government has no meaningful indigenous character.

Worse, if the new governments do not embody a notion of power that is appropriate to indigenous cultures, the goals of the struggle will have been betrayed. Leaders who promote non-indigenous goals and embody non-indigenous values are simply tools used by the state to maintain its control. The spiritual connections and fundamental respect for one another and for the earth that were our ancestors' way and the foundations of our traditional systems must be restored. Resistance to foreign notions of power and control must become a primary commitment—not only as a posture in our relations with the state, but also in the way Native community governments treat their own people. The state's power, including such European concepts as taxation, citizenship, executive authority, and sovereignty, must be eradicated from politics in Native communities. In a very real sense, to remain Native—to reflect the essence of indigenous North Americans—our politics must shift to give primacy to concepts grounded in our own cultures.

In fact, traditional philosophy is crucially relevant to the contemporary indigenous situation. In the Rotinohshonni tradition, the natural order accepts and celebrates the coexistence of opposites; human purpose is the perpetual quest for balance and harmony; and peace is achieved by extending the respect, rights, and responsibilities of family relations to other peoples. Even stripped down to a skeleton, these teachings speak with power to the fundamental questions that a philosophy of governance must address. There is a widespread cultural ideal among the original peoples of this land to achieve respectful coexistence as a tolerant and harmony-seeking first principle of government. Diametrically opposed to the possessive individualism that is central to the systems imposed on our communities, this single principle expresses the hope that tradition offers for a future beyond division and conflict. With this heritage, why do we indigenous people so often look away from our own wisdom and let other people answer the basic questions for us?

At the core of the crisis facing our nations is the fact that we are being led away from our traditional ideals by the people with the authority to control our lives. Some of these people—lawyers, advisers, consultants, managers, government agents—are not Native and therefore cannot be expected to understand us or share our ideals. Others, however, are the very people we count on to provide leadership and embody the values at the heart of our societies: to love and sacrifice for their people. Instead, these self-centred, corrupt politicians are easily seduced by the mainstream. Not all Native leaders are bad. More and more, however, we find our leaders looking, sounding, and behaving just like mainstream politicians.

There is unquestionable pathos in the material and social reality of most reserves. Yet, above all, the crisis we face is one of the mind: a lack of conscience and consciousness. Material poverty and social dysfunction are merely the visible surface of a deep pool of internal suffering. The underlying cause of that suffering is alienation—separation from our heritage and from ourselves. Indigenous nations are slowly dissolving with the continuing loss of language, land, and young people. Although the indigenous peoples of Turtle Island—the land now called Canada and the United States—have survived the most severe and extended genocide in human history, the war is not over yet. Our bodies may live without our languages, lands, or freedom, but they will be hollow shells. Even if we survive as individuals, we will no longer be what we Rotinohshonni call Onkwehonwe— the real and original people—because the communities that make us true indigenous people will have been lost. We will be nothing but echoes of proud nations floating across a landscape possessed by others.

From the outside, the intensity of the crisis is obscured by the smoke-screen of efforts to reduce the most obvious signs of social deprivation and increase the material wealth within Native communities. It is commonly thought that allowing indigenous people a reasonable standard of living will solve all their problems. But there is more to justice than equity. Of course, indigenous people have a right to a standard of living equal to that of others. But to stop there and continue to deny their nationhood is to accept the European genocide of five hundred years. Attempting to right historical wrongs by equalizing our material conditions is not enough. To accept the simple equality offered lately would be to forget what indigenous nations were before those wrongs began. There have been many clumsy attempts by the government to force us into a state of fatal amnesia, such as the Indian residential school apology and the compensation payout scheme negotiated by the Assembly of First Nations head Phil Fontaine and his lawyers. The scheme focuses on the gross abuses of residential school authorities toward individuals in an attempt to make us forget that the schools were part of an attempted psychological and cultural assassination inflicted on our people as a whole. Our people cannot and will not forget this history.

It is the central argument of this manifesto that the key to surviving and overcoming this crisis is leadership. Our teachings tell us that it is essential to sustain an ideal of leadership and to bring (ritually and ceremoniously) special individuals into the culture of leadership so that they can play their crucial role in achieving peace, power, and righteousness on the collective level. Yet the traditional culture of leadership has become just another artifact, and the people who dominate in most Native communities and organizations today model themselves on the most vulgar European-style of power-wielding. The kind of revival we need cannot be accomplished by using business school textbooks for bibles or by employing *Robert's Rules of Order*. Instead of mimicking the bad character and greed of mainstream politicians, Native leaders must aspire to embody traditional values.

There is great diversity among Turtle Island's indigenous peoples: hundreds of languages, a broad range of customs in the social and political realms, and a complex variety of spiritual beliefs that have yet to be understood by outsiders. Nevertheless, we share a common bond that makes it possible to speak of a "Native American" political tradition: a commitment to a profoundly respectful way of governing based on a world view that values autonomy but also recognizes a universal interdependency and promotes peaceful coexistence among all the elements of creation. There may be five hundred different ways of expressing these values, but, in our singular commitment to them, we find what is perhaps the only pan-Indian commonality. Despite the vast geographic and cultural space between them, the Wet'suwet'en people from the west and Kanien'kehaka from the east share both concepts and process in what the Wet'suwet'en call *Saldai* ("keepers of the law") and the Kanien'kehaka call the *Kaienerekowa* ("the great law of peace"). The challenge before us today is to recognize the common elements in the indigenous tradition of governance and develop them into a coherent philosophy: a bulwark against assimilation to foreign values.

This book focuses on Native communities. It attempts to grasp and convey a knowledge situated in and respectful of the shared experiences of our peoples. This approach reflects the fact that what makes an individual "indigenous" is her situation within a community. In fact, it is impossible to understand an indigenous reality by focusing on individuals or discrete aspects of culture outside of a community context. However knowledgeable and rooted the individual, one cannot be truly indigenous without the support and inspiration, as well as the reprobation and stress, that a community provides. Ideas transform when they make the journey from the mind of one person into the collective consciousness. And our peoples' reality is communal. To know indigenous people, those seeking knowledge must interact with indigenous communities, in all their past and present complexity. It is the dynamic interaction between the individual and the group that creates Native American cultures, and this interaction cannot be replicated or properly expressed by a single person "objectively" studying isolated parts of the reality.

I have written previously on my own community, the Mohawks of Kahnawake, and used the particular experience of one indigenous nation to gain an understanding of the historical development of what I termed an *ideology of Native nationalism*. Shifting from local to more broad-based issues, I intend with *Peace, Power, Righteousness* to lay the groundwork for a universal understanding and reconstruction of social and governmental institutions embodying traditional indigenous cultural values. I hope that, with this knowledge, indigenous peoples everywhere will be better equipped to understand, promote, and defend the philosophical principles at the core of their own struggles for self-determination.

The goal of promoting a better understanding of tradition within Native communities comes together with an academic interest in the central philosophical questions concerning political leadership. At the most basic level, there are two questions: Is one form of leadership intrinsically better than another? By what criteria can we discern a leader of quality? These two questions form the theoretical subtext of this book. I will recommend a set of political and social values drawn from the basic teachings of traditional indigenous cultures, and in so doing I will pay tribute to the general contribution made by our peoples to the philosophy of societal and governmental organization.

This book is inspired by, and draws its structure from, the ritual songs of the Rotinohshonni condolence ceremony. Although it does not strictly replicate the ritual, neither does it conform to academic convention. In fact, its form is central to the goal of conveying the logic of our traditions. I am convinced that it is futile to attempt to take abstract knowledge from the traditional teachings without making reference to their narrative form. The message must be heard in its entirety if we are to grasp its coherence and power. The logic of our traditions has developed over countless generations of experience. Following a communicative method of such antiquity and strength brings us closer to the core message of respect for the interrelatedness of word, thought, belief, and action. The meanings of our traditional teachings are embedded in the structure of the narrative as much as in any words one might write to explain them.

The task I have undertaken is a daunting one: to attempt to draw out and communicate an interpretation of the traditional teachings that is relevant to the contemporary situation. The text can be read on one level as a scholarly essay on the key political issues facing indigenous peoples in North America today and on another level as a traditionally rooted philosophical reflection intended to give voice to a long-silenced wisdom. The conjunction of ancient and contemporary realities is deliberate. The problems and challenges facing our peoples today raise questions that have motivated political philosophy in every age. The answers developed by our ancestors hold power today as they did fifty generations ago. It will be necessary, in time, to adapt those traditional answers to the contemporary reality. However, this is secondary to the primary task: to grasp the deep meaning of the traditional teachings and to understand their complex logic as a political philosophy whose power has been diminished not by time but by our own lack of faith. The important issues we face today are the next steps in the movement to free ourselves from colonialism. How do we create a political philosophy to guide our people that is neither derived from the Western model nor a simple reaction against it? In the Rotinohshonni tradition, when the people have become confused, we are told to go symbolically "back to the woods" and find ourselves again.

Working within a traditional framework, we must acknowledge the fact that cultures change and that any particular notion of what constitutes tradition will be contested. Nevertheless, we can identify certain common beliefs, values, and principles that form the persistent core of a community's culture. It is this traditional framework that we must use as the basis on which to build a better society. I am advocating a self-conscious traditionalism, an intellectual, social, and political movement that will reinvigorate those values, principles, and other cultural elements that are best suited to the larger contemporary political and economic reality. Not only has the indigenous voice been excluded from the larger social and political discourse, but even within our own communities it has been supplanted by other voices. The notion of traditionalism I am promoting demands cultural give and take with non-indigenous people—respect for what both sides have to contribute and share. It also demands self-respect and the confidence to build on what we know to be good and right for our own people. As a movement to gain respect for indigenous people, this form of traditionalism is not predicated on racially constructed conflict. It is a matter not of red versus white, but of right versus wrong, considered within the broad framework of values we all share: freedom, justice, and peace.

That is the intellectual context in which I hope this essay will help to move our thinking forward. I acknowledge, however, the paucity of my own knowledge. I can only aspire to share what little I have learned of our traditional teachings. In attempting to persuade people to consider drawing on our traditional teachings to create an appropriate framework for governance, I am only adding my voice to an ancient discourse.

It will become abundantly clear that I am Onkwehonwe, shaped by my upbringing in Kahnawake and my political life among the Rotinohshonni, and that I take my responsibilities as a bearer of this tradition seriously. I draw inspiration and purpose from the heritage of the great Rotinohshonni warriors and statesmen: a supreme confidence in the universal truth of the message brought to our people long ago by the prophet, Tekaniawítha. Like my forebears, I believe that leadership calls for invoking the power of reason, and that the human capacity to achieve harmony is best developed through pacification and persuasion. The Rotinohshonni cultural imperative is to spread the message of peace, power, and righteousness—and to struggle vigorously against those who would impose a disrespectful and unjust order.

In a culture deeply respectful of individual autonomy, the only real political power exists in the ability to persuade. For a people convinced that their vision of peace can save the world from strife and conflict by restoring harmony and balance, the development of powerful oratorical abilities is imperative. The late John Mohawk, a respected and influential Rotinohshonni historian, said of our oratorical tradition,

> all human beings possess the power of rational thought; all human beings can think; all human beings have the same kinds of needs; all human beings want what is good for society; all human beings want peace.... Out of that idea will come the power ... that will make the people of the [Rotinohshonni] among the most influential thinkers in the history of human thought.... The basic fundamental truth contained in that idea is that so long as we believe that everybody in the world has the power to think rationally, we can negotiate them to a position of peace.

Traditionally, the condolence ceremony represents a way of bringing people back to the power of reason. *Peace, Power, Righteousness* draws on the spirit of condolence to advance the development of a powerful and unifying rationality to help us overcome the evils of colonization that haunt our lives. Its substance reflects the wisdom contained in the teachings, updated and—I hope—made relevant to the contemporary era. I explained the condolence ceremony to a friend and tried to show how the book would relate to its main themes.

The first part is called "On the Journey." It begins when the people first come together. The condolers, or visitors, or those seeking peace, would be standing there singing their songs with wampum belts hanging off their arms to announce that they're coming in peace to express sympathy or to consecrate a new relationship. There was kind of a pragmatic reason for this, to announce that their intentions were peaceful. But it was also important to show respect to the community by announcing they were coming. In the ceremony, this section also served to remind everyone of the proper names and roles of all the chiefs in the Confederacy, so they would walk along to the meeting place and recite all the different titles.

The second section, "Welcome at Wood's Edge," is where the visitors are welcomed by the people receiving the condolence, or the other party to a treaty. Reciprocal demonstration of respect was very important. In terms of the progress of the ceremony, the visitors have announced themselves and now they're going to be welcomed. In the book, I'll be focusing on three main things. The first is what's called "Rejoicing in Our Survival." (All this terminology is drawn from the ceremony itself.) The point here is how strong we are despite all the troubles we've come through. So I won't be starting out on a negative note, just complaining about our leadership. In essence, I'll be talking about the fact that surviving has made us strong—showing the ways we are strong and what we have to celebrate. The next stage in the ceremony is "Recognizing Our Pain and Sorrow." This is where we say, "All right, we're strong and we're proud, but let's also be realistic about our problems and the responsibility we have to address them." A big part of this is the third stage "Recognizing Our Responsibility to Our Ancestors." This responsibility is incumbent not only on the leaders but on all of us. If we ever want to return to health as a community, we have to address these issues even though they are painful and cause sorrow. That's how you get ready to make change.

Now, once your mind is set, the heart of the ceremony begins. This is what's called the "Requickening." If you look it up in the dictionary, "quickening" means "bringing something to life or adding life." So requickening means bringing something back to life. It starts with the rhetorical gestures that we call the "rare words": wiping the eyes, cleansing the throat, and unblocking the ears. These are symbolic gestures to pacify grieving people, or the former adversary in a treaty process. The reason you have to pacify those people is that they are in pain: They can't see properly; they can't hear; and they don't speak the truth. Something serious has happened to them, and the challenge for the strong-minded, the peacemakers, is to take them beyond the pain to a place of peace. What happened to bring them pain? In the ritual—and all your life, if you desire peace—you have to figure out a way of saying something to those people, doing something, or giving them something that will make them capable of seeing, hearing, and speaking their way back to peace.

That's the first part of the "Requickening." There are twelve others. The next few relate to the society, to what needs to happen. The first three have to do with recognizing the discomfort in our body. Here again the question is, What's wrong? This overlap in the traditional ritual is deliberate, and it's consistent with the way knowledge was conveyed in oral cultures. The question being addressed here is, What's wrong in our community? What is the fundamental concern that we're dealing with as a people? That's why at this stage I will begin to talk about leadership.

Next comes the section called "Damage to Our Space." The term space I take to mean "nationhood, or our community as a whole." Traditionally, this idea was expressed metaphorically: as if one chief were sitting there, in his proper space, and another nation, or another set of chiefs, came too close. Then, there would be a problem. You need your space; each person and every nation shares the proper allotment in the circle, and that's how our nationhood was expressed. Part of the problem now is that our space hasn't been respected, that we've had structures and ideas imposed on us. We need to reclaim our intellectual, political, and geographical space.

Following the ritual, in the book I talk about the loss of consciousness—consciousness here being our sense of indigenous nationhood. In fact, a lot of our Native people imagine themselves to be Canadians. And that's not true. In the words of the ritual, those Canadianized Indians are "in the darkness." They've had their eyes shut to their true being; they can't envision a future in which we are nations. They can't see a positive future. They're wallowing in the pain of being dependent wards of the Canadian state. Then, in the ritual, "the sun is lost." This is another metaphorical statement of the truth.

The next teachings in the "Requickening" address the leaders as individuals. In effect, this section tells them what they have to do to be real leaders. You have to commit to acting for the betterment of your nation. You have to free your mind from all harmful influences and negative things that are going on in your life and in your society. You have to have a clear mind to think for yourself and to do the best for your people. You have to work toward unity: You're not a divisive person; you don't try to create factions; and you don't focus on personal or divisive issues. Your imperative is to unify the people and work co-operatively. At the same time, you have to be aware of what the ritual calls "lurking dangers"—that is the actual phrase used to refer to dangers that are always there, waiting. In Peace, Power, Righteousness, this is where I begin to talk about co-optation—how people come to be co-opted or used by other governments to create divisions.

Now, the ritual goes on to talk about a number of duties that are culturally specific to my people. In the book, I'll talk instead about leadership in terms of the necessary skills and characteristics.

The next phase of the ritual is called "Beware the Magic!" In our language, "magic" refers to witchcraft. I take this to be a metaphor for watching your back when you're a leader. In the contemporary context, the magic could be money or bribes, whatever magical things people may offer you when you are a leader, to turn you away from your responsibilities. The "Requickening" finishes with "Lighting the Torch." This is the traditional metaphor for communication. So, in traditional terms, as a leader, you are the one who holds the torch, the one responsible for bringing knowledge to the people, for ensuring good communication within the community and with other communities.

The final part of the traditional condolence ritual includes a section called "Sacred Songs." In the ceremony, these songs are very sacred. So, out of respect for their nature and meaning, in the book, I will draw on their role in the overall ritual but not go into the songs themselves. Instead, I'll adapt this part to present a concluding restatement of all the major themes, just as in the ritual the songs are chanted repetitions of important teachings. In these ritualized songs, I see the reference to "warriors" as a metaphor for teachings intended for our youth. The issue here is young people and their role in the society. What do we need to do that is relevant to them?

The ritual concludes with a set of teachings called "Keep Listening to Them," which includes a reference to "the grandfathers." The message here—and this will come through strongly in the book—is that whatever you are doing, you need to keep the traditional teachings in your heart and mind. Adapt, change, go forward, but always make sure you're listening to the traditional knowledge at the same time. Commit yourself to uphold the first principles and values. We have to refer to both the past and the future in our decision-making. This is where we get the concept of the "seven generations": We're supposed to be listening to our grandfathers, our ancestors, but we also need to listen to the grandfathers yet to come. These teachings blend into the last set, called "Over the Great Forest" and "Adding to the Rafters." In the past, they realized that once the condolence council or treaty council ended, people would have to face some great physical dangers to get home again. On the way, there were enemies, and all kinds of things could happen. So, traditionally, this part of the ritual was intended to wish you well, to tell you what you needed to know, and to inform you of how to confront the challenges that you were going to face.

The diverse themes that make up this text are linked by the understanding, central to each, that the answer to our problems is leadership based on traditional values. There are many things to say and many ways of saying them, and a voice that hopes to speak to all people must shift according to both the issue and the audience. Thus, the style of the text shifts as necessary to reflect the complexity of the argument and to respect the people who will listen to it.

Peace, Power, Righteousness treats thirteen themes grouped in three parts, corresponding to the organization of the Rotinohshonni condolence ritual. The first section, "Peace," concentrates on initiating a dialogue. Like "On the Journey" and "Welcome at Wood's Edge," the sections that begin the ritual, it is largely a lament for the loss of knowledge, acknowledging what indigenous people had in the past. It recognizes the vastness of the task ahead and prepares the ground by invoking the healing spirit of the condolence in offering words that will allow people to approach the subject with a clear mind and a good heart. It seeks to clear away misconceptions and dispel cloudy emotional reactions to our losses in favour of a strong and honest appraisal of the situation we face.

The second section, "Power," is expressly political, focusing on what indigenous political culture and leadership values ought to be. It follows the condolence ritual's "Requickening" section in organizing its themes into three movements: pacification, context, and duties. These themes, which reflect key elements within the condolence itself, have formed the basis of my political and cross-national philosophical perspectives on these issues.

Finally, the "Righteousness" section restates the main themes, bringing them into the contemporary context and applying them to the most important challenges facing indigenous peoples today: the temptation to sell out for money, the state's efforts to extinguish indigenous nations through what it calls "self-government" and "treaty-making," and the growing alienation of our youth from the corrupt colonial form of most Native politics today. Like the condolence's closing, "Keep Listening to Them—Over the Great Forest," it offers reassurance in the face of the difficult task ahead and begs for a continuing commitment to the indigenous path.

A final word on the overall intent. This book reflects an explicit attempt to create a relevant text within both the indigenous and Western traditions. Its unconventional structure reflects a self-imposed demand for accessibility, particularly among Native people. It is shaped by concerns, issues, and demands for guidance arising from within Native communities, together with a commitment to searching within indigenous traditions to find the answers we need to move forward.

If we are to effect real change, however, non-indigenous people must come to share the objective of justice. Hence, *Peace, Power, Righteousness* must also be accessible to non-Native readers and convincing as a work of scholarship. If I am successful in conveying some of the wisdom inherent in our cultures, perhaps that wisdom will help others as well to deal with dysfunctional aspects of their own societies and to live better lives, both collectively and individually.

In a way, this book is an extension of the work I began with *Heeding the Voices of Our Ancestors*, a study of Kahnawake's history and Kanien'kehaka nationalism. The text of *Heeding the Voices* was shaped so that Native readers needed to penetrate a fairly thick layer of academic convention and language to gain access to knowledge that could help them understand their past and present conflicts. This book starts from the opposite perspective. It asks non-indigenous people to join in an indigenously oriented dialogue aimed at moving beyond those conflicts. As an academic project, it is an extended exercise in the self-critical study of indigenous political cultures. As is evident in the subtitle, my goal is to prepare the philosophical ground for the eventual development of a broad "indigenous"—as opposed to narrow tribalist—critique of politics and the state. However, these theoretical and philosophical elements are only two among many layers of meaning that I hope will emerge from this manifesto's rhetoric, which is rooted in indigenous ground.

A Note on Terminology

Whenever possible, I will use terms from indigenous languages, out of respect for the people's struggle to free their minds. In the past thirty years, most indigenous people have rejected the definitions imposed on them by white society. Today, we recognize the significance and symbolic value of terminology, and the use of our own recovered languages is important not only for the purposes of communication but as a symbol of our survival. In addition, it helps us all avoid insult and injury.

As Native people today relearn the languages stripped from us in the past, we are coming to realize the gross insult of most common "Indian" names. It hasn't been that long since terms such as "squaw" were banished from use—at least in polite public conversation. But before Native people objected to the common and derogatory use of that Algonkian word, the implicit and subtle dehumanization of its usage was a fact of our lives. The struggle to break the bonds placed on our minds and spirits by derogatory or ignorant labels is ongoing.

In broader discussions, I will use various terms: "Indian" (as it is a legal term still in use among some indigenous people in North America), "Native" (in reference to the racial and cultural distinctiveness of individuals, and to distinguish our communities from those of the mainstream society), "American Indian" (in common use and a legal–political category in the United States), "Aboriginal" (a legal category in Canada), and "indigenous" (in global contexts and to emphasize natural, tribal, and traditional characteristics of various peoples). All are appropriate in their contexts and are used extensively by Native people themselves.

Notes to the text of *Peace, Power, Righteousness*, keyed to page numbers, can be found on pages 182–189.

Peace

The clear-minded ones will take to the road, walking to the place where they are in mourning, and there at the edge of the ashes, one will stand up saying words of sympathy to raise their spirits. At once they will begin to feel relieved, the mourners, and they will resume the path of the great peace.

—from the *Kaienerekowa*

Native American Political Traditions

Native American community life today is framed by two value systems that are fundamentally opposed. One, still rooted in traditional teachings, structures social and cultural relations; the other, imposed by the colonial state, structures politics. This disunity is the fundamental cause of factionalism in Native communities, and it contributes significantly to the alienation that plagues them. What those who seek to understand and remedy the problems that flow from it often don't realize is that this separation was deliberate. Without a good understanding of history, it is difficult to grasp how intense the European effort to destroy indigenous nations has been, how strongly Native people have resisted, and how much we have recently recovered. Not to recognize that the ongoing crisis of our communities is fuelled by continuing efforts to prevent us from using the power of our traditional teachings is to be blind to the state's persistent intent to maintain the colonial oppression of the first nations of this land.

Indigenous people have made significant strides toward reconstructing their identities as autonomous individual, collective, and social beings. Although much remains to be done, the threat of cultural assimilation to the North American mainstream is no longer overwhelming, because substantial pride has been restored in the idea of being Native. The positive effects of this restoration in terms of mental, physical, and emotional health cannot be overstated. But it is not enough. The social ills that persist are proof that cultural revitalization is neither complete nor in itself a solution. Politics matters: The imposition of Western governance structures and the denial of indigenous ones continue to have profoundly harmful effects on indigenous people. Land, culture, and government are inseparable in traditional philosophies; each depends on the others, and this means that the denial of one aspect precludes recovery for the whole. Without a value system that takes traditional teachings as the basis for government and politics, the recovery will never be complete.

Indigenous people have successfully engaged Western society in the first stages of a movement to restore their autonomous power and cultural integrity in the area of governance. This movement—which goes by various names, including "Aboriginal self-government," "indigenous self-determination," and "Native sovereignty"—is founded on an ideology of Native nationalism and a rejection of models of government rooted in European cultural values. It is an uneven process of re-establishing systems that promote the goals and reinforce the values of indigenous cultures against ongoing efforts by the Canadian and United States governments to maintain the systems of dominance imposed on Native communities in the last century.

Since the 1980s, there has been limited progress made toward ending the colonial relationship and realizing the ideals of indigenous political thought: respect, harmony, autonomy, and peaceful coexistence. Some communities have worked to disentangle themselves from paternalistic state control in areas of government that are important to them. Many more are currently engaged in substantial negotiations over land and governance, which they believe will give them significantly greater control over their own lives. Perhaps because of this perception of progress, people in the communities are looking beyond the present to envision a post-colonial future. However, that future raises serious questions in the minds of those people who remain committed to systems of government that complement and sustain indigenous cultures.

To many of these traditionalists, it seems that, so far, all the attention and energy has been directed at the cumbersome and expensive process of decolonization—the mechanics of removing ourselves from direct state control and the legal and political struggle to gain recognition of an indigenous governing authority. Almost no attention has been paid to the end goals of the struggle. What will Native governance systems be like after self-government is achieved? Few people imagine that they will be exact replicas of the systems that governed Native communities in the pre–colonial past. Most acknowledge that all Native structures will have to incorporate modern administrative techniques and technologies. But the core values on which the new government systems will be based remain a mystery.

The great hope is that those systems will embody the underlying cultural values of the communities. The great fear is that they will simply replicate non-indigenous systems—intensifying the oppression (because it is self-inflicted and localized) and perpetuating the values dichotomy at the root of our problems.

What follows will be considered a bold assertion in government and academic circles, although its truth is widely recognized in Native communities. The fact is that neither the state-sponsored modifications to the colonial–municipal model (imposed in Canada through the Indian Act and in the US through the Indian Reorganization Act) nor the corporate or public-government systems recently negotiated in the North constitute indigenous governments at all. Potentially representing the final solution to the white society's "Indian Problem," they use the co-operation of Native leaders in the design and implementation of such systems to legitimize the state's long-standing assimilationist goals for indigenous nations and lands. The results of the creation of the territory of Nunavut in the Arctic support this: Inuit people are now the titular heads of government, but the apparatus of government is staffed and controlled mainly by white southerners, and it operates in much the same way as the Canadian territorial government did in the period of open colonization, although with increasingly insecure legitimacy as this fact becomes more evident. The rapid opening of the Arctic to resource-extraction industries that fail to provide economic benefits to Inuit themselves and the increase in psychosocial stress within the communities since the "handover" of administrative control of the territories demonstrates that it is indeed the form of governance more than the people at its head that determines the outcome of supposed decolonization processes.

Most non-indigenous people have always seen indigenous people in problematic terms: as obstacles to the progress of civilization, wards of the Crown, relics of savagery, the dregs of modern society, criminals, and terrorists. Over the centuries, indigenous people themselves have consistently defended their nationhood as best they could. They have sheltered and nurtured their cultures, keeping the core alive despite all manner of hostility and degradation. It would be a tragedy if generations of Native people should have suffered and sacrificed to preserve what is most essential to their nations' survival only to see it given away in exchange for the status of a third-order government within a European–American economic and political system.

Has anything changed in the way white society looks at Native people? It is still the objective of the Canadian and US governments to remove Indians, or, failing that, to prevent them from benefiting, from their ancestral territories. And by insisting on their ownership of traditional territories, cultural autonomy, and self-determination, the original people of this land remain a problem for the state. Particularly in Canada, where the legal title to large portions of the land is uncertain, the policy goal is to extinguish Aboriginal title and facilitate the exploitation of the natural resources on or under those lands. In the area of culture, folklore and the arts are promoted while traditional political values are denied validity in the process of nego-tiating new relationships, and the state defends its "right" to create Native communities and determine their membership. In politics, indigenous nations continue to face denial of their international rights to autonomy, imposed wardship status, and intensive efforts to co–opt community lead-ers. In fact, nothing has changed. Why, then, are Aboriginal communities now so accepting of what Canada and the United States have to offer?

Throughout the process of supposed decolonization, many Native politi-cians have steadily moved away from the principles embedded in tradi-tional cultures, toward accommodation of Western cultural values and acceptance of integration into the larger political and economic system. It is as if they stopped believing that their indigenousness is a holistic state of being. Rather, contemporary Native politicians seem to assume that indige-nousness can be abstracted and realized in convenient (and profitable) ways, that being indigenous does not have an inherent political dimension and is simply a matter of looking the part—possessing indigenous blood, singing traditional songs, or displaying tribally correct behaviour. They ignore the basic traditional teaching that just as we must respect and hon-our our songs, ceremonies, and dances, so, too, we must honour the insti-tutions that in the past governed social and political relations among our people, because they are equally part of the sacred core of our nations. As long as this is the case, the underlying values dichotomy will remain.

An indigenous existence cannot be realized without respecting all facets of tradition: culture, spirituality, and government. Mystics who ignore pol-itics and live their identity only through ritual and the arts are just as lost as materialists whose lives are devoid of spirituality. This is not to say that people need to immerse themselves in all aspects of tradition in order to fully embrace their indigenousness—simply that the basic values and prin-ciples of traditional political philosophy must be respected to the same degree as cultural and spiritual traditions.

Should we as indigenous people consider ourselves as individuals, or as representatives of our cultures and members of our nations representing distinct and identifiable values and world views? Many people recognize the obvious injustices and misuses of power, and the absence of traditional values, in the new structures, but they can only point to the problems. The lack of any coherent strategy to solve them suggests that Native people need to go beyond the divisive electoral politics and Western-style institutions recommended by most scholars and develop solutions for themselves from within their own cultural frameworks, reuniting themselves as individuals with their collectivity. Human beings do not exist in isolation—the influence of cultural groups and structures is constant and profound. By ignoring traditional teachings, Native people risk losing what they most need to survive as indigenous people, and move closer still to the cultural vortex of the other, foreign, collectivity.

The alternative to cultural annihilation begins with acknowledging the erosion of pre-contact indigenous cultures and becoming fully aware not only of post-contact history, but also of the shifting, evolving nature of culture itself. Knowing the history of European colonialism in North America demands recognition of the damage that has been done to the vitality of our traditional cultures. But we must also honour the fact that indigenous peoples have survived: The frameworks of their values systems remain intact and vital. Indigenous governance systems embody distinctive political values, radically different from those of the mainstream. Western notions of dominion (human and natural) are noticeably absent; in their place, we find harmony, autonomy, and respect. We have a responsibility to recover, understand, and preserve these values, not only because they represent a unique contribution to the history of ideas, but also because renewal of respect for traditional values is the only lasting solution to the political, economic, and social problems that beset our people. To bring those roots to new fruition, we must reinvigorate the principles embedded in the ancient teachings, and use them to address our contemporary problems.

Within just a few generations, Turtle Island has been devastated and degraded. The land there has been shamefully exploited, indigenous people have borne every form of oppression, and Native American ideas have been denigrated. Recently, however, Native people have come to realize that the main obstacle to recovery from this near total destruction—to the restoration of peace and harmony in our communities and the creation of just relationships between our peoples and the earth—is the dominance of European-derived ideas. In the past two or three generations, we have seen efforts to rebuild social cohesion, gain economic self-sufficiency, and develop structures for self-government within Native communities. We have also seen renewed interest in the wisdom of the traditional teachings that sustained the great cultural achievement of respectful coexistence. Indigenous people have begun to appreciate that wisdom, and much of the discussion about justice within Native communities today revolves around the struggle to recover those values. Yet, among non-indigenous people, there has been little movement toward understanding or even recognizing the indigenous tradition.

In fact, it is one of the strongest themes within Native American cultures that the modern colonial state could not only build a framework for coexistence but cure many of its own ills by understanding and respecting traditional Native teachings. The wisdom encoded in the indigenous cultures can provide answers to many questions; many seemingly intractable problems could be resolved by bringing traditional ideas and values back to life. Pre-contact indigenous societies developed regimes of conscience and justice that promoted the harmonious co–existence of humans and nature for hundreds of generations. As we move into a post-imperial age, the values central to those traditional cultures are the indigenous contribution to the reconstruction of a just and harmonious world.

Indigenous people have many different perspectives on what constitutes tradition, and what is good and bad about traditional ways. My own views have been shaped by life in Kahnawake, a Kanien'kehaka (Mohawk) community of over 9000 people located on the south shore of the St Lawrence River outside Montreal. Our people have come a long way toward recovering their identity and power in recent years, but during my childhood, in the 1960s and early '70s, we were fractured, dysfunctional, and violently self-destructive—colonized and controlled to a large degree by white men. Yet that period was also a revolutionary time. As my generation awakened politically in the late 1970s, we refused to participate in our own colonization and embarked on the path of tradition, rejecting the identities and power relations that characterized us as a dominated people. It has been an enormous, costly, and sometimes violent struggle, and it is ongoing. But, today, the Kahnawakero:non are part of a re-emergent nation, self-confident and assertive in the promotion of our goals. We are not yet free from the effects of colonization on our people, nor have we yet reunified or recovered our lands, but we do not hesitate to contest our colonization. In this short time, we have accomplished the rebirth of a sense of ourselves as *Onkwehonwe* in Kahnawake. The transformation of the community in terms of personal, familial, and collective empowerment has been profound.

Yet the return to indigenous values and identities is not consistent within the community nor is it uniform among Native peoples, either in its pace or in its intensity; it is not even universally accepted as an objective. To gain a better understanding of how different nations are dealing with the internal and external conflicts that are inherent in the process of decolonization, in the summer of 1997, I spoke with a 33-year-old Kwa'kwa'ka'wakw woman living in Victoria, British Columbia, who has worked extensively in various Native political organizations and is active in the revival of traditional culture among her people. We talked about the effects of colonization and shared thoughts on the most serious problems undermining the health and security of indigenous people today. We also considered the lessons and strategies represented in this book and explored the relevance of a message drawn from the Rotinohshonni tradition to the situations of other indigenous peoples. Our conversation pointed to the particularity of each community's struggle, but also to the underlying similarities that make it possible to speak of a Native American perspective rooted in traditional values. The words we shared captured some of the complex intensity that seems to motivate all those committed to a traditionalist critique of the prevailing colonial structure and mindset.

Now that I've explained the traditional Condolence ritual, I'd like to know your thoughts about your own traditions and nation. Remember that in "Adding to the Rafters," there is a reminder that the longhouse—as a metaphor for our teachings—sometimes needs additions. As the present generation, that's our responsibility: We have to add sections to the longhouse. That's where we're failing now, in my view, and in the book I will deal with that by projecting this traditional perspective onto some key contemporary issues. We have the rafters—the traditions that our grandmothers and grandfathers, great-grandfathers and great-grandmothers built. But there is an explicit instruction in the teachings that some day we will have to add to those rafters. Now, it seems, we're so jealous and protective of our traditions that we aren't thinking about that, in my nation anyway. From what I've seen in my travels, it's much the same in other nations. We're afraid to change, to update. As in the ritual, that's where I want to leave off, by concluding that what we really need to do is embark on a creative rethinking of ourselves, rooted in tradition.

In relation to the first part—the rhetorical lament for the loss of traditional knowledge—what do you think we have lost as a society? I look around our communities and there's something missing. What is it?

What I keep doing is looking at the causes of the losses. You know, when you look back on the smallpox and tuberculosis and all the different things that contact with white people brought, I don't think the implications of those things over the generations are anywhere near being understood.

Even among our own people?

Among our own people, that's true. Think about how contact and everything that came with it affected the transference of knowledge. We don't have the skills that we would have learned if everything had stayed the same. People's experience in residential schools is a good example. On one level, the family gets broken up; on the next level, the community gets broken up. That's a big factor. But on the individual level, it's even worse. If you don't have the benefits of the nurturing and the teachings in the first place, when you come out of the school, you still don't know how to learn, let alone how to teach. You end up going back home and it's as if the community had blown up, as if a bomb had been dropped in the middle of the village and we were just salvaging the leftover pieces, just trying to stick them back together. But because nobody has the real internal, individual knowledge, nobody's able to work together. So there are all kinds of fragments floating around. When you talk about what's missing—it's some very basic individual, healthy sense of self.

You notice this in a lot of communities because you do a lot of travelling, right?

Right. I've noticed it more this last time around because we were talking about education and traditions, and I became interested in knowing how different parts of the province, different tribal groups, had handled things. Everyone talked about learning from the elders, but on the other hand, they recognized that not all elders are the same—some are respected, but there are others who have fallen victim to the system. These elders have been victims in a really bad way for their whole lives and ended up sort of "faking it." Now, they're trying to appear knowledgeable, to sound knowledgeable, but all you have to do is put a couple of their statements together and you realize that they don't know what they're talking about, because it doesn't make sense. The way people were talking about all the things we've been trying to do—economic development, community development, self-government, the whole treaty process.... I don't think it's going to work because people, at an individual level, don't understand where they're supposed to be going anyway. On a very personal level, people don't know what you mean when you talk about "jurisdiction." They don't know what you're talking about when you say "control"—other than the negative idea of control that they have from their own direct experience of government in the communities. People don't know what it means to really have self-respect. I've talked to lots of women out in the communities who tell me that our young people don't know what it means to make a statement like, "I'm going to make a choice about getting involved in drugs or not, and my choice is based solely on the fact that I have enough self-respect that I wouldn't do that to myself." There's always another reason; it's always because "my family says so." It's always very external. The only thing that's holding people together is that, peripherally, they're seeing another way. They see something is there but they don't know what it is, they are just seeing this shadow that kind of follows them around. People keep trying to look at what it is, but they don't have enough … I don't know what the words are …

What is it for you, that thing?

I think maybe it's intuition. No. It's not so much intuition itself, as the ability to recognize intuition. And to trust it—to be able to trust yourself and your own choices based on your intuition and your knowledge. It's as if all those little things are sitting there waiting for you, but it's hard getting the connecting factors and finding how they all work together inside. So that's what we're up against.

I'm thinking about our treaty process. I walk in there and I don't know where to begin. You'd have to go through every individual and wipe out all of the superficial ideas that people have about what treaties are going to bring them and get down to what they believe in, philosophically. When I was up in North Island [Vancouver Island] I asked people, "Philosophically, why are we doing this? Why do you want to negotiate a treaty?" They'd answer, "Because it's the only game in town," and other external reasons, or maybe mention some really cerebral kinds of ideas about what they want to do. You know, it was interesting when you mentioned "seven generations." I asked people at home and in several communities, "What do you really mean by seven generations?" I was sure that that sort of thinking, wherever it comes from, has a full story behind it. But I kept hearing everybody use the words, when it was clear that nobody knew what the hell they were talking about. Yeah, that sounds like a nice buzzword, "seven generations" from now!

Penetrating that superficiality is one of the things I want to do, because what you just described is certainly a problem in our communities as well. Everybody seems to use that expression, because it comes directly from the ceremonies, but we don't really think about it—it just sounds good. The principle of "seven generations" involves children, some foresight, and all of that. But as for living it as a person, either in a treaty or even in your own life, I get the sense that not a lot of people have thought about how it applies, what it actually means. That's one of the things that I want to get at.

In the past, everyone knew who he or she was in relation to one another. I look at the medicine wheel and its message about the different races, and I think that, somewhere, our teachings probably talk about who we are as the red people in the medicine wheel, that there is a spiritual link. When you look at our ceremonies in the big house, the cedar bark, and things like the spiritual creature that comes from the north end of the world—all those things contain messages that we haven't figured out how to interpret today; but I think it's all there in our songs. The answer to who we are in relation to everybody else is sitting there, and has been sitting there for many generations now, but nobody has quite deciphered what it means because no one has thought to put a little energy into it. And that's because people think, "We're in the 1990s and we've got our potlatches; at least we still have our language, our culture." They think they can just take in whatever else is going on around them and stay true to their traditions, too. But if we don't get a sense of who we really are from the old teachings, then all this tradition stuff is just going to become watered down in a couple of generations.

So you think that this might be the gap in the traditional movement— that people are singing the songs without looking at what they really mean?

Yep. For a while, it was just surface, then we got a little bit beneath the surface, but nobody's gone any deeper than that. So the traditional movement has the appearance of something that's going to carry on, that's going to last. But the traditional culture is only going to last, I think, as if it were in a glass box. It's all recording, videos—now we have internet connections. All of that doesn't mean anything. The culture is going to sit in a little glass box that we'll all go to the museum and see one day, just the way we look at all our other stuff right now.

Well, that's what I call folklore. It's all just folklore unless you act on it. In fact, that's a criticism that's been directed at some "traditionalists." They act as if they're traditional and they sort of parrot what they're supposed to be doing, but then they go and live their lives totally differently and ignore the inconvenient messages—the ones that don't conform to their own choices in life. They ignore the important teachings that they don't like, and then they try to give the impression that those sections are obsolete. I would argue that they aren't obsolete at all. All the basic teachings are part of a unified whole that's crucial to understanding the tradition and the wisdom; we have to understand the way they all interrelate. You can't just ignore sections of it. If you haven't ever got to the real meaning, then I agree with you—in two or three generations it'll just be folklore.

Nobody understands the bottom line, basic principles that form the framework for everything. All the other stuff—the fact that we use button blankets, the fact that we're recording songs—those are just little tools that we've adapted along the way. "The basic principles"—people keep saying those words but nobody's living them. They're not saying that the bottom line is doing what I do in my life with respect and humility and understanding and honour. If I'm doing these things in a serious way, then anything that blossoms out of it is going to be right. Everyone figures, you know, that if we go to enough ceremonies and get seen enough and have a presence and visibility and appear to be involved in all this culture stuff, then we're truly balancing both worlds. But you don't have to balance both worlds. What you have to do is know your basic principles in the first place, and then blend the contemporary and traditional together—but you have to have the principles right. I grew up watching some people at ceremonies thinking they had all the knowledge, and then when I got into my mid-twenties, I went back to ask them what it means. I said, "I watched you do that when I was a kid; I saw you do that in a potlatch." But they didn't even know why! Now, I'm finding out in the last five or six years that all along they were just following what they were told or mimicking what they had seen themselves. They don't know why they're doing anything.

Do you fault them for that?

No.

Or do you see it as an evolutionary thing?

Yeah, I think that there were a lot of factors in the 1950s and '60s that affected that generation. Everyone in that era had a whole bunch of other things to deal with that we're not dealing with now: the right to vote, all the civil rights stuff happening south of the border, the American Indian Movement, and then the Indian Act here. In the late 1960s and early '70s, actually getting band offices and our own councils in the first place, and having our own Native people sitting in Department of Indian Affairs offices serving as Indian agents. And they believed at that time that we were going to become white. So if there was a potlatch and they were told by their elders, "Here's how you do the dance, just go do it," they did what they were told because they had had enough of the old teachings to know that they had to. But they still weren't getting the consistent, everyday exposure that they would've had in the past. When it came around to potlatch time, they would get into it and go through the motions. But every other day of the rest of their lives, it was just—you know—go out, get a job, participate in the economy, make some money and have a big house.

Some of which might be contrary to the values and the objectives of the potlatch in the first place.

I think it brought about an interesting way of thinking—and I ended up being on the receiving end of it. In the potlatch system, there are various ranks—in effect you've got noble people and commoners, and the whole range in between—but everybody has a role, and everybody is acknowledged in that role and you don't actually look down on people, and you don't treat them poorly. In the mentality of the 1960s and '70s, if you potlatched in a really big way, you had the right to call anyone down because you were so great. You were so humble that you would never do it, you had too much respect to do it—but you knew that you could. Another reason I think it happened was that people were getting mixed messages about whether they were Indian or white. They would equate participation in the potlatch with material wealth, as being one and the same. Meaning that if you didn't have a big house, plus a fishing boat, plus $100,000 per year coming in from your job, then you were poor. You were poor materially and poor in the potlatch system.

I think that's one of the differences between our cultures, even today. Yours is much more hierarchical and divided among families. I believe ours is much more egalitarian. When I was growing up, our identity was always "Mohawk" and not really defined by clan or family. Whenever any of us did something good, people would say, "Way to go, Mohawk!" You know, it was "for the nation." When someone did something good, I would always identify with it. At home, it's still that way. People get upset when someone claims to speak as a Mohawk but isn't really part of the society, because, for us, when someone says they're speaking as a Mohawk, we expect the message and the perspective to be consistent with what the community thinks. In my basic identification, I don't say I'm from the "Alfred" family, or from Kahnawake, or this clan or that clan. I say I'm Kanien'kehaka, Mohawk. And that's it, there's only one group. Whereas out here, on the West Coast, it seems to me that identity is family or clan-based. It's very different.

Yes it is. And residential schools are a big part of life out here, too. It's not just a generational thing either; it's not just the individuals who actually went to the schools. It's their entire families. Their parents feel guilty for sending their kids in the first place and finding out it wasn't such a good place after all. So, first, there are the parents, and then the kids, and then all their children. This "recognizing pain and sorrow" that you talk about, people don't know how to do that. They don't know how to name it, they don't know what to call it, and they don't know what the spinoff effect is when you deprive yourself of the opportunity to grieve. And all the grieving that never happened around the losses from disease.... If you don't go through the process of acknowledging what you've lost, you don't have a way to come back and get it ... get it back again.

Do you feel that some of the efforts that are under way now, with the social work or social services approach, are helping?

I think it's all a pile of crap.

Why don't you tell us how you really feel? Try not to hold back, okay? (laughter) Why is that so? I don't like the dominant social work approach either. I think they're using a foreign set of assumptions, goals even, to address the problem. But why do you think it's crappy? Maybe it comes from experience?

I'll have to smoke on that one. But I'll tell you the image I get in my mind when I think about social work, all the self-help groups, therapy, and all. I think of us trying to make a bike wheel: We've already got the outside rim, we know where the spokes need to go, and all of those spokes are possible, but people have to work together to make them a reality. And everyone has to have an understanding of that, right?

Is that our traditional culture, the wheel that you're talking about?

Everyone describes it in a different way, or visualizes it in a different way. For me, it's as if everyone has to understand where the spokes need to go before we can get anywhere, but the information about where the spokes go is scattered right now. So if all the people who understand where just one spoke needs to go came together and put their one spoke on the wheel, we'd have something. But instead, what social work and all these self-help things try to do is create more spokes. And they keep putting them in the wrong place—they're all on one side of the wheel. The social work approach is taking what's already fragmented and fragmenting it even more. They've got all these spokes on one side of the wheel, and they get frustrated with us because they can't understand why, after they've given us all these spokes, we haven't been able to make the wheel turn. Well, one, it doesn't have any of our spokes, and, two, they're all on one side. White people are just starting to discover that, yes, we do have a lot of answers, and we did have really elaborate, complex systems that spoke to every aspect of life.

Excuse the pun, eh?

What pun?

"Spoke" to …

At the end of the day, any social workers who've been in our communities for twenty years or more have resigned themselves to the fact that the discipline of social work, or psychology, doesn't have a clue.

I'd like to shift over and talk about the role of women in Native societies, both traditionally and today. In your life right now, you're involved in politics; you're involved with the culture. Is there respect for women?

To be really honest, no. I think that men who are in their forties, fifties, and sixties say the words. But only a rare few really know what it means to show respect and to actually demonstrate it.

How would someone do that? You could give me a positive or a negative example. How would someone disrespect women—if you're comfortable talking about it?

On the positive side, there's one man at home, in particular, that comes to mind. He was brought up with the old people; he understands the language, understands the culture. His words are so carefully orchestrated, and I don't think that's because he's trying to appear respectful; he is respectful, and it comes out in the way he speaks. Because he has such an understanding of Kwa'kwa'la language, when he translates to English, he does it in a very eloquent way. As for guys who aren't respectful, I always hear them talk about "our women." "Our women" as if we were possessions still. They keep saying, "We have respect for our women." The biggest insult, to me, is that they go through the motions in the big house, but then when we come out of the big house into our contemporary lives, they don't show any of that respect.

What about the young guys?

I think among the young people that I'm spending the most time with, it's about an 80 percent to 20 percent split. There's 20 percent or so that have had the benefit of the band school, hearing the language in the home or learning the values and the principles in the home or through the potlatch. So they're okay, they're on the right path, even though they're still being distracted by the contemporary influences. The other 80 percent are doing what the previous generations have done, in that they're using whatever works for them, whatever will serve their personal agenda. A couple of years ago, when a bunch of us women started getting together at night for dance practices and singing practices in the big house, some young guys— 16 or 17 years old—were saying things like "First of all, there should be no women sitting up at the log singing" or "Women shouldn't be learning the songs anyway" or "When we have our pot-luck dinners or when we have feasts, we should be served first."

"We" being the men?

They haven't been taught that you will be shown respect when you give respect in the first place. So the women in the community here in Victoria started getting together and thinking about how we could address this.

Because we realized that we hadn't succeeded in teaching these boys everything they needed to know. We hadn't carried out our responsibilities either. At first, we just thought their families should have done more. Then we started realizing, "Holy cow! We've got residential schools, and alcoholism, and all kinds of issues around adoption and families getting back together." There were too many things happening at once for any of us to assume that anyone was doing anything outside of our own activities. So we started, just over the last couple of years, rebuilding the whole scheme. We focus first on the young kids, because we can't afford to lose this time with them—they need to learn it the fastest now. A bunch of us are going to focus on that, and some of us are going to take a look at what we are learning in the way of contemporary skills—doing projects, workshops, healing kinds of things. There're some of us who are proposal writers, ideas people. So we'll sit and think about things. And then, over time, whenever we feel like we need to, we'll just get together and brainstorm, piece it together, make it happen.

Who's the leader that you respect most and why? I'm asking you now what you would consider to be a leader. In spite of everything that you've talked about, there are obviously still people, men and women, whom you would respect. What is it about them that makes them true leaders? Or maybe I'm making a big assumption. Maybe it's not the case ...

There are some, but they're very few, and they are all elders. Agnes Cranmer, who just passed away recently, was a hell of a leader because she knew that her upbringing in the potlatch, her understanding of the potlatch, was right. That's all there is to it. She never thought, "Maybe I'm wrong about this." She believed she was right. There was also, in the same time period, a woman we all called Granny. Those two women, along with lots of women in that generation, just believed that it was right to do what they were doing. Regardless of whether there was funding, regardless of whether there was a hall or a place to go and do things, they just kept doing them. They kept teaching their kids; they made sure their kids were brought up in the potlatch way and that they understood what basic principles are, no matter what happened. They lived through the potlatch ban.

It was Mrs Cranmer's husband, Dan Cranmer, who threw the potlatch on Village Island where everybody got arrested and thrown in jail. They lived through all of that, and saw the worst of it, but they kept doing it anyway, because they believed it.

Did she embody all the traditional values ...?

She lived them. I think that's what the neat thing was, considering the era she lived in. She made it through the potlatch ban, she lived through the 1960s, and '70s and '80s, and, throughout all of that, she was still carrying on the culture. She opened up her own corner store and pool hall. She ran a business and, at the same time, she was working with the community to teach children in the nursery school. She did all these incredible things, and none of them ever interfered with one another; they actually complemented one another. So, even though she was very much participating in the local economic activity, she was still one of the foundations of our culture in everything that she did. There was another lady who was I don't know how much older than Agnes. She never involved herself much in contemporary economic stuff, but she supported those who did. She gave them enough common-sense information to go out there and look at business as though it was a traditional activity: "As long as you follow these basic principles you'll be fine." To me, that's all of it right there. I never watched how the old men conducted themselves. To me, it was simple: I just had to follow the path that those women led. I'm not going to be able to do what those men do. I'm not a speaker; I'm not a singer; I'm not any of those things, so I didn't pay attention to any of that—just to what those ladies did.

But there are men whom you would respect in that category, as well?

The man from home I spoke about earlier. What I think is neat about him is that when he's wrong he comes right out and admits it. He doesn't try to make excuses. He just says, "This is what happened; this is what I understood at the time to be true; this was my action as a result of my thinking. It turned out that it wasn't correct, and now I stand corrected." Then he goes through the traditional way to correct it. I don't know how many male "leaders," or people who are sitting in political positions now, do that. I've not heard any of them admit they were wrong and really mean it. I've seen them do it for the sake of appearing to be humble. And I've seen them do it because if they didn't admit it, the repercussions would be worse, and they stood to lose more in terms of material things. So I've seen them do it. But, you know, you can tell when they're just faking.

So how do these internal issues that we've been talking about affect our status rel-ative to other peoples? How have they affected the strength of our nation vis-à-vis others? Has our "sovereignty" been undermined? Has our nation lost power in a real way because of these problems? Or is it more a matter of other people doing things to us? That's another question I want to address in this book. What is the relationship between our problems and those that have been imposed on us? Maybe we haven't responded well. If so, does that have ongoing implications? Can we rebuild our nations in the midst of these internal issues? Or do we have to resolve those issues first, and then confront the outside?

Well, I think one of the simplest things it comes down to is this: If you don't respect yourself, no one else will. As for rebuilding internally and externally, I think they can be done simultaneously. In fact, they have to be done simul-taneously, the healing and the rebuilding. If we stop nation-building now and do nothing but healing, then the whole treaty process—which is going down the tubes anyway—will be down the tubes even faster, because all the resources will get scooped up while we're all busy trying to heal. There is a lot of healing to be done. But the flip side is that there's so much strength; the fact that we're still here is testimony to the fact that we've got some good coping skills. Why don't we pat ourselves on the back for what we've done well? It's amazing that we've managed to survive this far. We should empha-size that instead of always saying, "I'm a victim of residential schools. I'm a victim of alcoholism." You can play that game for a few years, but you're wasting time. In the meantime, you could be learning a little bit about how to run a home-based business and get self-sufficient. If you don't understand what self-sufficiency is in your home, you can't contribute that to the nation. Why would you think you can contribute something to the nation, when you have no concept of it in your own life? That's why I think the rebuild-ing has to happen simultaneously, inside the community and outside.

In terms of nations, what would be the ideal relationship between your nation and the rest of Canada once things get back on track? If you compare the mili-tancy of Mohawk politics with things here in BC, where do you stand?

Well, I like to look at all sides of the question. I do think there's a need for us to get militant again, in a big bad way. I think we have to. But, at the same time, there are people who are nowhere near ready for that. They're scared. And they'll sabotage things for the militants because they're afraid—afraid for a lot of reasons. I'm close to the militant extreme, because I really believe that we have to nail this down—just get on with it. But I know from the people I've talked to around the province that there are many people who couldn't physically, emotionally, or intellectually bring themselves to that level. They're not prepared to die. Whereas, personally, I remember that when Oka flared up, I was thinking, "If this is how it has to be, I'm prepared to die." But lots of people I worked with were saying, "What the hell are the Mohawks doing? They're gonna get us all in shit!"

Are you a Canadian?

No. Actually, I've tried to search for the moment in time when Canada decided legally—at least legally—that we were considered citizens. Which is kind of a joke, because as I've heard someone say, "Legally, yes, we are regarded as citizens. Yet the same legislation—the Indian Act—is always there to remind us that we're not." To me, you can't look at the Indian Act, and look at the precedents in the courts, and then draw the conclusion that we're citizens.

Well, I think legally they gave Indians the vote in the 1960s. Formal citizenship came before that, but not much before. It wasn't asked for: It was given because they realized that in order to tax and do the things they wanted to do for Indians—or to Indians—they needed them to be citizens. They resisted as long as they could, then they made Indians second-class citizens and imposed the Indian Act on them. I'm not a Canadian. I don't believe in that. I think that if you're strong in your nation, then that's what you are. If you have a good relationship with Canada, fine, so much the better.

Some of my best friends are Canadians (laughter). No, I do not regard myself as a Canadian. You see all the things like the Olympics, the Commonwealth Games, all those things that people get excited about. For what? These people are going to go off to—where is it, Bosnia?—and the government is going to give them $15 million. Somebody just died on one of our reserves this week—someone died on every reserve this week—of malnutrition or infection, because of poor conditions. Oh yeah, we're citizens.

They gave $2 billion to China, to buy nuclear reactors, and they complain about $58 million for a Royal Commission on Aboriginal Peoples.

I was surprised, the commentaries in the papers on the Royal Commission's recommendations were not that bad. They were even a little bit support-ive. Got to watch out for that though. Watch out for ... what is it again?

"Beware the magic."

The magic, and the lurking dangers.

Is there a fundamental or inherent difference between indigenous and white society? This is a relevant question, given the tendency of the dominant Western tradition to draw racial distinctions. Indigenous traditions, by con-trast, include all human beings as equal members in the regimes of conscience. Yet some Native people have been influenced by the divisive European approach. Representing this perspective in an academic context, Donald Fixico has claimed that white people can never come to terms with indigenous val-ues because they "come from a different place on earth." He writes,

> Anglo-Americans and Natives are fundamentally different. These dif-
> ferences in worldview and in the values that go with them mean that
> there will always exist an Indian view and a White view of the earth.

I believe, on the contrary, that there is a real danger in believing that views are fixed (and that cultures don't change). Fixico's polarization of Indian and European values suggests he believes that white people are incapable of attaining the level of moral development that indigenous societies pro-mote among their members with respect to, for example, the land. Not only does this dichotomization go against the traditional Native belief in a uni-versal rationality, but it offers a convenient excuse for those who support the state in its colonization of indigenous nations and exploitation of the earth. If Fixico is right, the state can't help it: The establishment's world view is preordained.

Challenging mainstream society to question its own structure, its acquis-itive, individualistic values system, and the false premises of colonialism is essential if we are to move beyond the problems plaguing all our societies, Native and white, and rebuild relations between our peoples. A deep read-ing of tradition points to a moral universe in which all of humanity is accountable to the same standard. Our goal should be to convince others of the wisdom of the indigenous perspective. Although it may be emotionally satisfying for indigenous people to ascribe a greedy, dominating nature to white people, taking such an approach leaves one in self-defeating intellectual and political positions. It is more hopeful to listen to the way traditional teachings speak of the various human families: They ask that we consider each one to be gifted and powerful in its own way, each with something different to contribute to the achievement of peace and harmony. Far from condemning different cultures, this position challenges each one to discover its gift in itself and realize it fully, to the benefit of humanity as a whole. It is just as important for Europeans as it is for Native people to cultivate the values that promote peace and harmony.

The value of the indigenous critique of the Western world view lies not in the creation of false dichotomies but in the insight that the colonial attitudes and structures imposed on the world by Europeans are not manifestations of an inherent evil: They are merely reflections of white society's understanding of its own power and relationship with nature. The brutal regime of European technological advancement, intent on domination, confronted its opposite in indigenous societies. The resulting near-extinction of indigenous peoples created a vacuum in which the European regime established its political, economic, and philosophical dominance.

The primitive philosophical premises underpinning that regime were not advanced or refined in the deployment of microbes and weapons. At their core, European states and their colonial offspring still embody the same destructive and disrespectful impulses that they did five hundred years ago. For this reason, questions of justice—social, political, and environmental—are best considered outside the framework of classical European thought and legal traditions. The value of breaking away from old patterns of thought and developing innovative responses has been demonstrated with respect to environmental questions. But, in fact, many of these and other pressing questions have been answered before: Indigenous traditions are the repository of vast experience and deep insight on achieving balance and harmony.

At the time of their first contact with Europeans, the vast majority of Native American societies had achieved true civilization: They did not abuse the earth; they promoted communal responsibility; they practised equality in gender relations; and they respected individual freedom. As the Wendat historian Georges Sioui put it in a lucid summary of the basic values of traditional indigenous political and social thought,

With their awareness of the sacred relations that they, as humans, must help maintain between all beings, New World men and women dictate a philosophy for themselves in which the existence and survival of other beings, especially animals and plants, must not be endangered. They recognize and observe the laws and do not reduce the freedom of other creatures. In this way they ensure the protection of their most precious possession, their own freedom.

The context of life has changed, and indigenous people today live in a materialistic world of consumerism and corporate globalization—a world diametrically opposed to the social and political culture that sustained our communities in the past. It may be difficult to recognize the viability of a philosophy that originated in an era unaffected by European ideas and attitudes. Nevertheless, revitalizing indigenous forms of government offers a real opportunity to inspire and educate mainstream society and to create and empower a genuine alternative to the current system.

In my own community of Kahnawake, as part of an effort to determine the cultural appropriateness of various social services in the early 1990s, people were asked to consider a list of statements about traditional values and to say whether they agreed that those concepts were still important today:

TRADITIONAL VALUE	PERCENTAGE WHO STRONGLY AGREE
Responsibility to all creation	97%
Importance of extended family	89%
Respect for inner strength or wisdom	88%
Importance of educating youth	88%
Sacredness and autonomy of children	78%
Importance of family unity	78%
Wisdom of the past	71%
Sharing and co-operation	71%

The survey points to the community's recognition of traditional values, despite the imposition of European culture. Indigenous people who seek to realize the goal of harmonious coexistence within their communities find that this is impossible within the mainstream political system as it is currently structured. The Lakota philosopher Luther Standing Bear, writing in 1933, presaged this frustration with Western values:

> True, the white man brought great change. But the varied fruits of his civilization, though highly colored and inviting, are sickening and deadening.... I am going to venture that the man who sat on the ground in his teepee meditating on life and its meaning, accepting the kinship of all creatures, and acknowledging unity with the universe of things was infusing into his being the true essence of civilization. And when native man left off this form of development, his humanization was retarded in growth.

Having had their freedom stolen and their civilizations crushed by colonialism, Native people are well aware of the social and political crisis they face. But the crucial goal of restoring a general respect for traditional values and reconnecting our social and political life with traditional teachings remains elusive. Standing Bear's thoughts on true civilization are echoed in conversations all over Indian country. So why have we not yet rejected the European ways that hurt us and rejoined the indigenous path to peace, power, and righteousness?

The answer to this question is the reason why, of all the important issues we need to address, the most crucial is leadership. Understanding leadership means understanding indigenous political philosophy: conceptions of power and the primary values that create legitimacy and allow governments to function appropriately and effectively. Good indigenous leadership ensures that government is rooted in tradition, is consistent with the cultural values of the community. This is a key element in restoring the necessary harmony between social and political cultures in Native societies. Non-indigenous political structures, values, and styles of leadership lead to coercive and compromised forms of government that contradict basic indigenous values and are the main reason our social and political crises persist.

We have not fully recovered from colonialism because our leadership has been compromised, and we will remain subject to the intellectual, political, and economic dominance of Western society until the leaders of our communities realize the power of indigenous philosophies and act to restore respect for traditional wisdom. Leadership is essential if we are to disprove the rule that societies must hit rock bottom before they begin to realize meaningful change. Is it not possible to reach into the depths of tradition and begin to build the future now?

Returning to indigenous traditions of leadership will require an intensive effort to understand indigenous political life within the moral and ethical framework established by traditional values. Without obscuring the distinctiveness of individual societies, it is possible to see fundamental similarities in the concept of "Native leadership" among indigenous cultures. Most agree that the institutions operating in Native communities today have little to do with indigenous belief systems and that striking commonalities exist among the traditional philosophies that set the parameters for governance. The values that underpin these traditional philosophies constitute a core statement of what indigenous governance is as a style, a structure, and a set of norms.

In their most basic values, and even to a certain extent their style, traditional forms of government are not unique. Similar characteristics can be found in other systems. The special nature of Native American government consists of the prioritization of those values, the rigorous consistency of its principles with those values and the patterns and procedures of government, as well as the common set of goals (respect, balance, and harmony) that are recognizable across Native American societies. Adherence to those core values made the achievement of the goals possible. It was because of the symbiotic relationship between the traditional values system and the institutions that evolved within the culture that balance and harmony were its hallmarks. Indigenous governance demands respect for the totality of the belief system. It must be rooted in a traditional values system, operate according to principles derived from that system, and seek to achieve goals that can be justified within that system. This is the founding premise of pre- and decolonized Native politics—and we are in danger of losing it permanently if the practices and institutions currently in place become any further entrenched (and, hence, validated).

On the west coast of Vancouver Island, I spoke with a Nuu-chah-nulth elder who recognized the danger of continuing to think of governance in the terms of the values system and the institutional structures that have been imposed on Native communities by the state. The late hereditary chief Moses Smith had served as a band councillor under the Canadian government's Indian Act system, but late came to recognize the harm that system did to his community. As a leader, he recommitted himself to teaching his people's traditional philosophy so that an indigenous form of government could be restored. Lamenting the loss both of traditional values and of the structures that promoted good leadership, Moses said that "In the old days leaders were taught and values were ingrained in hereditary chiefs. The fundamental value was respect." In his view, contemporary band councils are not operating according to traditional values, and Native leadership premised on traditional power and knowledge will vanish forever unless "the traditional perspective is taken up by the new generation."

In choosing between revitalizing indigenous forms of government and maintaining the European forms imposed on them, Native communities have a choice between two radically different kinds of social organization: One based on conscience and the authority of the good, and the other on coercion and authoritarianism. The Native concept of governance is based on what Russell Barsh, a great student of indigenous societies, has called the "primacy of conscience." There is no central or coercive authority, and decision-making is collective. Leaders rely on their persuasive abilities to achieve a consensus that respects the autonomy of individuals, each of whom is free to dissent from, and remain unaffected by, the collective decision. The clan or family is the basic unit of social organization, and larger forms of organization, from tribe through nation to confederacy, are all predicated on the political autonomy and economic independence of clan units through family-based control of lands and resources.

A crucial feature of the indigenous concept of governance is its respect for individual autonomy. This respect precludes the notion of "sovereignty"—the idea that there can be a permanent transference of power or authority from the individual to an abstraction of the collective called "government." The indigenous tradition sees government as the collective power of the individual members of the nation; there is no separation between society and state. Leadership is exercised by persuading individuals to pool their self-power in the interest of the collective good. By contrast, in the European tradition, power is surrendered to the representatives of the majority, whose decisions on what they think is the collective good are then imposed on all citizens.

In the indigenous tradition, the idea of self-determination truly starts with the self; political identity—with its inherent freedoms, powers, and responsibilities—is not surrendered to any external entity. Individuals alone determine their interests and destinies. There is no coercion, only the compelling force of conscience based on those inherited and collectively refined principles that structure the society. With the collective inheritance of a cohesive spiritual universe and traditional culture, profound dissent is rare and is resolved by exemption of the individual from the implementation and implications of the particular decision. When the difference between individual and collective becomes irreconcilable, the individual leaves the group.

Collective self-determination depends on the conscious coordination of individual powers of self-determination. The governance process consists in the structured interplay of three kinds of power: individual power, persuasive power, and the power of tradition. These power relations are channelled into forms of decision-making and dispute resolution grounded in the recognition that beyond the individual there exists a natural community of interest: the extended family. Thus, in almost all indigenous cultures, the foundational order of government is the clan. And almost all indigenous systems are predicated on a collective decision-making process organized around the clan.

It is erosion of this traditional power relationship and the forced dependence on a central government for provision of sustenance that lie at the root of injustice in the indigenous mind. Barsh recognizes a truth that applies to institutions at both the broad and the local level: "The evil of modern states is their power to decide who eats." Along with armed force, they use dependency—which they have created—to induce people's compliance with the will of an abstract authority structure serving the interests of an economic and political elite. It is an affront to justice that individuals are stripped of their power of self-determination and forced to comply with the decisions of a system based on the consciousness and interests of others.

The principles underlying European-style representative government through coercive force stand in fundamental opposition to the values from which indigenous leadership and power derive. In indigenous cultures, the core values of equality and respect are reflected in the practices of consensus decision-making and dispute resolution through balanced consideration of all interests and views. In indigenous societies, governance results from the interaction of leadership and the autonomous power of the individuals who make up the society. Governance in an indigenist sense can be practised only in a decentralized, small-scale environment among people who share a culture. It centres on the achievement of consensus and the creation of collective power, bounded by six principles:

- Governance depends on the active participation of individuals.
- Governance balances many layers of equal power.
- Governance is dispersed.
- Governance is situational.
- Governance is non-coercive.
- Governance respects diversity.

Contemporary politics in Native communities is shaped by the interplay of people who, socially and culturally, are still basically oriented toward this understanding of government, with a set of structures and political relationships that reflect a very different, almost oppositional, understanding.

The imposition of colonial political structures is the source of most factionalism within Native communities. Such institutions operate on principles that can never be truly acceptable to people whose orientations and attitudes are derived from a traditional value system. But they are tolerated by cynical community members as a fact of their colonized political lives. As a result, those structures have solidified into major obstacles to the achievement of peace and harmony in Native communities, spawning a non-traditional or anti-traditionalist political subculture among those individuals who draw their status and income from them.

The effort needed to bring contemporary political institutions, and the people who inhabit them, into harmony with traditional values is very different from the superficial and purely symbolic efforts at reform that have taken place in many communities. Symbols are crucially important, but they must not be confused with substance. When terminology, costume, and protocol are all that change, while unjust power relationships and colonized attitudes remain untouched, such "reform" becomes nothing more than a politically correct smokescreen obscuring the fact that no real progress is being made toward realizing traditionalist goals. Cloaking oneself in the mantle of tradition is no substitute for altering one's behaviour, especially where power is concerned. In too many Native communities, adherence to tradition is a shallow facade masking a greed for power and success as defined by mainstream society. Recognizable by its lack of community values, this selfish hunger for power holds many Native leaders in its grip and keeps them from working to overturn the colonial system.

The indigenous tradition is profoundly egalitarian; it does not put any substantial distance between leaders and other people, let alone allow for the exercise of coercive authority. Yet these are fundamental features of the political systems imposed on Native people. The hard truth is that many of those who hold positions of authority in Native communities have come to depend on the colonial framework for their power, employment, and status. How many of them would still hold their positions if the criteria for leadership reflected indigenous values instead of an ability to serve the interests of mainstream society? Very few contemporary Native politicians can honestly claim to possess the qualities and skills needed to lead in a non-coercive, participatory, transparent, consensus-based system. The hunger for power, money, and status prevents many people from seeing what is best for the community in the long run. But even when the people who seek that power do so with the best intentions, for the good of the people, the fact remains that holding non-consensual power over others is contrary to traditional values. Whatever the purpose behind the use of arbitrary authority, the power relationship itself is wrong.

Proponents of an indigenous form of government aim to overturn that unjust power relationship along with the government systems that have been imposed on our communities since colonization. Those systems cannot be defended on grounds of history (they are foreign), morality (they are intended to destabilize), or even practice (they do not work). Yet many people who are entrenched politically or bureaucratically within them resist any attempt to recover the traditional basis for governmental organization. Their defence of the status quo reflects a need to preserve the power relationships of contemporary Native politics. This is both a political and philosophical problem, a corruption that must be addressed if the values embedded in the European/American political system are not to form the general criteria for status, prestige, and leadership in our communities.

Efforts to recover the integrity of indigenous societies are not new. The first post-European Native cultural revival, at the start of the nineteenth century, was aimed largely at expunging cultural influences that were seen to be destructive. Various social and religious movements, including the Ghost Dance, Peyoteism, and the Code of Handsome Lake, sought to overcome the loss of spiritual rootedness and refocus attention on Native values systems. Experience since then has shown that cultural revival is not a matter of rejecting all Western influences, but of separating the good from the bad and of fashioning a coherent set of ideas out of the traditional culture to guide whatever forms of political and social development—including the good elements of Western forms—are appropriate to the contemporary reality. It is this rootedness in traditional values that defines an indigenous people; a culture that does not reflect the basic principles of the traditional philosophy of government cannot be considered to be indigenous in any real sense.

In lamenting the loss of a traditional frame of reference, we must be careful not to romanticize the past. Tradition is the spring from which we draw our healing water; but any decisions must take into account contemporary economic, social, and political concerns. We seek the answer to one of the basic questions any society must answer: What is the right way to govern? For generations, foreigners have provided the answer to this question. Our deference to other people's solutions has taken a terrible toll on indigenous peoples. A focused recommitment to traditional teachings is the only way to preserve what remains of indigenous cultures and to recover the strength and integrity of indigenous nations. At this time in history, indigenous people need to acknowledge the losses suffered and confront the seriousness of their plight. There is no time left to wallow in our pain. Instead, we should use it as a measure of how urgent the challenge is. The power of our most important traditional teachings will become evident as they begin to ease our suffering and restore peace.

Reorienting leaders and institutions toward an indigenous framework means confronting tough questions about the present state of affairs. It would be unrealistic to imagine that all Native communities are willing and able to jettison the structures in place today for the romantic hope of a return to a pre-European life. But it would also be too pessimistic to suggest that there is no room at all for traditional values. Mediating between these extremes, one could argue that most communities would simply be better served by governments founded on those principles drawn from their own cultures that are relevant to the contemporary reality. In a practical sense, this is what is meant by a return to traditional government.

The persistence of political apathy, ignorance, and greed does not mean that traditional forms of government are not viable. These problems simply demonstrate that imported forms of government do not work in Native communities. Those places that have embarked on a traditionalist path and still find themselves plagued by these problems show that there is still too much distance between the idea of traditional government and the reality of the issues that need to be addressed. In both cases, traditional knowledge has to be brought forward and translated into a form that can be seen as a viable alternative to the imposed structures—as the culturally appropriate solution to fundamental political problems.

Some may be tempted to ask why it is so important to return to a traditional perspective. Aren't there are other paths to peace, paths that would take us forward rather than backward? Some may even see the problems besetting Native communities as the product not of colonialism, but of the people's own failure to adapt to a modern reality shaped by forces that traditional values cannot comprehend, let alone address. Tradition, in their view, is a dream no more grounded in reality than clouds that disappear on the first wind—a beautiful dream, unsuited to the harsh realities of the world.

Such people are mistaken. Rediscovering the power of the traditional teachings and applying them to contemporary problems is crucially important to the survival of indigenous people. There is more than one Native in this world who dreams in the language of her ancestors and wakes mute to them, who dreams of peace and wakes to a deep and heavy anger. If a traditionally grounded nation is a dream, it is one worth pursuing. It has been said before, and it bears repeating: Sometimes dreams are wiser than waking.

Native Political Elites

In the midst of the current crisis, there are still people who embody the traditional virtues of indigenous cultures. There are generous men and women who hold fast to the traditional way and who know its power to bring people together. These are the true leaders—the ones to whom communities should be looking to take them beyond the division and greed of contemporary politics. But it is rare for such people to obtain positions of authority or influence within the current colonial structure. Often, the qualities that make them leaders in the traditional sense are not sufficiently appreciated. As well, many of them make a conscious decision to withdraw from a foreign political system. Either way, the public sphere comes to be dominated by people who conform to the criteria for leadership imposed on Native communities, while those who meet the indigenous criteria for leadership remain secluded in the private realm of traditional life in the communities. There is a division between those who serve the system and those who serve the people. In a colonial system designed to undermine, divide, and assimilate indigenous people, those who achieve power run the risk of becoming instruments of those objectives.

Most of those who possess authority delegated by the Canadian or United States government are less leaders (with apologies to the rare exceptions) than tools of the state. This does not necessarily mean they are total sellouts. Some are simply blind to the reality of their co-optation; others, however, are complicit in the political subjugation of legitimate leaders.

Near the end of his tenure, the former Assembly of First Nations head Ovide Mercredi made a bitter admission: "I'm not going to run interference for the white government. I've done that already. And the white politicians have done nothing to help in return." Apparently, the style of politics practised by the present indigenous political elite includes the cynical manipulation common to non-indigenous systems. In the mid-1990s, seeking to block revision of the Canadian government's Indian Act legislation—one of the Indian Affairs minister's major initiatives—Mercredi sought approval for a new, more militant posture from his organization at its annual meeting. The meeting was attended by only about 150 of the 633 band council chiefs in Canada, and fewer than 80 were even present for the vote on the new stance. So with the support of perhaps one in every ten band council chiefs—whose own legitimacy is questionable, given the very low rates of political participation in the community—Mercredi claimed that he had gained the "consensus" of Native people in Canada! Mercredi's successor, Phil Fontaine, went even further in standing with Canadian police agencies and government officials to publicly denounce community-based activists who would threaten the submissive and pleading tone of his so-called "National Day of Action" for social justice by staging contentious protests and confrontations across the country in June 2007.

Those who challenge the status and style of the entrenched elite may do so on a moral basis, as the Native Women's Association of Canada (NWAC) did during the 1992 negotiations to revise Canada's Constitution, when they were excluded by the Assembly of First Nations (AFN). But they lack an indigenous philosophical base. And without a solid grounding in traditional values, such critical opposition is incapable of asserting indigenous rights; it becomes just a lever for those who want to replace the entrenched leaders and wield power themselves, still within a non-indigenous framework. The efforts of NWAC and other politically marginalized groups to combat the AFN's exercise of its claimed authority as the Native representative exemplified this futile "mainstreaming" of dissent—and, indeed, under the leadership of its recently appointed president Beverley Jacobs, NWAC has abandoned its contentious stance and merged with the AFN politically, joining the list of mainstream Aboriginal groups serving as consultative tools for legitimating Canadian government policy.

There is a difference between indigenous and Western forms of leadership. From a Native standpoint, it simply is not enough to gain control of an institution. It is the quality and character of that institution that are of primary concern to indigenous people. Noel Dyck has described how indigenous youth in the 1970s were quick to recognize the distinction between true indigenous organizations and ones fronted by "brown bureaucrats." As Dyck observed, "brown and bureaucrat, or put another way, Indian and government, represent two different and opposing categories of social organization.... In the culture and experience of the [association], the two categories are not compatible."

The idea that "indigenous" and "bureaucratic" are mutually exclusive categories has been rethought since the 1970s. But even with the focus now on values and intentions as the criteria for determining whether or not an organization is good for the community, structure still matters. Working for the system in a political arm of the Canadian or US government almost always means working against your own people. There are a few rare cases where communities have decolonized their local governments and people have set up their own systems of representation. But the sad reality is that it's still difficult to justify working directly for the state.

So why do people do it? Jack Forbes has described a spectrum of identities, from a very firmly rooted Native nationalism to an opportunistic minority-race identification. Forbes's spectrum points to the lines of cleavage that the state manipulates in its efforts to legitimize its own institutions among Native people. In the war against indigenous nations, the state first alienates individuals from their communities and cultures and then capitalizes on their alienation by turning them into agents who will work to further the state's interests within those communities.

Adapting Forbes's analysis to the present situation, we can mark four major points along the spectrum of identity:

1. The **traditional nationalist** represents the values, principles, and approaches of an indigenous cultural perspective that accepts no compromise with the colonial structure.
2. The **secular nationalist** represents an incomplete or unfulfilled indigenous perspective, stripped of its spiritual element and oriented almost solely toward confronting colonial structures.
3. The **tribal pragmatist** represents an interest-based calculation, a perspective that merges indigenous and mainstream values toward the integration of Native communities within colonial structures.
4. The **racial minority** ("of Indian descent") represents Western values—a perspective completely separate from indigenous cultures and

supportive of the colonial structures that are the sole source of Native identification.

It goes almost without saying that state agencies recruit their Native people among the latter two groups. For people with a traditionalist perspective and a little cultural confidence, co-optation by the state is difficult. Undeniably, many Native people who work in state institutions, or in state-sponsored governments within communities, see themselves as working in the interests of their people. There is a strong, although fundamentally naive, belief among them that it is possible to "promote change from within." In retrospect, those who have tried such an approach have failed to see that belief for what it is: more of a justification than a reason. There are many political identities across Native America, and even within single communities the dynamics of personality and psychology produce varying responses to the colonial situation. The people who choose to work for or with the colonial institutions have constructed a political identity for themselves that justifies their participation. This is no excuse for being wrong—and they are—but it indicates the dire need for a stronger sense of traditional values among all Native people. In the absence of a political culture firmly rooted in tradition, and a common set of principles based on traditional values, it is not surprising that individuals will tend to stray toward mainstream beliefs and attitudes.

The co-optive intent of the current system is clear to anyone who has worked within it, as is the moral necessity of rejecting the divisive institutions and leaders who emerge from a bureaucratic culture. It is one thing to seek out the heart of whiteness in order to prepare yourself for future battles—"know thine enemy" is still good advice. But it is quite another thing to have your own heart chilled by the experience. Whether in a bureaucratic context or an indigenous one, individual conduct and values are crucial in determining who the real leaders are.

To plant a tree of peace, power, and righteousness, the ground must be prepared.

"Rejoicing in Our Survival"
The strength and quality of indigenous peoples' greatest accomplishment is almost buried under the weight of the problems they confront. That accomplishment consists in their survival. Indigenous peoples have every right to celebrate their continued existence and to draw strength from the fact that

their nations live on despite the terrible losses of the past five hundred years. Today's challenge must be shouldered proudly because it is no less than the sacred heritage passed on by generations of ancestors who sacrificed and died to preserve the notion of their being. For all the chaos and pain brought by colonization, and for all the self-inflicted wounds, the first step in getting beyond the present crisis must be to celebrate the inherent strength that has allowed indigenous people to resist extinction. That strength must then be turned to a different purpose, because beyond mere survival lies a demanding future that will depend on indigenous peoples' confidence, pride, and skill in making their right of self-determination real. The lesson of the past is that indigenous people have less to fear by moving away from colonialism than by remaining bound by it. In their resistance, they demonstrate an inner strength greater than that of the nations that would dominate them.

"Recognizing Our Pain and Sorrow"

With confidence in the integrity and power of their traditions and faith in their ability to overcome the worst, indigenous people must face the reality that much of their pain and sorrow today is self-inflicted. What is the legacy of colonialism? Dispossession, disempowerment, and disease inflicted by white society, to be sure. The ongoing struggle consists mainly in an effort to redress such injustice. Yet a parallel truth—and, in most cases, it is almost unspeakable—is that the injustice and sickness are perpetuated and compounded from within.

The only way to erase this pain and sorrow is to confront it directly. Most Native life is a painful burden that is the result of colonialism. Yet the real tragedy is that many Native people are left to wander aimlessly for want of the inspiration that a healthy, supportive, and cohesive community could provide. Cultural dislocation has led to despair, but the real deprivation is the loss of the ethic of personal and communal responsibility. The violence and hate directed at our own people and ourselves that is so prevalent in Native communities is what the Sto:lo writer Lee Maracle has called "a cover for systemic rage" common among colonized peoples. Her poem "Hatred" exposes this often ignored reality: "Blinded by niceties and polite liberality/We can't see our enemy/so, we'll just have to kill each other." Yet the enemy is in plain view: residential schools, racism, expropriation, extinguishment, wardship, welfare. In fact, the problem is not so much blindness as it is aversion to the truth that although "they" began our oppression "we" have to a large degree perpetuated it.

Long-term subjugation has a series of effects on both the mind and the soul. We must recognize and take seriously the effects of colonial oppression on both individual and collective levels. In many people's view, political and economic problems are less urgent than the damage to our psychological health. As the psychologist Eduardo Duran has characterized the problem,

> Once a group of people have been assaulted in a genocidal fashion, there are psychological ramifications. With the victim's complete loss of power comes despair, and the psyche reacts by internalizing what appears to be genuine power—the power of the oppressor. The internalizing process begins when Native American people internalize the oppressor, which is merely a caricature of the power actually taken from Native American people. At this point, the self-worth of the individual and/or group has sunk to a level of despair tantamount to self-hatred. This self-hatred can be either internalized or externalized.

Could there be a clearer statement of the essential problems besetting Native communities? Denied, medicated, rationalized, ignored, or hated, this is a reality that affects all indigenous people to one degree or another.

Men bear a special guilt. Many men have added to Native women's oppression by inflicting pain on their wives, daughters, mothers, and sisters. Once we fully understand the idea of oppression, it doesn't take much further insight to see that men's inability to confront the real source of their disempowerment and weakness leads to compound oppression for women. This is a deep and universal problem that continues to exist despite the positive economic and political developments that have taken place in indigenous communities during the last two generations. Internalized oppression manifests itself in various ways. Women as well as men express it in many kinds of self-destructive behaviour. For a lot of indigenous men, however, rage is externalized, and some cowards take out their frustration on women and children rather than risk confronting the real (and still dangerous) oppressor. The 1995 film *Once Were Warriors* about spousal abuse among the Maori of Aotearoa (New Zealand) captures the essence of this problem for all indigenous people. Gendered violence is endemic in most societies, but the fact that our cultures were founded on gender equality and respect makes it a special betrayal in Native communities. That the violence perpetrated by Native men on Native women constitutes a further subjugation compounds the gravity of the crime.

We are entitled to lay blame but not to make excuses. Colonization created the conditions of material and social deprivation, but the failure to confront them is our own. Why have we directed our anger at ourselves and our families rather than its source? There are three prerequisites for recovery: awareness of the pain's source; conscious withdrawal from an isolated, unfocused state of rage; and development of a supportive community and the courage to begin attacking the causes of discontent and deprivation.

"A Responsibility to Our Ancestors"

It is incumbent on this generation of Native people to heal the colonial sickness through the re-creation of sound communities, individual empowerment, and the re-establishment of relationships based on traditional values. This is the burden placed on young shoulders by the elders and ancestors who carried the torch through many years of darkness. It is not enough to survive and heal; there is also a responsibility to rebuild the foundations of nationhood by recovering a holistic traditional philosophy, reconnecting with our spirituality and culture, and infusing our politics and relationships with traditional values.

> I pray that I can take care of myself until the day I go, because I see so many elders being badly abused by their families. This is a loss of culture, a loss of identity, and a loss of tradition. One of the things I find is that people will fall back on how they were raised and what happened to them, saying, Well, my father was a cruel man, and I have low self-esteem, and I can't comprehend what you are teaching me about love and kindness and giving. And I say, Do not fall back on that kind of garbage. The Creator gave you a sound mind and an incredible spirit and a way of being so that you can do anything right now! You can change that attitude same as you wake up in the morning and it's a new day. Your mind and everything else can be new. I've lived through hardships and horror, and I'm a loving, caring, giving person because I choose to be that way. I choose to listen to the other side to guide me. We all have the ability with our spirit to change things right now.
>
> —Osoka Bousko, Woodland Cree
> (Johnson, ed., *The Book of Elders*, 60)

The gradual transformation of Native communities from threatened to confident, from sick to healthy, from weak to strong, will be a collective effort. But the collective will require the shining lights of leadership provided by individual guides and mentors. This kind of leadership will be the most crucial element in our recovery from colonial oppression.

Native people can't cry their way to nationhood. Fulfilling the responsibility to reconstruct the nation means moving beyond the politics of pity. A sensitive pragmatism is needed to reinfuse our societies with the positive energy required to confront the continuing injustice, protect what remains, and build our own future. Mainstream self-help and "new age" esteem work is not enough. Without a foundation in the traditional teachings and a connection to community development, such efforts represent nothing more than self-centred escapism and denial of the fundamental problem. It is not enough to think of individual healing. As the Cree educator Roslyn Ing told me, if we are to "honour what our ancestors went through and died for," we have "a responsibility ... to want to exist as Cree people and to carry on."

The time for blaming the white man, the far away and long ago, is over. People should recognize that the real enemy is close enough to touch. As a chief of the Ehattesaht tribe on North Vancouver Island told me,

> People don't appreciate traditional values, and don't live according to them. They have more immediate concerns and have neglected the important things. The biggest problem is that people have developed a victim mentality and blame everyone else for their oppression rather than doing the work to raise themselves out of it. The culture of dependency and the feeling of defeat are our biggest problems.

As long as the federal government works to keep Native people politically and economically dependent, leaders will need to resist the state's efforts to undermine the integrity of the culture and prevent the reclamation of the traditional ways that are the keys to empowerment.

But what does it mean to reclaim traditional ways? One kind of "retraditionalized" leadership has been defined with reference to indigenous women who have extended "traditional caretaking and cultural transmission roles to include activities vital to the continuity of Indian communities within a predominantly non-Indian society":

American Indian women have achieved success by exhibiting independence, leadership, confidence, competitiveness, and emotional control. Without ignoring their cultural heritage, losing acceptance among their people, or forfeiting the ability to behave appropriately within Indian cultures, Indian women leaders have increased respect and status for Indian people and gained professional recognition for themselves.

These people are to be respected for their abilities and their success in challenging racism within the professions of the establishment. However, there is a substantial difference between this type of activity and the perspective on leadership that I am advocating. While gaining the respect of mainstream society is perhaps a necessary element in the decolonization process, it is essentially individualist. What the authors of the passage above would term a Native "leader" is actually a person who has become successful in European/American society by mastering the skills, knowledge, and behaviours required for white success. To become a role model and contribute to the mainstream society while still maintaining a respected position in one's nation is very fine, but it is not leadership in the truest sense.

This notion of retraditionalized Native leadership lacks one essential component: participation in, and support for, the nation's collective struggle. It is the duty of Native leaders to satisfy not mainstream but indigenous cultural criteria. To be sure, making a positive contribution is an important aspect of leadership, but individual success is not enough. To become a true leader, one must go far beyond.

Is it possible to be prominent and esteemed in one world without being marginal in the other? Is it possible to compromise, to meet the demands of both worlds? Ultimately, I think the real question is, "Can Native people afford to lose even one potential leader to the pursuit of success as defined by the mainstream society?"

Brothers and Sisters:

These words are a prayer of hope for a new
path to wisdom and power.

Anguished hearts, minds, and bodies
are the profound reality of our world.
We have lost our way
and the voices of our ancestors go unheeded.

This is our ordeal.

There are those who remember
what has had meaning since time began
but we are deaf to their wisdom.

Why do we not hear them?
Suffering; the dragons of discord.

Wipe the tears from your eyes
Open your ears to the truth
Prepare to speak in the voice of your ancestors.

This is a discourse of condolence.
A prayer of hope for a new path.

Power

The chiefs ... shall be mentors of the people for all time. The thickness of their skin shall be seven spans nine, which is to say that they shall be proof against anger, offensive action, and criticism. Their hearts shall be full of peace and good will, and their minds filled with a yearning for the welfare of the people.... With endless patience, they shall carry out their duty. Their firmness shall be tempered with a tenderness for their people. Neither anger nor fury shall find lodging in their minds and all their words and actions shall be marked by calm deliberation.

—from the *Kaienerekowa*

In Native American cultures, empowerment means requickening the traditional spirit of leadership. In the political tradition of the Rotinohshonni, upon the death of a leader, the spirit of the nation must be brought back to life. A new leader must be brought forward who will make a grieving nation whole again by reconnecting its members with the past and the ancient way of peace, power, and righteousness.

Metaphors of death and recovery through reconnection tend to resonate with indigenous people generally, sharing as they do a history of loss. That resonance attests to the need to make tradition more than an artifact—to bring traditional values and approaches to power back to life as guiding principles for contemporary governance. We need to realize that ways of thinking that perpetuate European values can do nothing to ease the pain of colonization and return us to the harmony, balance, and peaceful coexistence that were—and are—the ideals envisioned in all traditional indigenous philosophies. In fact, it is not possible to reach those goals in the context of Western institutions at all, because those institutions were designed within the framework of a very different belief system, to achieve very different objectives.

We had no places to practice freedom of religion. No place where we could build a fireplace and sweat lodges and worship the Creator in the way that we needed to connect with Him. We need that connectedness

> to feel like living again. To stop feeling suicidal, wanting to kill ourselves with alcohol and drugs. We had to find our connection again, and we found it in our ancient ceremonies, which are still valid today as they were way back then. People say you can't go back in the past and live in a tipi, but the living laws that we were taught are still with us today.
>
> —Janet McCloud, Tulalip (Johnson, ed., *The Book of Elders*, 60)

For example, consider the question of justice—the source of the notions of right and wrong that underpin all discussions of the nature and use of power. The dominant Western conception of justice is rooted in a fundamentally individualistic, materialistic ideal of equity or sameness. By contrast, indigenous notions of justice arose within the context of belief in a universal relationship among all the elements that make up our universe. Native ideas centre on the imperative of respectful, balanced coexistence among all human, animal, and spirit beings, together with the earth. Justice is seen as a perpetual process of maintaining that crucial balance and demonstrating true respect for the power and dignity of each part of the circle of interdependency.

Injustice is perceived as dysfunction—an erosion at some point that disturbs the crucial balance. In the sphere of politics and social relations, for example, dysfunction may result from the degeneration of a person's or a community's natural power through neglect of traditional wisdom, or through disrespect for the dignity of creation (other people, other beings, nature, or oneself), upsetting the balance of power, of peace and harmony. The goal of indigenous justice is best characterized as the achievement of respectful coexistence—restoration of harmony to the network of relationships and renewed commitment to ensuring the integrity and physical, emotional, and spiritual health of all individuals and communities. Indigenous ideas of justice differ from Western ideas in three basic ways: (1) They are not concerned primarily with questions of equity in treatment or distribution; (2) There is no universalizing or levelling imperative that may be used to justify the limitation of freedom; and (3) The cultural framework that determines whether or not power is used appropriately includes not only the set of human relationships that form our society, but all other relationships as well.

Consider the intimate relationship among politics, morality, and economies. Whereas Western concepts of justice treat these separately, in indigenous societies right or wrong is determined by the broad effect of a specific action on all elements of the universe. Justice consists in maintaining the state of harmonious coexistence that is the goal of all political, spiritual, and economic activity.

In the indigenous view, determination of right and wrong cannot be abstracted from the particular context of the action or person in question, because re-establishing harmony requires not only consideration of all the elements concerned but their active participation in resolving the issue. That resolution involves dialogue, explanation, and repair of the fabric of the particular relationship—that is, healing. Justice is the process of healing relationships so that each element in creation can live its natural power and fulfil its responsibility.

The difference between indigenous and Western concepts of justice can be seen in their approaches to conflict resolution. Injustice in the indigenous sense is the absence of balance and harmony. It does not consist in the commission of a particular act, however defined; acts may be seen as unjust, but only in their effect. Sanctions are not unknown to indigenous societies; but, whereas in Western justice systems they are used for punishment, in indigenous systems their purpose is to restore harmony—to re-establish peaceful coexistence with respect for the integrity of each element in the particular set of relationships that make up the context of the issue in question.

One of the major differences between the Western and indigenous conceptions of power and justice is that the cultural values that determine fairness in the Western conception are limited (with a few rare exceptions) to human society. Among indigenous people, the cultural framework used to determine whether or not power is used appropriately includes not only human social relationships but all other relationships as well. The indigenous conception of justice goes beyond humanism and environmentalism to touch the realm of the spirit. It considers each natural element in the universe to have an integral power and purpose that must be recognized and respected. In effect, there is a sacred relationship not only among human beings or between human beings and the physical world, but among all creatures and elements and extending to the realm of the spirit. Each one of these relationships must be honoured and preserved if human purpose is to be fulfilled. Justice is the achievement of balance in all these relationships and the demonstration in both thought and action of respect for the dignity of each element in the circle of interdependency that forms our universe.

This concept of justice requires that people have an intimate knowledge of traditional teachings. It is holistic in the truest sense. Justice embodies the state of balance that exists when a community has achieved harmony in all the relationships out of which it is formed, on both individual and collective levels. The entire circle is broken and the universe is amiss if one aspect or elemental relationship is unbalanced or disrespected. The objective can be achieved only through the promotion of healthy minds, bodies, and souls among individuals, who then make sound families and build strong nations.

Thus, the philosophical premises underpinning indigenous notions of justice and power differ radically from those that support most Western formulations. Acknowledging the existence of power in all the elements that make up the universe, indigenous philosophies teach us to respect and accommodate that power in all its varied forms. The principles of respect and coexistence guided indigenous peoples for countless generations. But their displacement as a result of colonization has created a need to confront new questions, and the truth and relevance of traditional philosophies are being tested against history.

Using traditional philosophy as the foundation of a new movement for indigenous governance will help us restore the lost harmony between indigenous people's social and political cultures. If political legitimacy flows from harmony between a community's cultural values and the values embedded within its political institutions, then this deep traditionalism is the key to overcoming the divisions and fractionalization that characterize Native politics today.

The Abuse of Power

One reason we have lost our way is that the materialistic mainstream value system has blinded us to the subtle beauty of indigenous systems founded on a profound respect for balance. Without that respect, the system fails. We must reorient our societies to provide leaders with a basis for conduct rooted in indigenous culture, to restore—bring back to life—traditional political cultures by abandoning the structures imposed on us and by exorcising the attitudes, beliefs, and values that perpetuate our colonization.

In his classic study *Leadership* (1978), James MacGregor Burns developed the concept of "moral leadership." Identifying a fundamental difference between what he called "power-wielders" and true leaders, he argued that the manipulation of resources to effect the personal will or interest of the manipulator is not leadership at all; leadership must be rooted in a set of personal values consistent with and supportive of the collective's values. Burns's concept of moral leadership complements indigenous ideas. In particular, his critique of "leaders" who are actually nothing more than politicians resembles the criticism expressed by many indigenous people with respect to their new leaders.

For Burns, the average politician in an electoral system is simply playing a power game in which he structures incentives to induce people to do what he wants: to vote for a certain party, to support a particular policy, to carry out a given order. There is no consideration of the deeper (non-economic) motives and desires of the target of the manipulation. As Burns puts it, there's "no engagement" between the power-wielder and the follower. Where the follower's goals are satisfied, it is only because interest groups have either threatened to take away the power-wielder's base of support or managed to convince him that the goal is in his interest as well; most often, the group that does see its goals satisfied happens to be the one to which the power-wielder will return when the electoral game is up.

Except for some emerging discursive forms of democracy, this description is true of contemporary politics generally, including the political systems that have been imposed in Native communities. The imposition of electoral politics in place of consensual models and the emulation of Western politicians has made Native politics just as much a matter of cynical manipulation of power as any other kind. More important, the disengagement of leaders from their collectives in these systems has undermined the integrity of indigenous communities to the extent that there appear to be two distinct cultures; the interests and attitudes of office-holders often differ radically from those of the rest of the group.

How can we reconnect Native power-wielders to their communities and traditions? We have to disentangle their interests from those of the state, and to replace the manipulative Western notion of leadership with one based on traditional indigenous values.

Traditional indigenous cultures are remarkably coherent and comprehensive moral and ethical systems; but, they have been damaged by colonialism and weakened by neglect. Strengthening traditional institutions means undertaking a conscious revitalization, relearning those systems and rediscovering respect for the values that support them. To transcend the corrupt politics of the mainstream, we must begin by rejecting the institutions and values that perpetuate it. As individuals, Native people—leaders and followers alike—must seek to develop the moral qualities that will allow their communities to avoid the cynical manipulation so prevalent in contemporary politics.

Power-wielding aside, leadership should reflect indigenous values. Beyond the simple imperatives to provide for safety and security, maintain law and order, and uphold the social contract, indigenous forms of government promote the realization of spiritual objectives and high values such as peace and harmony. In this context, leadership has nothing to do with tests of will or adversarial power games; rather, it involves sensing the common good and guiding people toward fulfilment of their needs within the parameters established by traditional cultural values. As Burns describes it in the context of a morally grounded Western society,

> The essence of leadership … is the recognition of real need, the uncovering and exploiting of contradictions among values and between values and practice, the realigning of values, the re-organization of institutions where necessary, and the governance of change.

As Burns points out, the true distinction among leaders is between those with a commitment to general values rooted in the culture and the responsibilities to which they give rise, and those concerned with lesser values and a more narrow, self-defined set of responsibilities. This brings us back to the difference between Native leaders who promote indigenous empowerment on individual and collective levels within a framework of traditional cultural values, and Native power-wielders who serve the interests of the state, and/or a narrow self-interest that conflicts with the general good of the community.

Re-empowerment

Under colonization, hundreds of indigenous nations that were previously autonomous and self-governing suffered a loss of freedom. Even today, the lives of their people are controlled by others. The problems faced by social workers, political scientists, physicians, and teachers can all be traced to this power relationship, to the control of Native lives by a foreign power. In the midst of Western societies that pride themselves on their respect for freedom, the freedom of indigenous people to realize their own goals has been extinguished by the state in law and, to a great degree, in practice. Above all, indigenous nationhood is about reconstructing a power base for the assertion of control over Native land and life. This should be the primary objective of Native politics.

The problem is that, at present, Native politics is still understood and practised in the context of the law as structured by the state. Within this context, the state has nothing to fear from Native leaders, for even if they succeed in achieving the goal of self-government, the basic power structure remains intact. From the perspective of the state, marginal losses of control are the trade-off for the ultimate preservation of the framework of dominance. What we need is a nationalist perspective that directly challenges that framework. A first step in developing that perspective is to understand the intellectual basis of the state's control over Native people. We must deconstruct the notion of state power to allow people to see that the settler state has no right to determine indigenous futures.

In the conventional Western understanding, a leader's power is based on control of certain strategic resources: for example, service provision, connections to the outside, and specific symbols with special meaning within the culture. It is exercised by manipulating various resources to secure changes in a target. Thus, power in the Western sense involves the imposition of an individual's will upon others. Even the most progressive non-indigenous notions of power, such as the one developed by Burns, still involve satisfying the personal motives of the leader. While Burns distinguishes between "naked power," in which there is no engagement of leader to follower, and real leadership, in which the goals of leader and follower are merged, power is still defined in terms of "securing changes in the behaviour of the respondent, human or animal, and in the environment." Especially for indigenous peoples—all too familiar with state power founded on coercion—Burns's naked power seems the norm.

Michel Foucault identified two ways of understanding state power. The first sees state sovereignty as being created through the contractual surrender of individual rights. In this view, it is the abuse of state power—its extension beyond the accepted legal framework—that results in "oppression" of individuals. Most of Western political theory concerns the tensions that arise within a constitutionally regulated matrix of political power.

The other, deeper, understanding of power proposed by Foucault sees the overextension of state power within a constitutional framework not as abuse but as the "mere effect and continuation of a relation of domination" that is fundamental—"a perpetual relation of force." Instead of defining oppression as an overextension of state power within a legal framework,

Foucault points to the continual domination by force necessary to maintain that framework itself. This approach is particularly useful for analyzing the relationship between the state and indigenous peoples—an approach in which not only the expression and extension of state power but the entire framework on which the sovereignty of the state depends is in question.

A critique of state power that sees oppression as an inevitable function of the state, even when it is constrained by a constitutionally defined social–political contract, should have special resonance for indigenous people, since their nations were never party to any contract and yet have been forced to operate within a framework that presupposes the legitimacy of state sovereignty over them. Arguing for rights within that framework only reinforces the state's anti-historic claim to sovereignty by contract.

By accepting that claim, we empower the state to dominate indigenous peoples. In this way, "perpetual relations of force" have become the norm. Indigenous people, of course, recognize the difference between the coercive state and their traditional systems. But, in seeking to empower themselves, do they run the risk of reproducing the power relations based on domination that Foucault recognized in the state? Is it possible to resist state domination in this regard?

The state attempts to rewrite history to legitimize its exercise of power (sovereignty) over indigenous peoples. Native people struggle to resist the co-optation of their historical sense. But the fact remains that in order to negotiate a withdrawal from the colonial relationship indigenous people must still interact with the state, which uses all kinds of incentives to prevent Native leaders from representing traditional understandings.

Traditionalists, recognizing the risk of intellectual co-optation, have adopted a traditional solution: focusing not on opposing external power, but on actualizing their own power and preserving their intellectual independence. This is an indigenous approach to empowerment. Unlike the statist version, this conception of power is not predicated on force. It does not involve coercing or inducing other beings to fulfil imperatives external to their own nature; thus, it is not inherently conflictual. Nor does it require a contractual surrender of power, leading to continuous tension between the individual and the state. Furthermore, it is consistent with Foucault's thoughts on the direction away from state sovereignty:

If one wants to look for a non-disciplinary form of power, or rather, to struggle against disciplines and disciplinary power, it is not toward the ancient right of sovereignty that one should turn, but towards the possibility of a new form of right, one which must indeed be anti-disciplinarian, but at the same time liberated from the principle of sovereignty.

The alternative to state power offered by the indigenous tradition transforms our understanding of power's meaning and use. There are many potential benefits to such a reorientation, not only within Native communities but as the foundation for building a post-colonial relationship with the state.

On the meaning of power, indigenous thought has traditionally focused on questions regarding the legitimacy of the nature and use of power, rather than its distribution. Within indigenous cultures, it is recognized that forms and levels of power vary, depending on the spiritual and physical resources available to the individual. There have always been two basic questions: (1) What kinds of power do individuals have? and (2) Are they using it appropriately? In other words, the traditional indigenous view of power and justice has nothing to do with competition or status vis-à-vis others. It focuses on whether or not power is used in a way that contributes to the creation and maintenance of balance and peaceful coexistence in a web of relationships.

The Tlingit people on the coast of the Northwest speak of power as shagóon: "ancestors, origins, heritage and destiny/supreme being." Unlike the English version, this is not an inherently oppositional concept. By understanding and embodying these ideas, a person contributes to the achievement and maintenance of the crucial balance. Power is the force needed by all to achieve peace and harmony. Where differences in the understanding of power come into play is in the various forms power can take, and the spiritual elements of the natural order that regulate and structure the expression of power in the temporal world. In the 1980s, the Okanagan elder, Harry Robinson, explained his understanding of power this way:

> *See?*
> *That's another power way.*
> *He's a powerful man, but—*
> > *he can tell what's coming coming to him*
> > > *in a certain time.*
> *But he can't stop it,*
> > *he can't beat it.*
> *So he die that way,*
> > *by the other power's order.*

Robinson's "powerful man" understands and respects other people's power as well as his own—he does not try to stop, or to beat, that which flows from an exercise of power within a natural order.

There is a fundamental consistency between this notion of power and the notions expressed in many other indigenous cultures. Among the Havasupai people of the American Southwest, the basic term is sumáaga: "a spirit or power in certain living things and natural phenomena." In the 1960s, the ethnomusicologist Leanne Hinton described how this notion of power was expressed in the Havasupai women's curative songs. Human beings gain access to a natural power source through ritual; in other words, power is summoned and hosted by human beings who become conduits for it. Humans become powerful by understanding the rituals. They obtain power by demonstrating respect for the forces that control nature and the universe. Without a connection to the spiritual resources—provided by sumáaje, spirit beings that communicate with humans through songs obtained in dreams—that are the most important and non–material elements in the universe, human beings are powerless.

The central concern is not about harnessing power, or taking it from nature, to use for a temporal purpose. As Hinton explains of the Havasupai, this concept of power (or what is more commonly thought of as a type of "medicine man" power) is concerned with creating engagement, maintaining a connection and celebrating the relationship between the people and the source of nature/power:

> It is the sumáaje himself, by his own intention, who brings about the powerful results of curing illness (or creating it, if the song is sung at the wrong time!), changing the weather, ensuring good crops, and generally affecting the course of natural events.

Among other traditional indigenous understandings of power, the Diné (Navajo) power concept of diyin offers a particularly complex view of the application of power in relations between human beings, and between human beings and their universe. In Diné culture, power exists along a continuum between two poles: báhádzid, or danger, and adziil, or strength—a form of power based on knowledge acquired through ritual learning. In other words, where there is power there is danger, but it can be mediated through knowledge. For the Diné, then, there is a progression of power from danger to goodness: "All beings in the universe, whether they are in the realm of diyinii, human beings, natural phenomena, or whatever, can be placed on this continuum and differentiated according to the particular knowledge and concomitant power they possess." A "powerful" human being is one who has become intimate with diyinii. There is no distinction between these people as humans and as beings in the spiritual realm. They hold power through their practice of ritual and by virtue of the knowledge they have obtained. At the height of power, there is a profound experience of oneness with nature and the spiritual realm.

A Diné battle song from the 1930s invokes the force of nature–power to inspire fear in the enemy:

Big Black Bear.
My moccasins are black obsidian.
My leggings are black obsidian.
My shirt is black obsidian.
I am girdled with a gray arrow snake.
Black snakes project from my head.
With zigzag lightning projecting from the ends of my feet I step.
With zigzag lightning streaming out from my knees I step.
With zigzag lightning streaming out from the tips of my fingers I work my
*   hands.*
With zigzag lightning streaming out from the tip of my tongue I speak.
Now a disk of pollen rests on the crown of my head.
Gray arrow snakes and rattlesnakes eat it.
Black obsidian and zigzag lightning streams out from me in four ways.
Where they strike the earth, bad things bad talk does not like it.
It causes the missiles to spread out.
Long life, something frightful I am.
Now I am.

To hold power, it is necessary to gain knowledge through life experience and directed learning from elders. A classic anthropological study of the Diné describes their belief that learning begins when one realizes the power of the diyinii to cause misfortune:

It is at this point, when one begins to believe but has no knowledge, that the world is most fearful. One then begins to learn the stories and the ceremonies in an effort to transcend this fear ... a point is reached where fear is no longer the predominant emotional coloring of one's relationship with diyinii. That fear is replaced with respect. This respect describes a relationship between equals or near equals, whereas fear characterizes a relationship of subordination.

A Paiute song told by the Acoma writer Simon Ortiz reflects a similar understanding of power:

That's the Indian way.
Singing,
That's the Indian way!
And pretty soon it's there.
You know it's all around, it's right there.
And the people are right there . . .
The people talking, telling the power to come to them
And pretty soon it will come, it will come,
The moving power of the voice,
The moving power of the earth,'
The moving power of the people.
That's the place Indian people talk about.

In traditional indigenous cultures, access to power is gained through balancing the diverse aspects of our being, harmonization with the natural forces that exist outside us, respect for the integrity of others and the diverse forms of power, and knowledge of ritual.

The Kanien'kehaka Kaswentha (Two-Row Wampum) principle embodies this notion of power in the context of relations between nations. Instead of subjugating one to the other, the Kanien'kehaka who opened their territory to Dutch traders in the early seventeenth century negotiated an original and lasting peace based on coexistence of power in a context of respect for the autonomy and distinctive nature of each partner. The metaphor for this relationship—two vessels, each possessing its own integrity, travelling the river of time together—was conveyed visually on a wampum belt of two parallel purple lines (representing power) on a background of white beads (representing peace). In this respectful (co-equal) friendship and alliance, any interference with the other partner's autonomy, freedom, or powers was expressly forbidden. So long as these principles were respected, the relationship would be peaceful, harmonious, and just.

It is with indigenous notions of power such as these that contemporary Native nationalism seeks to replace the dividing, alienating, and exploitative notions, based on fear, that drive politics inside and outside Native communities today. This goal differs significantly from the revolutionary objectives of earlier phases of the Native movement. Not only is revolution in the classic sense unworkable, given the relatively small numbers of indigenous peoples in North America today, but it is contrary to the basic principles of traditional indigenous philosophies. Indigenous peoples do not seek to destroy the state, but to make it more just and to improve their relations with the mainstream society. The principles embedded in cultural ideals such as the Kaswentha are in fact consistent with some Western principles that have been nearly forgotten in the construction of the modern hegemonic state—among them, the original principle of federalism. Indigenous empowerment involves achieving a relationship between peoples founded on the principles of autonomy and interdependence. To accommodate indigenous notions of nationhood and cease its interference in indigenous communities, the state need only refer to the federal principle.

In traditional systems, it was essential for communities to cultivate relationships with their neighbours that would allow for ongoing dialogue and dispute resolution. This principle was embodied in numerous confederal unions that promoted harmony and co-operation. Today, in many cases, such co-operation is hindered by political, racial, and legal differences between neighbouring communities. The time has come to recognize our mutual dependency, to realize that indigenous and non-indigenous communities are permanent features of our political and social landscape, to embrace the notion of respectful co-operation on equal terms, and to apply the peacemaking principles on which were based both the many great pre-contact North American confederacies and the later alliances that allowed European societies to establish themselves and flourish on this continent.

In addition, we must recognize that we can never achieve the goal of peaceful coexistence as long as we continue to accept the classic notion of sovereignty as the framework for discussions of political relations between indigenous peoples and the state. The late Vine Deloria, Jr, a highly respected and influential Dakota scholar, distinguished between the indigenous concept of nationhood and the statist concept based on a sovereign political authority (sovereignty). Deloria saw nationhood as distinct from "self-government" (or the "domestic dependent nations" status accorded indigenous peoples in the United States). The right of "self-determination," unbounded by state law, is a concept appropriate to nations. By contrast, delegated forms of authority, such as "self-government" within the context of state sovereignty, are appropriate to what we might call "minority peoples," or other ethnically defined groups within the polity as a whole.

Beyond the question of the source of authority and its implications for nationhood, however, there are practical drawbacks to implementing a form of government based on sovereignty in communities with completely different perspectives on the nature and appropriate use of power. According to Deloria, provisions for "self-government" and other state-delegated forms of authority in indigenous communities are not wrong; they are simply inadequate because they do not take into account the spiritual needs of indigenous societies:

> Self-government is not an Indian idea. It originates in the minds of non-Indians who have reduced the traditional ways to dust, or believe they have, and now wish to give, as a gift, a limited measure of local control and responsibility. Self-government is an exceedingly useful concept for Indians to use when dealing with the larger government because it provides a context within which negotiations can take place. Since it will never supplant the intangible, spiritual, and emotional aspirations of American Indians, it cannot be regarded as the final solution to Indian problems.

I would go even further than Deloria on this point. "Sovereignty" as it is currently understood and applied in indigenous–state relations cannot be seen as an appropriate goal or framework, because it has no relevance to indigenous values. The challenge before us is to detach the notion of sovereignty from its current legal meaning and use in the context of the Western understanding of power and relationships. We need to create a meaning for sovereignty that respects the understanding of power in indigenous cultures, one that reflects more of the sense embodied in such Western notions as "personal sovereignty" and "popular sovereignty." Until then, sovereignty can never be part of the language of liberation.

My principal cause is freedom. I'm old enough to remember what it was like to be free. Free from harassment by police, free from harassment by fisheries. And so it's difficult for me to give up the struggle because I want to be there when we win our freedom. When I speak about freedom, that means I want the recognition of our sovereignty, as the first people not only of Canada but of the States. I believe that we should be recognized as indigenous people, with the right to make our own decisions and govern ourselves. To once again take control of our lives, our lands, and our resources.... People talk about this country being a free country. They have no idea of freedom. If you ever had the taste of freedom that I have known, you would never give it up, you'd fight for it like I do.

—Thowhegwelth, Haida (Johnson, ed., *The Book of Elders*, 190–93)

Sovereignty: An Inappropriate Concept

The concept of sovereignty as Native leaders have constructed it thus far is incompatible with traditional indigenous notions of power. Nevertheless, until now, it has been an effective vehicle for indigenous critiques of the state's imposition of control. By forcing the state to recognize major inconsistencies between its own principles and its treatment of Native people, it has pointed to the racism and contradiction inherent in settler states' claimed authority over non-consenting peoples. In fact, it has become obsolete mainly because of the success the best Native leaders have had in creating the space required for greater assertion of self-governing powers.

Even so, the suitability of sovereignty as the primary political goal of indigenous people has gone largely unquestioned. It is taken for granted that what indigenous peoples are seeking in recognition of their nationhood is essentially what countries such as Canada and the United States possess now. In fact, most of the current generation of Native politicians see politics as a zero-sum contest for power—just the way non-indigenous politicians do.

There is real danger in the assumption that sovereignty is the appropriate model for indigenous government. The Canadian scholars Menno Boldt and Tony Long have described that danger in the context of their work among the Blood and Peigan peoples:

By adopting the European-Western ideology of sovereignty, the current generation of Indian leaders is buttressing the imposed alien authority structures within its communities, and is legitimizing the associated hierarchy comprised of indigenous political and bureaucratic elites. This endorsement of hierarchical authority and a ruling entity constitutes a complete rupture with traditional indigenous principles.

Traditional indigenous nationhood stands in sharp contrast to the dominant understanding of "the state": There is no absolute authority, no coercive enforcement of decisions, no hierarchy, and no separate ruling entity. In accepting the idea that progress is attainable within the framework of the state, therefore, indigenous people are moving toward acceptance of forms of government that more closely resemble the state than traditional systems. Is it possible to accomplish good in a system designed to promote harm? Yes, on the margins. But, eventually, the grinding engine of discord and deprivation will obliterate the marginal good. The real goal should be to stop that engine.

Instead of treating nationhood as a value rooted in traditional indigenous philosophy, many Native politicians seem to regard it as a lever to gain a better bargaining position. As the former Assembly of First Nations' head Ovide Mercredi said in 1996, "I'm not going to allow my philosophy of sovereignty to interfere with the working relationship that can produce the results we're working for. That's all it is, a philosophy." For such politicians, there is a dichotomy between philosophical principle and politics. They don't really believe in a sovereign right for indigenous peoples; it is simply a bargaining chip, a lever for concessions within the established constitutional framework. The problem is that if Natives don't believe in it, no one else will—which explains the consistent failure to achieve recognition of a "sovereign" Native power.

Because shallow-minded politicians do not take the concept of sovereignty seriously, they are unable to grasp that asserting a right to sovereignty has significant implications. In making a claim to sovereignty—even if they don't really mean it—they are making a choice to accept the state as their model and to allow indigenous political goals to be framed and evaluated according to a "statist" pattern. Thus, the common criteria of statehood—coercive force, control of territory, population numbers, international recognition—come to dominate discussion of indigenous peoples' political goals as well.

This is not only a movement away from traditional indigenous philosophies and values, but it is also transparently disingenuous in terms of the sovereignty model itself. Who would believe that indigenous nations could ever successfully challenge Canada and the United States to win their sovereignty? No one, apparently, because even those who advocate sovereignty as a goal seek only a limited form of autonomy, not independence; the goal relates only to powers of self-government within a framework of constitutional law and authorities delegated by the state. Canada's Mercredi has described his goal of sovereignty in terms of the limited authority granted to American Indian tribes by the US Congress:

> We are not talking about secession. We are talking about essentially gaining and regaining control of our lives. American Indians do not have to negotiate their powers of self-government because their internal political authority is recognized by the Supreme Court of the land.

Thus, the Native sovereigntist must modify the concept of sovereignty to fit his limited goals. But the simple act of framing the goal in terms of sovereignty is harmful in itself. "Sovereignty" implies a set of values and objectives in direct opposition to those found in traditional indigenous philosophies. Non-indigenous politicians recognize the inherent weakness of assertions of a sovereign right for peoples who have neither the cultural framework nor the institutional capacity to sustain it. The problem is that the assertion of a sovereign right for indigenous peoples continues to structure the politics of decolonization, and the state uses the theoretical inconsistencies in that position to its own advantage.

A case in point is the issue of land claims. The resolution of such claims (addressing the legal inconsistency of Crown or state title to indigenous lands) is generally seen by progressive non-indigenous people as a step in the right direction. But without a fundamental questioning of the assumptions underpinning the state's approach to power, the counterfactual assumptions of colonialism will continue to structure the relationship between the state and indigenous peoples. Within this framework, any progress made toward justice will be marginal; in fact, it will be tolerated by the state only to the extent that it serves, or at least does not oppose, the interests of the state itself.

In Canada, for example, the ongoing definition of the concept of "Aboriginal rights and title" by the Supreme Court since the 1980s is widely seen as progress. Yet, even with a legal recognition of collective rights to certain subsistence activities within certain territories, indigenous people are still subject to state control in the exercise of their inherent freedoms and powers. They must also meet state-defined criteria for Aboriginal identity in order to gain access to these legal rights. Given Canada's shameful history, defining Aboriginal rights in terms of, for example, a right to fish for food and traditional purposes is better than nothing. But to what extent does that state-regulated "right" to food-fish represent justice for people who have been fishing on their rivers and seas since time began?

To argue on behalf of indigenous nationhood within the dominant Western paradigm is self-defeating. To frame the struggle to achieve justice in terms of indigenous "claims" against the state is implicitly to accept the fiction of state sovereignty. Indigenous peoples are by definition the original inhabitants of the land. They had complex societies and systems of government. And they never gave consent to European ownership of territory or the establishment of European sovereignty over them (treaties did not do this, according to both historic Native understandings and contemporary legal analysis). These are indisputable realities based on empirically verifiable facts. So why are indigenous efforts to achieve legal recognition of these facts framed as claims? The mythology of the state is hegemonic, and the struggle for justice would be better served by undermining the myth of state sovereignty than by carving out a small and dependent space for indigenous peoples within it.

The need to perpetuate a set of fictive legal premises and fact-denying myths is apparent in every legal act of the state. To justify the establishment of non-indigenous sovereignty, aboriginality in a true sense must necessarily be excluded and denied. Otherwise, it would seem ridiculous that the original inhabitants of a place should be forced to justify their existence to a crude horde of refugees from another continent. As the European scholar Fae Korsmo has pointed out, the loss of collective memory is an essential requirement for creating a colonial reality:

> The people already living in or near the area have no role in the new myths, except perhaps as enemies or a dying race. They represent a noble yet doomed past that must be prevented from becoming a present-day threat. Insofar as the colonial mythology has put the burden on the indigenous societies to justify their claims in terms of their origins and hardy continuity, the doctrine of aboriginal title is part of colonialism and therefore dooms the indigenous claimants to failure.

To summarize the argument thus far, sovereignty is an exclusionary concept rooted in an adversarial and coercive Western notion of power. Indigenous peoples can never match the awesome coercive force of the state; so long as sovereignty remains the goal of indigenous politics. Therefore, Native communities will occupy a dependent and reactionary position relative to the state. Acceptance of Aboriginal rights and title in the context of state sovereignty represents the culmination of white society's efforts to assimilate indigenous peoples.

Framing indigenous people in the past as "noble yet doomed" relics of an earlier age allows the colonial state to maintain its own legitimacy by preventing the fact of contemporary indigenous peoples' nationhood to intrude on its own mythology. Native people imperil themselves by accepting formulations of their own identities and rights that prevent them from transcending the past. The state relegates indigenous peoples' rights to the past, and constrains the development of their societies by allowing only those activities that support its own necessary illusion: that indigenous peoples today do not present a serious challenge to its legitimacy. Thus, the state celebrates paint and feathers and Indian dancing, because they reinforce the image of doomed nobility that justified the pretense of European sovereignty on Turtle Island. Tribal casinos, Indian tax immunity, and Aboriginal fisheries, on the other hand, are uncomfortable reminders that—despite the doctrine of state sovereignty—indigenous identities and rights continue to exist.

Native leaders have a responsibility to expose the truth and debunk the imperial pretense that supports the doctrine of state sovereignty and white society's dominion over indigenous nations and their lands. State sovereignty depends on the fabrication of falsehoods that exclude the indigenous voice. Ignorance and racism are the founding principles of the colonial state, and concepts of indigenous sovereignty that don't challenge these principles, in fact, serve to perpetuate them. To claim that the state's legitimacy is based on the rule of law is hypocritical and anti-historic. There is no moral justification for state sovereignty. The truth is that Canada and the United States were established only because indigenous peoples were overwhelmed by imported European diseases and were unable to prevent the massive immigration of European populations. Only recently as indigenous people have learned to manipulate state institutions and gained support from other groups oppressed by the state has the state been forced to change its approach. Recognizing the power of the indigenous challenge and unable to deny it a voice, the state has attempted to pull indigenous people closer to it. It has encouraged them to reframe and moderate their nationhood demands to accept the *fait accompli* of colonization, to collaborate in the development of a "solution" that does not challenge the fundamental imperial lie.

By allowing indigenous peoples a small measure of self-administration, and by forgoing a small portion of the money derived from the exploitation of indigenous nations' lands, the state has created incentives for integration into its own sovereignty framework. Those communities that co-operate are the beneficiaries of a patronizing false altruism that sees indigenous peoples as the anachronistic remnants of nations, the descendants of once independent peoples who by a combination of tenacity and luck have managed to survive and must now be protected as minorities. By agreeing to live as artifacts, such co-opted communities guarantee themselves a role in the state mythology, through which they hope to secure a limited but perpetual set of rights. In truth, the bargain is a pathetic compromise of principle. The reformulation of nationhood to create historical artifacts that lend legitimacy to the political economy of the modern state is nothing less than a betrayal.

What do traditionalists hope to protect? What have the co-opted ones forsaken? In both cases, the answer is the heart and soul of indigenous nations: a set of values that challenge the destructive and homogenizing force of Western liberalism and free-market capitalism, and that honour the autonomy of individual conscience, non-coercive authority, and the deep interconnection between human beings and the other elements of creation.

Nowhere is the contrast between indigenous and (dominant) Western traditions sharper than in their philosophical approaches to the fundamental issues of power and nature. In indigenous philosophies, power flows from respect for nature and the natural order. In the dominant Western philosophy, power derives from coercion and artifice—in effect, alienation from nature.

A brief detour to consider the relationship of human beings to the earth may serve to illustrate the last point. Indigenous philosophies are premised on the belief that earth was created by a power external to human beings, who have a responsibility to act as stewards; since humans had no hand in making the earth, they have no right to "possess" it or dispose of it as they see fit—possession of land by humankind is unnatural and unjust. The stewardship principle, reflecting a spiritual connection with the land established by the Creator, gives human beings special responsibilities within the areas they occupy as indigenous peoples, linking them in a "natural" way to their territories.

The realities of capitalism make this concept problematic both for the state and for indigenous peoples. But the perceptions of the problem are different. Non-indigenous people may suspect that traditionalist Natives would oppose the types of uses and activities promoted by the state in their nations' territories. In fact, this is not the case. Most Native people do not reject modernization or participation in larger economies. However, traditionalists recognize a responsibility to participate in the economy with the intent of ensuring the long-term health and stability of people and the land; in this context, development for development's sake, consumerism, and unrestrained growth are not justifiable. It is the intense possessive materialism at the heart of Western economies that must be rejected—for the basic reason that it contradicts traditional values aimed at maintaining a respectful balance among people and between human beings and the earth.

The form of distributive or social justice promoted by the state today depends on the development of industry and enterprises to provide jobs for people and revenue for government institutions. Most often—especially on indigenous lands—those industries and enterprises centre on the extraction of natural resources. Trees, rocks, and fish become commodities whose value is calculated solely in monetary terms without reference to the spiritual connections between them and indigenous peoples. From a traditional point of view, this is an extreme devaluation of nature.

Yet, in a world economy dependent on resource exploitation that is structured so that such exploitation seems the only means of survival, what are indigenous peoples committed to traditional values to do? All societies must take their sustenance from the land; however, we must also recognize that the earth has an inherent value, beyond human needs. The situation now, and in the framework of conventional economic development models, is that a small minority of the white population of the earth go far beyond sustenance to take extravagant wealth from indigenous lands. Very little in terms of either employment or wealth comes back to the indigenous people themselves. The modern reality demands that indigenous people use the land much more intensively and in very different ways than their ancestors did. However, traditionalists believe that Native people must assert their consciousness of nature and power by demanding that their territories be used in ways that respect indigenous notions of justice, not simply for the short-sighted generation of wealth for others.

The only position on development compatible with a traditional frame of mind is a balanced one, committed at once to using the land in ways that respect the spiritual and cultural connections indigenous peoples have with it and to managing the process so as to ensure a primary benefit for its natural indigenous stewards. The primary goals of an indigenous economy are to sustain the earth and to ensure the health and well-being of the people. Any derogation of that principle—whether in qualitative terms or with reference to the intensity of activity on the land—should be seen as upsetting the balanced ideal that lies at the heart of Native societies.

Returning to the issue of nationhood, we must acknowledge that, unlike the earth, social and political institutions were created by men and women. From the indigenous perspective, this means that people have the power and responsibility to manipulate those institutions. Whereas the human–earth relationship is structured by the larger forces in nature, beyond the capacity of humans to change, the human–institution relationship gives rise to an active responsibility in human beings to use their own powers of creation to achieve balance and harmony. Governance structures and social institutions should be designed to empower individuals and reinforce tradition in order to maintain the balance found in nature.

In this view, sovereignty is not a natural phenomenon but a social creation—the result of choices made by men and women located in a particular social and political order. The unquestioned acceptance of sovereignty as the framework for politics today reflects the triumph of a particular set of ideas over others—and is no more natural to the world than any other human-made object.

The kind of justice that indigenous people seek in their relations with the state has to do with restoring a regime of respect. This ideal stands in clear contrast to the statist notion, still rooted in the classical notion of sovereignty, which, in the name of equity, may direct more material resources to indigenous people, but which preserves the state's superior position relative to them and to the earth. The indigenous conception of justice builds a framework of respectful coexistence on the fundamental acknowledgement of the integrity and autonomy of the various elements that make up the relationship. It goes far beyond even the most liberal Western ideas of justice in advancing the cause of peace, because it explicitly allows for difference while promoting the construction of sound relationships among autonomous elements.

The Western view of power and human relationships is so thoroughly entrenched that it appears valid, objective, and natural. It has become what Jens Bartelson has called "the unthought foundation of political knowledge." The challenge, then, is to "de-think" the concept of sovereignty and replace it with a notion of power that is based on more appropriate premises.

One of the most progressive Western thinkers today, James Tully, has recognized the obstacle to reconciliation posed by intellectual demands for conformity to a single language and way of knowing. In his view, the "imperial" demand of uniformity is obsolete and unachievable in the (ethnically, linguistically, and racially) diverse social and political communities characteristic of modern states. Justice demands recognition—intellectual, legal, and political—of the diversity of languages and knowledge that exists among people, indigenous peoples' ideas about relationships and power commanding the same respect as those that used to constitute the singular reality of the state. Creating a legitimate post-colonial relationship means abandoning notions of European cultural superiority and adopting a mutually respectful stance. The idea that there is only one right way to see or do things is no longer tenable:

> One of the important discoveries of the twentieth century is that such a comprehensive language or point of view is an illusion. There is no view from no where. No matter how comprehensive such a language may appear to be … it will always bring to light some aspects of the phenomenon it is employed to comprehend at the expense of disregarding others.

Indigenous thinkers from around the world have had some success in undermining the intellectual credibility of state sovereignty as the only legitimate form of political organization. Scholars in international law are now beginning to see the vast potential for peace in indigenous political philosophies. The international attention focused on the Rotinohshonni *Kaienerekowa* (Great Law of Peace) is indicative of the growing recognition given to indigenous models as post-colonial alternatives to state sovereignty. According to the most comprehensive and authoritative legal text on indigenous peoples in international law,

> The Great Law of Peace promotes unity among individuals, families, clans, and nations while upholding the integrity of diverse identities

and spheres of autonomy. Similar ideals have been expressed by leaders of other indigenous groups in contemporary appeals to international bodies. Such conceptions outside the mold of classical Western liberalism would appear to provide a more appropriate foundation for understanding humanity.

But the state will not easily release its grip on *control-power* and accept the alternative of *knowledge-power*. The traditional values of indigenous peoples directly threaten the monopoly of control-power currently enjoyed by the state. Some scholars have interpreted the violence that occurs when the state confronts indigenous traditionalism as a natural statist reaction to such threats. For example, Arthur Kroker believes that the state is determined to eliminate the intellectual threat posed by the idea of a politics beyond state sovereignty and to that end is prepared to use terror—including not only physical force but the intellectual violence inherent in state policies. In the wake of Canada's conflicts with the Kanien'kehaka and other indigenous nations in the 1990s, Kroker asked whether "the indefinite occupation ... and the ceaseless police raids into other aboriginal territories [were] not an indefinite preparation for war in another way ... a violent warning to all First Nations people?" The same question might be posed with respect to the intellectual violence done to indigenous people through the continued denial of their reality in the dominant mythology.

Hope for moving beyond the intellectual violence of the state is offered by the emerging concept of legal pluralism, which is reflected in the limited recognition afforded indigenous principles in recent legal argumentation. That concept must be taken to its logical conclusion. As the Canadian legal scholar Alain Bissonnette has put it, the courts must develop the ability to think "in multiple terms." In other words, they must develop what Native people have maintained all along is the necessary precondition to peace and justice: respect for others. Bissonnette sees great potential for preserving the Canadian state's legitimacy in the respect and recognition of indigenous rights:

Judges should break with a knowledge of the law that does not allow them to assimilate or master this new legal reality, especially since the recent constitutional recognition ... informs them that over the years, these rights "were virtually ignored" and, on the other hand, requires them in future to protect these rights by using a form of legal reasoning different from that which prevailed before.... If they take this approach they will no doubt gradually be able truly to legitimize the whole of the Canadian legal system, which in future will be based on the recognition or creation of a common cultural code that rejects in advance any symbolic violence against the historical, social and cultural reality of the Aboriginal peoples.

Within Native communities themselves, people are seriously questioning the identities shaped by the colonial reality, in an effort to construct intellectual and political strategies that will both resonate within the communities and present an effective challenge to the state's latest strategies to perpetuate its dominance. I asked Audra Simpson, a Kanien'kehaka anthropologist, to comment on some of these issues. Her responses shed light on the depth of the examination now under way, as well as on the significance attached to the process of constructing a post-colonial identity among politicized people in our communities.

Is there a difference between the Native concept of "nationhood" and "sovereignty" in the legal sense, or as you understand it?

These concepts are quite different. I find it hard to isolate, define, and then generalize what a "Native" concept of nationhood would be without its sounding contrived. This is a tired point: We are all different people, different nations, and would have different ideas about what nationhood is and what it means to us. The Sechelt conception or Northern Cree conception will certainly depart from Mohawk ideas about who we are. Each people will have a term in their own language that will mean "us." I think that is what our concept of nationhood is.

My opinion is that "Mohawk" and "nationhood" are inseparable. Both are simply about being. Being is who you are, and a sense of who you are is arrived at through your relationships with other people—your people. So who we are is tied with what we are: a nation.

Now, sovereignty—the authority to exercise power over life, affairs, territory—this is not inherited. It's not a part of being, the way our form of nationhood is. It has to be conferred, or granted—it's a thing that can be given and thus can be taken away. It's clearly a foreign concept, because it occurs through an exercise of power—power over another.

This is not to say that the valuing of sovereignty, of having control over territory, has not been indigenized. We've used it in a rhetorical and political way time and time again. But I think there is a difference between the being of who we are—Mohawk—and the defence mechanisms that we have to adopt in the neo-colonial context—sovereignty.

But in terms of the substance of who we are, the nature of our "being," is it necessary to be self-conscious in defining and maintaining our tradition as a support for either cultural nationhood or political sovereignty?

This "self-conscious traditionalism," like the culture concept, cannot be thought about, or written about, enough. To be Native today is to be cultured: to possess culture, to exercise it, to proclaim it, to celebrate it. But we cannot have just any culture. It has to be "traditional" culture—defined, isolated, reflected upon, relearned, and then perfected. Our very sovereignty—in the European sense—depends on it, as we must continually prove our difference in order to have our rights respected. We see this with land-claims cases and in day-to-day life—our day-to-day experiences do not suffice when making claims to difference, as these claims are always made to others outside of our communities.

This traditionalism is, therefore, very important in the context of the neo-colonial present, because it is the basis of our claim to difference, and difference is tied to sovereignty. However, I fear that, in the long run, we might lose who we really are in order to perfect a dance that looks great, feels good at the time, but is done largely for the benefit of others—to meet somebody else's standards of Indianness.

I sought an alternative perspective on these same questions from Vine Deloria, Jr, the highly influential Lakota scholar and American Indian activist.

Is there a difference between the Native concept of "nationhood" and "sovereignty" in the legal sense?

I think that "sovereignty" was a European word that tried to express the nationhood of a people who could think with one mind. Since the king was the ruler, he was sovereign in the sense that he was supposed to represent what the people of his nation wanted. Indians had spread out the idea of governing to include all activities of life—thus, at times, medicine people would be influential and, at other times, warriors, or hunters, or scouts would be influential. Many tribes did not have "laws" or "religion," but a single belief system that was described as "our way of doing things."

Sovereignty today, unfortunately, is conceived as a wholly political–legal concept. I would prefer that social processes determined how the people feel about things and whether they are willing to act as a single unit. If they could all boycott a store, bank, or social function of the whites and just be content with a more closed society, people would have to pay attention to them.

The Six Nations' [Rotinohshonni] arrangement of chiefs in their meetings is a very good way of ensuring that real sovereignty exists and is protected—that the political actions of a people reflect their consensus. We should think about the process they developed a lot more. The Sioux used to be more formal and dignified, but, now, they shout and carry on in meetings until you don't want to attend them anymore!

What about the "co-optation" of Native leaders, both in their minds and as a process?

It's relatively easy to co-opt Indian leaders—but it's easy to co-opt everyone else also. The problem people face is gaining access to the levers of power, and that requires co-operating with the people who control things. You have to have an enormous amount of power to oppose co-optation. Indians could do a lot more for themselves if they stood by certain principles. It is noteworthy that in those instances where Indians have stood firm on something, they have been more successful.

One of the loosely related problems is that Indians won't criticize other Indians no matter how bad they are. This enables people who are basically rip-offs to have the same kind of status as devoted leaders. So there is a group of Indians frantically trying to buy into the system, and they clog up the analysis of our problems because they seem to be co-opted, but they are really just selling out. One way to avoid that is to have a council governing the tribe and have it choose a particular person as spokesman for different occasions. Many tribes practised that successfully with similar institutions. The Sioux used to appoint people to make different speeches, without vesting the power to negotiate in any of them. The Cheyenne had peace chiefs and war chiefs—no warrior as such was allowed to be either, as I understand it.

I agree that we need to return to a traditional mode. Has your experience given you any ideas on how to make the first practical steps toward that goal?

Since we live in a world that has many forms of communication, it is impossible to speak to a small group—like the old tribal circles—without everyone knowing what you are saying. So I think we should institute new customs, and have some nights set aside to do storytelling, some to discuss the future of the tribe or community, every so often. We should also teach the old clan and kinship responsibilities, and make deliberate efforts to carry them out, perhaps even set up deadlines to accomplish certain kinds of goals—calling people within the family by the relative name, like "father" or "sister," and reviving the customs of doing things for them. Then we can move on to more complicated things. There was a sense of civility that the old traditional ways brought that we do not have now, and we should return to them.

What is the role of a leader in this? Or, more generally, what are the duties and traits of a real Native leader?

Well, in the old days, a leader made certain that the camp, or longhouse, did not have petty problems that festered. Many a chief called the two parties who were quarrelling together and tried to get them to make up. Sometimes, he had to give them his own horses or some other gift to put everything right.

So I think that the Indian leader, insofar as [it's] possible, should be a figure of reconciliation and futuristic vision. And I think we are getting some people elected now who are acting that way. But a leader also should look at the community, evaluate where the strengths and weaknesses are, and develop a cadre of people who can work together on things—making sure that everyone comes together once in a while to get the general feeling that the community as a whole is moving forward. A leader probably ought also to be someone who enables processes to happen, who realizes that sometimes people are not ready to do things, and [will take the time] to gently educate them, to prepare them. Many of the old tribal chairmen of the 1960s did that, and they were very powerful leaders.

Is it still possible to hold our current leaders to a traditional standard of accountability to the people?

Well, before Western individualism took over, people were held accountable by their family, clan, and community. And they used shame to bring people around. As you know, the Cherokees executed some of their chiefs who signed away lands—an extreme form of accountability. Today, we are so polarized between Indian and white that no one dares criticize an Indian leader publicly, so we let them get away with murder.

Back in the 1960s, when I first got into this stuff, there was a core group at NCAI [the National Congress of American Indians] that had worked together for years, through the hardest years of termination [the former US policy aimed at extinguishing indigenous nations]. They acted as a committee to enforce accountability. Unfortunately, after we had rebuilt the NCAI in 1967, the "out" group won the election, and then corruption on a large scale set in. I remember some of the crooks asking some of us who had lost the election to help throw out the others. But the honest, elected officers wouldn't take action against the crooks for fear they would lose the next NCAI election. So we began to lose accountability, at least on the national level, around 1969–70. I think that's when AIM [the American Indian Movement] came to prominence, because tribal leaders wouldn't speak out. Poverty funds ruined integrity at the national and tribal level and we have never been able to restore much of it—people would do anything for a dollar, or an appointment to a national committee.

Maybe, once the funds dry up and we have to live by our wits, people will take offence at the squandering of tribal assets and demand accountability again. But look at the Navajos: Peter McDonald was looting the tribe, trying to skim millions from his own people, and the Navajos petitioned for [President] Clinton to pardon him. If we don't want to punish anyone for wrongdoing, how can we have accountability?

In spite of their national, gender, experience, and age differences (and very different styles), both Simpson and Deloria express the same core critique of sovereignty, the colonial power structure, and the intellectual justifications that have been used to perpetuate it. Their views represent those of many indigenous people who have managed to see through the state's facade of legitimacy and recognize the destructive implications—both intellectual and political—of remaining within a colonial structure and mindset.

Colonial Mentalities

Despite all the wisdom available within indigenous traditions, most Native lives continue to be lived in a world of ideas imposed on them by others. The same set of factors that creates internalized oppression, blinding people to the true source of their pain and hostility, also allows them to accept, and even to defend, the continuation of an unjust power relationship. The "colonial mentality" is the intellectual dimension in the group of emotional and psychological pathologies associated with internalized oppression. Just as harmful to the society as self-hate and hostility are to individuals, the colonial mentality can be thought of as a mental state that blocks recognition of the existence or viability of traditional perspectives. It prevents people from seeing beyond the conditions created by the white society to serve its own interests.

The colonial mentality is recognizable in the gradual assumption of the values, goals, and perspectives that make up the status quo. The development of such a mentality is almost understandable (if not acceptable), given the structural basis of indigenous–state relations and the necessity for Native people to work through the various institutions of control to achieve their objectives. Native professionals, for example, find it hard to resist the (assimilative) opportunity structure created by the range of state strategies designed to co-opt and weaken challenges to the state's hegemony.

The structural integration and professionalization of Native politics within a bureaucratic framework controlled—financially and politically—by the state is the main reason for the persistence of the colonial mentality. In the Native context, all local governments, regional bodies, and national representative organizations are chartered and funded by the state. In Canada, for example, band councils, tribal councils, and the Assembly of First Nations are all creatures of the federal government. The fact that the very existence of government institutions within Native communities depends on an essentially foreign government goes largely unexamined and unchallenged by Native politicians. This dependence imposes a set of parameters that constrains the actions and even the thoughts of those working within the system.

Attempting to decolonize without addressing the structural imperatives of the colonial system itself is clearly futile. Yet most people accept the idea that we are making steady progress toward the resolution of injustices stemming from colonization. It may take more energy, or more money, than is currently being devoted to the process of decolonization, but the issue is always discussed within existing structural and legal frameworks. Most Native people do not see any need for a massive reorientation of the relationship between themselves and the state. This is symptomatic of the colonial mentality.

Not having been forced to accept domination by a foreign power, most outside observers would no doubt recognize the contradiction inherent in asserting nationhood rights within a colonial legal framework. The most fundamental right of a people is the one that empowers them to determine their own identity. Yet, in Canada, it is the state that determines who is considered indigenous under the law. Despite the Canadian Constitution's protection for "all existing aboriginal and treaty rights" (section 35), the Canadian government's policies deny Native governments the legal right to set their own membership criteria, and impose a primarily individualist conception of rights upon indigenous nations by insisting on the application of the Charter of Rights and Freedoms.

Resistance to this form of control is futile. The state has consistently demonstrated that it will not respect indigenous nations' inherent right to determine their own membership and that it will use Canadian law to support individuals who challenge community definitions of membership. Moreover, some indigenous communities do not see the futility of arguing for recognition of nationhood rights within a framework founded on the legal and political supremacy of the state.

In the 1995 Twinn case, heard by the Federal Court of Canada, three Indian band councils in the province of Alberta argued that section 35 of the Constitution gave them the right to make whatever laws they wanted concerning membership. The band leaders neglected to consider that a subparagraph of the same section places firm restrictions on the range of action allowed band councils under the law. The court pointed out the discrepancy with cutting logic in its original judgment against the bands:

> The plaintiffs are firmly caught by the provisions of s. 35 of the Constitution Act which they themselves invoke. The more firmly the plaintiffs bring themselves into and under s.s. 35 (1) the more surely s.s. 35 (4) acts upon their alleged rights pursuant to s.s. 35 (1)....

Then, as if to make the point clearer still, the judges went on to express their belief that the fundamental right to determine their own membership is explicitly denied indigenous peoples in Canadian law: "Even if control of … membership had been a real Aboriginal right, it was extinguished by clear and unambiguous legislation."

Another Canadian example demonstrates the inappropriateness of efforts to use colonial law to undermine the existence of a colonial relationship. The band council for Six Nations of the Grand River evicted a white woman, who was residing on the reserve against the community's will. In 1996, the Federal Court upheld the band's right to control residency (and evict non-members) on the basis of what it called "historical factors," but nevertheless allowed the woman to remain on the reserve because eviction would cause "disruption" in her life! Thus, even when the Native people have a clear right within the colonial law, the colonial system regards white interests as superior.

The tortured logic of colonization is also clearly evident in the United States, where the common law provides for recognition of the inherent sovereignty of indigenous peoples (who are considered "domestic dependent nations") but simultaneously (and hypocritically) allows for the limitation of its sovereignty—even potential extinguishment—by Congress. As the Lumbee scholar David Wilkins notes in his analysis of the exercise of tribal sovereignty in the context of US federal law,

> The continuing and still virtually unlimited federal power over indigenous sovereignty (conceptualized by federal law as "domestic-dependent" sovereignty), tribal property (conceived by federal policy makers and administrators as "subject" territory susceptible to confiscation in certain situations and treated as being of an inferior title to that of the United States), and treaty rights (understood as being subject to the Supreme Court's plenary interpretive power) remains largely intact. This effectively leaves tribes without any substantive protection from the very government branches legally and morally charged with protecting and enforcing indigenous rights.

Clearly, any notion of nationhood or self-government rooted in state institutions and framed within the context of state sovereignty can never satisfy the imperatives of Native American political traditions. Harmonious cooperation and coexistence founded on respect for autonomy and the principle of self-determination are precluded by the state's insistence on dominion and its exclusionary notion of sovereignty.

Co-optation

Pete Standing Alone of the Blood tribe once said of a respected elder: "He was a real good Indian, the kind that don't take no shit from a white man." Most indigenous people are proud to know a few "real good Indians." But the unfortunate reality is that most of us have to put up with all too much "shit," lip, and ignorant attitudes every day of our lives. This is so true that, to some, it seems normal.

The co-optation of our political leadership is a subtle, insidious, unde-niable fact, and it has resulted in a collective loss of ability to confront the daily injustices, both petty and profound, of Native life. Politically and eco-nomically, all Native people are in a vulnerable position relative to the supe-rior power of the state. This is the reality with which all must cope. But individual people respond to this unjust power relationship in different ways. Some actively resist; some co-operate. These people rationalize and participate actively in their own subordination and the maintenance of the Other's superiority. They become co-opted.

The validity of individual responses to colonization must be judged with great sensitivity to each person's experience. All colonized people must find ways to survive the experience, and not everyone is capable of active resist-ance. Co-operation with colonialism, however, is most certainly wrong, espe-cially where leaders are concerned. The undeniable fact that, as indigenous people, we are politically subordinate means that the entire governmental, social, and economic framework is necessarily co-optive. The challenge, and the hope, is for each person to recognize and counteract the effects of colo-nization in her own life, and thus develop the ability to live in a way that con-tests colonization. We are all co-opted to one degree or another, so we can only pity those who are blind or who refuse to open their eyes to the colonial reality, and who continue to validate, legitimate, and accommodate the inter-ests of that reality in opposition to the goals and values of their own nations.

In his insightful book on non-white urban leadership in Canada, *The Governance of Ethnic Communities*, Raymond Breton explains how the state actively works to prevent community leaders from furthering the goals of their own people, and instead manipulates them into satisfying its own objectives. Without fail, when the objectives of any community differ from those of the entrenched interests that determine state policy (as is certainly the case with indigenous communities), community leaders are pressured to co-operate with state power. Political, social, psychological, and economic pressures are brought to bear on community leaders, to persuade or entice them to use the sources of power available within the community to serve the interests of the state.

Such co-optation is especially difficult for indigenous people to resist because of the political and cultural distance between indigenous and state cultures, and the vigour with which the state endeavours to undermine the territorial, cultural, and political integrity of their nations. The complexity of indigenous–state relations gives agents of the state many opportunities and mechanisms to move indigenous leaders away from their communities, politically and ideologically, and toward the state. Directly and indirectly, external agents seek to weaken indigenous nations by influencing patterns of thought and action among their leaders. No energy or expense is spared in the state's efforts to make the power of indigenous leaders work for the state rather than for the community—in short, to co-opt them.

As Breton shows, the state has found that the most effective way of co-opting the power of community leaders is to embrace them:

> Co-optation is a process through which the policy orientations of leaders are influenced and their organizational activities channeled. It blends the leader's interests with those of an external organization. In the process, ethnic leaders and their organizations become active in the state-run interorganizational system; they become participants in the decision-making process as advisors or committee members. By becoming somewhat of an insider the co-opted leader is likely to identify with the organization and its objectives. The leader's point of view is shaped through the personal ties formed with authorities and functionaries of the external organization.

Co-optation strategies are regularly used by state officials at every level of interaction with Native leaders. While most people who have served in positions of responsibility recognize the most blatant attempts of other governments to sway them, more subtle efforts may not be so evident. This is the danger: Without a comprehensive understanding of co–optation strategies, leaders lack the critical perspective they need to ensure that their decisions promote their own people's goals rather than those of the state.

What methods do state agents use to co-opt Native leaders? Native people will be familiar with at least some of the following strategies (adapted from Breton's analysis):

1. **Influence the composition of community leadership.** One of the primary ways in which outside governments influence Native politics is by acting indirectly to determine the political representation of Native communities. In the insecurely rooted and contentious systems in place within Native communities today, state governments consistently promote and support those people who pose the least threat to the status quo, and who do not challenge the assumed power of the state in any serious way.

   To ensure that Native communities are formally represented by co-opted leaders, the state relies on four main tactics: (i) it legitimizes desirable people by giving them formal recognition or legal status (similarly, at the infrastructural level, it promotes colonial frameworks over traditional ones, as in the legal recognition of band councils in Canada or tribal councils in the United States); (ii) it ignores certain individuals or bypasses their authority in favour of dealing with more desirable people (similarly, governmental processes may be structured so that Native communities must rely on the expertise and representation of non-Native people); (iii) it marginalizes undesirable people by drawing attention to the inequalities that exist within the community and labelling certain groups or perspectives as extremist; and (iv) it diverts attention and energy away from addressing core issues, toward managing the symptoms of colonization.

2. **Divide and conquer.** In its efforts to influence the composition of leadership, the state plays on and amplifies existing social, political, and economic divisions within the community. It can then use these cleavages to prevent the community from achieving the unity and solidarity that are essential if it is to effectively challenge state power.

3. **Generate dependency.** Communities that lack the basic capacity for self-sufficiency cannot make a strong assertion of nationhood. With this in mind, the state prevents the development of an economic base for Native communities and encourages dependency on external forces. With near-complete personal and communal dependency on funds transferred from the state, Native communities are subject to perpetual coercion and can challenge state power only at the risk of extreme economic and social deprivation.

4. **Incorporate.** Focusing on the co-optation of individual leaders, this strategy exploits the widespread misperception that the system can be changed from within. Assuming certain commonalities of values and goals, as well

as training, among those Native people who seek to serve as links between their communities and others, it manipulates the leader into a position where there is a significant degree of conflict between his own positions, values, or interests and those of the community. In other words, the state works to close the gap between the state and the person and widen the gap between the person and home, to the point where the person's identity is shaped not so much by the tension between the mainstream and the home community as by the process, policies, or institutions with which he has come to be associated. Breton describes the outcome:

> Leaders and their organizations become part of an interorganizational system with a number of common interests. They become participants in a policy field in which organizations of the larger society play, in all likelihood, a leading role. To some degree, they become agents of state policies.

Even if it is not possible to change the system from within, an individual's actions within the system do matter. We can accept or reject, promote or hinder the state's agenda. But without a sufficient grounding in traditional perspectives, it becomes very easy to acquiesce to the state's agenda. For this reason, it is the responsibility of Native leaders to adopt what I would term a *contentious* posture in relation to the state.

Contention is the opposite end of the reaction spectrum from co–optation. It is a non-cooperative, non-participatory position vis-à-vis the state, its actors, and its policies. In terms of action, it calls for disagreement with the kind of marginally progressive halfway measures put forward by the state to appease the less committed among us. Contention demands accountability for the underlying power relationship and the state's domination of our existence. It refuses to be drawn into maintaining the colonial system, and takes a firm stand (intellectually, politically, and physically) in defence of the principles, institutions, and lands that form the core of indigenous nations.

In the absence of a widespread commitment to contention as a political posture among Native leaders, there are many different responses to the state's efforts at co-optation. These responses are recognizable in a number of political personas, which are effectively identified by certain common caricatures.

At one pole, most Native leaders will admit to having felt, at one time or another, like a "Hang Around the Fort"—one of those old-time Indians who would pitch a tent right up against the walls of the stockade and survive by begging and running errands for the soldiers and Indian Agents. The contemporary version is the person who is completely dependent on the established order for his political survival, and whose contribution consists mainly in scrounging for government handouts. Like the Hang Around the Forts who conspired in the suppression of their own people, this person needs the conditions of poverty and marginalization to guarantee his status and role.

At the other end of the spectrum is the "Mystic Warrior," who thinks every day is a good day to die. For this type of person, Indianness consists in conflict, and the only way to exist as an Indian is to withdraw into the mythic spiritual past and attack any semblance of modernity as a betrayal. The attraction of this uncompromising persona is very powerful for people frustrated (as they inevitably are) by the effort to maintain a principled position in relations with non-indigenous governments—until the reality sets in that simply causing hell and discontent for white society cannot be a life purpose.

In between these two is the "Apple": the person whose thin red skin masks a mushy core of a shade closely resembling white. Typically, these people have "seen too much pain" in their lives and cannot stomach any more conflict. This persona is recognizable in the consistent favouring of compromise to ensure the primary goal of non-conflict at any cost. The person's self-defined role is to help white people "understand" Natives so that things can be better for everyone.

Inevitably, all Native leaders at one time or another during their careers are forced to adopt each of these personas, and, at various times and places in their lives, the personas actually feel authentic—when the community is not in control of its own reality, the Native leader can only react to situations and issues that are determined by others. So it becomes a fact of life that leaders respond in sometimes predictable ways. Although a few people have personalities so strong that they consistently determine what their relationship to the system will be, most people active in colonial institutions shift between personas according to the demands and pressures facing them at a particular moment.

The long process of colonization has had an impact on our way of thinking. People have been turned into the tools of their own oppression. We need to recognize and acknowledge the co-optation and to locate our own roles within the system. On one side, there are indigenous nations with their traditions and values; on the other side, there is mainstream society. We all live somewhere in between. But if our thoughts and actions consistently further the other society's objectives rather than our own, or if progress toward justice for our people is sacrificed to satisfy the "Other's" imperatives, then the degree of co-optation is unacceptable.

Native people cannot withdraw from the larger world that surrounds them. In fact, it is essential to engage white society and challenge the state at every level and in every way. The commitment to take on colonialism's every manifestation is reflected in the advice offered to me at the start of my own career by Vine Deloria, Jr. He agreed with my perception that most white people in positions of authority had to be prodded simply to recognize injustice in their dominance over indigenous people. He reflected on the fact that Native American academics were still marginalized when it came to designing solutions to the problems facing their people and in shaping the academic discourse on their own history and societies:

> You are absolutely right about white people positioning themselves to become dominant in making Indian policy. I've fought against it all my life and you will do the same. The first problem is that there are just too many of them; second, they have access to the white world as whole personalities ... simply because they are white—hence credible; third, Americans need to feel a "little guilty," but certainly don't want to be indicted; fourth, whites who come to dominate Indian policy believe they are helping by being a sympathetic voice—in fact, they don't ask for any justice, merely that they be regarded as the authorities.

His advice and observations are still valuable to Native people attempting to work within (and against) a system that remains essentially colonial:

> You have to be a keen observer and watch where power seems to reside among them—quietly make friends and you will be able to bounce your ideas from one to another and work your way into a position where you will have to be consulted about things.
>
> When I was young, we had a group of tribal chairmen who knew the law and knew how to manipulate the attitudes of whites who insisted on being in the field. Today we are at ground zero—Indians have had so many opportunities that many of them have never known a hostile congress or administration—so we have to start all over again and build up experience on how to deal with the power structure.
>
> At your age, you and others should get on committees, be consult-

ants, serve on boards, and set down a network of allies, Indian and white, that can understand the parts of your agenda that you want them to accomplish. Always maintain good relationships with opinion-makers of the tribe, because people will try and knock out your local base by rumor and innuendo. I have had all kinds of people attack me as an urban Indian, but have also had enough people at home defend me, since I go to help them when they are in need of someone to talk with.

Deloria made clear that successful resistance to the mental effects of colonialism also requires a consistent perspective and a long-term view, with a patient commitment to restoring justice and getting back what is rightfully ours:

> Remember to look far into the future and conceive what you want Indians to be, and how you want things to be shaped, and try to direct your energies toward that goal. You will do all right but you will have to work very hard. Read up on history—everything is buried there and you can have access to it by studying it.

There is a fine line to walk between playing the system and being played, and leaders must be concerned with achieving balance in their political lives. But our goals will never be achieved without

1. self-reflection, to determine the degree to which co-optation has affected our thought processes;
2. serious analysis of government in our communities, to determine whether the state has succeeded in structuring the situation to prevent the achievement of our objectives; and
3. revision of our decision-making processes to infuse them with an indigenous logic based on traditional teachings.

Freeing ourselves from co-optation comes down to acknowledging the unbalanced power dynamic that we exist within (and not making excuses for its continuation) and to holding ourselves apart from the institutions and people that actually constitute colonialism. Colonialism is not an abstract notion but a set of real people and relationships and structures that can be resisted and combatted by placing our respect and trust where it belongs: in indigenous people, relationships, and structures.

I am supposed to uphold the Indian message to try to promote their teachings. I consult with their elders, and if necessary, go off and communicate with the spirits of the ancestors in the area to try and find out what the original language was, where the original homeland territory was, and how they conducted their religion.... I encourage people to consider Thomas Banyacya's four words: "Stop, consider, change, and correct." Stop what you are doing. Consider the effects of what you are doing. Is it upholding life on this land? Or is it destructive to the life on this land? If it is destructive, then change your value system and your actions. We are not supposed to be subduing the earth, treading it underfoot, vanquishing the earth and all its life. We are supposed to be taking care of this land and the life upon it. So it's up to you to consider which side you are going to be on.... I was sent clear around the world, and I found Indians everywhere. They didn't all have brown skin; they weren't all what they call "red men." But they had their sacred original instructions, and they were diligently trying to follow them.

—Craig Carpenter, Kanien'kehaka
(Johnson, ed., *The Book of Elders*, 105)

Self-Conscious Traditionalism

Returning the politics of Native communities to a wholly indigenous framework means nothing less than reclaiming the inherent strength and power of indigenous governance systems and freeing our collective souls from a divisive and destructive colonized politics.

This process of decolonization is personal as well as public. At the more personal level, it means adopting patterns of thought and action that reject colonial premises in favour of a self-conscious traditionalism. However wrong, colonialism is a familiar reality that provides a certain security for some people. The final steps to decolonization can be truly frightening as Native people are jarred from that familiar reality and forced into a new one—even if it is of their own making. The post–colonial reality is fearsome in its demands, responsibilities, and burdens. There is no one to turn to except ourselves. There is no one else to blame.

Hence, the absolute necessity of reconstructing traditional communities to foster and support the kind of leadership I am urging (an idealized leadership, admittedly, but a utopian realism is necessary). It would be naive to think that individuals could achieve change without the support and co-operation of their communities. It is not possible for a single man or woman to reform a whole community and impose a traditional order on people who do not share the same basic objective. The type of leadership described here can be achieved only within a community that is itself committed to traditionalism.

It is precisely when the traditional social system has broken down that individuals skilled at manipulation wield the most influence. The erosion of traditional community values opens the door to abuse of power. An unstable social and political system invites corruption of the traditional ideal. Yet social chaos and separation from traditional cultural values are the reality in many indigenous communities. In this context, how do we recover sufficiently to create a social and political environment that promotes true leadership and discourages the selfish manipulation of power?

In my previous book, *Heeding the Voices of Our Ancestors* (1995), I analyzed Kahnawake's political revitalization and described the process of self-conscious reflection and selective readoption of traditional values that have been central to the re-establishment of a traditional political culture among the Kanien'kehaka. This self-conscious traditionalism has allowed Kahnawake to begin to make traditional values and principles the foundations of its political discourse. By bringing forward core values and principles from the vast store of our traditional teachings, and selectively employing those aspects of their tradition that are appropriate to the present social, political, and economic realities, the community has begun to construct a framework for government that represents a viable alternative to colonialism and that respects Native traditions.

Kahnawake is just one example of how people can begin to act to free themselves from colonialism by thinking through tradition. Members of that community did not inherit a pure and unbroken traditional culture—far from it. Many people relearned the traditional teachings, and, over the span of thirty years, have worked to recover the most important elements of the Rotinohshonni culture and make them the foundations of the community's political culture. This approach represents the potential experience of any Native community that seeks to relearn its traditions and place them at the centre of social and political life.

Communities that commit themselves to self-conscious traditionalism will find that, in translating and adapting traditional concepts to modern realities, they will come to embody the characteristics that make up the contemporary ideal of a strong indigenous nation:

- **Wholeness with diversity.** Community members are secure in knowing who and what they are; they have high levels of commitment to and solidarity with the group, but also tolerance for differences that emerge on issues that are not central to the community's identity.
- **Shared culture.** Community members know their traditions, and the values and norms that form the basis of the society are clearly established and universally accepted.
- **Communication.** There is an open and extensive network of communication among community members, and government institutions have clearly established channels by which information is made available to the people.
- **Respect and trust.** People care about and co-operate with one another and the government of the community, and they trust in one another's integrity.
- **Group maintenance.** People take pride in their community and seek to remain part of it; they collectively establish clear cultural boundaries and membership criteria and look to the community's government to keep those boundaries from eroding.
- **Participatory and consensus-based government.** Community leaders are responsive and accountable to the other members; they consult thoroughly and extensively and base all decisions on the principle of general consensus.
- **Youth empowerment.** The community is committed to mentoring and educating its young people, involving them in all decision-making processes, and respecting the unique challenges they face.
- **Strong links to the outside world.** The community has extensive positive social, political, and economic relationships with people in other communities, and its leaders consistently seek to foster good relations and gain support among other indigenous peoples and in the international community.

Indigenous people who reject the assumptions that legitimatize their subjugation have made the first step toward achieving self-determination and building sound communities. But there is a whole set of beliefs and attitudes, ingrained over years of tacit acceptance, which prevents indigenous people from recognizing that subjugation. Reasonable, realistic, and agreeable in the present reality, these beliefs and attitudes are crucial to the state's control over indigenous people. Clouding over the clarity of indigenous truth, they are designed to justify state control. The beliefs and assumptions that shape our present reality are "true" only to the extent that they consciously shape our thoughts and actions to fit the framework desired by the state. They are the myths of the colonial mindset.

Of all those myths, the greatest is the idea that indigenous peoples can find justice within the colonial legal system. People who have studied history know that it teaches a lesson about the law: "In periods of calm the law may shape reality, in periods of change the law will follow reality and find ways to accommodate and justify it." The myth is designed to induce tranquillity even in the face of blatant injustice. The task is to foment turmoil, force the law to change, create new parameters, and make indigenous goals an integral part of the new reality.

Another myth concerns labelling. What does it mean to be called an "Aboriginal" people? In Canada, there has been a turn toward politically correct, non-offensive terminology that attempts to assuage the guilt of colonialism, but, in fact, it is only a cover for the state's continuing abuse of indigenous peoples. What good does it do indigenous people to be called "Aboriginal" if the state continues to deny them legal recognition as the owners of their lands? What good does it do to be called a "First Nation" (a popular term in some Canadian provinces) when the governing structure is no more than a band council that is legitimized by the Indian Act? The only value in the wordplay is for the white establishment, most of whom do not have to face the racism built into the structure of their supposedly enlightened country. Natives face the same conditions and suffer the same abuses, except that now the problem is less obvious because, instead of being Indians governed by the state as wards under the Indian Act, they are now recognized as "Aboriginal" peoples with an "inherent right" to "self-government." Go to a reserve, look around, and ask yourself if Indians are any better off because white society has relieved itself of its terminological burden.

Intellectual dishonesty is one of the essential elements of colonialism. We need to stop believing the lies that have been perpetuated by Euroamericans to normalize the tempest of ruin it has inflicted on other peoples. Native people have become wrapped up in these lies; now, we are hostage to the status quo, unable to move. We must cut through white society's myths and begin to act on our own truths. We must shout a refrain to the strong and true words of Luther Standing Bear:

> The attempted transformation of the Indian by the white man and the chaos that has resulted are but the fruits of the white man's disobedience of a fundamental and spiritual law.... The attempt to force conformity of custom and habit has caused a reaction more destructive than war, and the injury has not only affected the Indian, but has extended to the white population as well. Tyranny, stupidity, and lack of vision have brought about the situation now alluded to as the "Indian Problem." There is, I insist, no Indian problem as created by the Indian himself. Every problem that exists today in regard to the Native population is due to the white man's cast of mind, which is unable, at least reluctant, to seek understanding and achieve adjustment in a new and significant environment into which it has so recently come.

The imposition of labels and definitions of identity on indigenous people has been a central feature of the colonization process from the start. Thus, another fundamental task facing Native communities is to overcome the racial, territorial, and "status" divisions that have become features of the political landscape. Factions and conflicts based on divisions between "status versus non-status," "enrolled versus non-enrolled," or "on-reserve versus urban" arise because our communities are still subject to outside controls. The practice of dividing Native people according to their status in the colonial law opposes the basic tenets of all indigenous philosophies. The extent to which these divisions continue to characterize Native communities indicates how deeply people have internalized the colonial mindset.

Who is indigenous? To have any value in promoting recovery from colonialism, the answer to this question must respect the integrity of indigenous nations and their traditions and must reject the divisive categories defined by the state. Neither the cold linearity of blood quantum nor the tortured weakness of self-identification—both systems designed and currently validated by the state—can sustain indigenous nations. When it comes to resolving questions of indigenous identity and determining membership, we ought to recognize the simple truth that indigenous nations are communities of human beings, and that, as such, they have the right to determine for themselves who they are. So there are no theoretical restrictions to the collective definitions that may be put forward by individual communities. The problem is that indigenous peoples are engaged with the state in a complex relationship in which there are varying degrees of interdependency at play, and history has created a range of definitions where formerly there were only those securely and collectively held by the communities themselves. In the old days, having an identity crisis meant that you couldn't find the spirit or ancestor living inside of you. The strength of indigenous societies at the time, and the clarity of the cultural boundaries among them, meant that people didn't have to think about their group affiliation—much less whether or not they were truly "Indian." But the breakdown of those traditional societies created in all Native people—even those consciously seeking recovery—many questions about belonging.

Today, there are many different ideas about what constitutes a Native person. We know what does not: pure self-identification and acting the part, however diligent the research or skilful the act. But arriving at a precise and accurate positive definition today is difficult. Maybe that is the problem. In fact, demands for precision and certainty disregard the reality of the situation: that group identity varies with time and place. The answer to the indigenous identity question depends on where you're located and when you ask the question. Only "process" issues (fairness, openness, regularity in the process of determining who is and who is not a member of the group) can be determined with any degree of certainty. Membership is a matter of blood and belonging determined through the institutions governing a community at a particular time. As outsiders to these self-determining communities, non-participant in their cultures, we must limit our concern to the institutional framework in which decisions are made. The substance of the collective decision on membership criteria, whatever it is, has to be seen as just so long as the decision-making process itself meets the general criteria for fairness and is internally equitable in its application and enforcement.

In the past, when traditional philosophies focused attention on the array of individual characteristics possessed by a person, membership was determined by beliefs and behaviour, together with blood relationship to the group. Both blood relations and cultural integration were, and are, essential to being Indian. Of course, collective views on culture and blood have shifted over time in response to the social, political, and economic forces that have affected the group's need for self-preservation. Returning to this framework and formulation will clarify the confusion introduced by imposed criteria, and result in a certain definition of membership for every community. The collective right of Native communities to determine their own membership must be recognized as a fundamental right of self-determination and respected as such. No individual has the right to usurp the identity of a nation simply by claiming it, much less when a collective decision has been made to the contrary. And no other nation (or state or organization) has the right to force an identity on another nation.

How would a return to an indigenous framework for determining membership resolve current conflicts, where the state has attempted to manipulate Native identities to destroy the original indigenous nations? Respecting the right of communities to determine membership for themselves would promote reconstruction of indigenous nations as groups of related people, descended from historic tribal communities, who meet commonly defined cultural and racial characteristics for inclusion. No doubt, this would exclude from the nations' circles many thousands of people who self-identify or people with minimal blood connections who have been told by the state that they are indigenous. But problems of misidentification arising out of the state's disrespect for indigenous collective rights and its manipulation of identity criteria are the state's to resolve. Bluntly speaking, Native communities should not be expected to clean up the mess created by white society and to further undermine their nationhood in order to accommodate people whose only connection to Native communities is a legal status ascribed to them by the state. The claimed rights of people who do not meet indigenous nations' own criteria for membership have no impact on the nations themselves.

Yet white society must do something to address the concerns of individuals who have been incorrectly associated with our nations. This issue is particularly relevant in Canada, where tens of thousands of self-identifying and minimal-blood persons who are excluded from membership in Indian communities are recognized as "Aboriginal" by Canadian governments, and receive benefits and legal entitlement to the resources of indigenous nations. It seems that white society feels some obligation to these people—probably because they are actually white, and, therefore, likely to co-operate with government efforts to eliminate indigenous nations as political forces. In any case, the problem can be resolved by recognizing that non-Indian "Aboriginals" are a strictly state-defined community, with rights and obligations deriving only from their membership in that community and having nothing to do with the treaty and political rights of members of indigenous nations. The state would then have one set of relationships with indigenous nations premised on their right of self-determination and a completely separate, presumably different, set with the communities that it created and sponsored. In political terms, and in relation to the dominant society, the first group is made up of colonized peoples and the second of oppressed racial or cultural minorities. Thus, the solutions to these problems are different: decolonization and self-determination for the first, and human and civil rights for the second.

In fact, until the two groups are separated, there can be no progress toward justice, because their conflation undermines cohesion, the foundation of group strength. Cohesion is an important factor in empowering any community, whether historic or contemporary. Uninformed people are always asking why Indians can't "get together" and build a political movement for positive change. The answer is that what many people mistakenly perceive as a common base for cohesion and solidarity among all indigenous peoples does not exist. There is a clear need for co-operation, and certainly there is a basis for building solidarity among our peoples, but cohesion and solidarity are two very different things.

Cohesion is the power that is created when a group of individuals come together as one to form a community that is self-conscious and secure in itself—when those people *cohere* around a set of beliefs and institutions, and gain fulfilment and strength in their association with one another. Roles and responsibilities are clear; there is both a common good and an agreed-upon process of dissent; and people protect and benefit from one another. Those things that can divide are consciously rejected, and those that bring people together and make them stronger are consciously embraced. This is unity—the prerequisite to peace and power in any community.

Solidarity is the power that comes from recognizing and respecting what all indigenous peoples have in common: the struggle for self-determination. We all support our fellow indigenous peoples because we understand that all Natives are linked in opposition to the injustice we face in our own lives. Yet, to show solidarity with other indigenous peoples, a community must first have its own strong identity and group cohesion. Having weak, fractured groups trading hollow noises about one another's pain will not move us forward. It is the communities that achieve cohesion around a set of values and institutions that become powerful in themselves and therefore capable of lending the strength of their voices and resources to others.

Both cohesion and solidarity mean coming together. The difference between the two is that cohesion is found among people of the same group and results in the strengthening of that group. Solidarity is found among people of different groups who recognize the value, even the necessity, of supporting other groups because of the similarities that exist among them.

People who ask why indigenous people can't "get together" are usually referring to a problem of cohesion. Why can't Indians in Canada get together and all support the national chief of the Assembly of First Nations? As we are often reminded by the ill-informed, there is power in numbers, and Indian people would really be a force to be reckoned with if they would only get over their tribal differences. Astute people, however, recognize that organizations such as the AFN consistently fail because they are predicated on the notion that a single body can represent the diversity of indigenous nations. The diversity of histories, cultures, interests, and goals among indigenous peoples in Canada and the United States means that there can never be a general cohesion. Indigenous organizations that are built to force unity among people in diverse situations are doomed to failure.

Some may ask whether there is any difference between this sort of forced pan-Indian unity—the movement to merge all into a single Indian identity—and a more authentic and powerful form of indigenism. There are similarities. All Indian peoples share certain commonalities that may serve a unifying function, particularly in efforts to explain the cultural basis of the movement's goals to non-indigenous people. Of course, each community will have its own tactics and strategies; but the foundations of the movement and the driving force behind it are shared by almost all indigenous people; and the values embedded within indigenous traditions are very similar.

Indigenism, as I use the term, is not a politically expedient kind of pan-Indianism, or the assimilative ideology of *indigenismo* common in Latin American countries. It brings together words, ideas, and symbols from different indigenous cultures to serve as tools for those involved in asserting nationhood. It does not, however, supplant the localized cultures of individual communities. Indigenism is an important means of confronting the state in that it provides a unifying vocabulary and basis for collective action. But it is entirely dependent on maintenance of the integrity of the traditional indigenous cultures and communities from which it draws its strength.

Indigenism and localized Native nationalism are not conflicting ideologies. In fact, they are mutually supportive, feeding each other's intellectual development as well as fostering political co-operation. Since mounting a successful challenge to colonialism demands activism at the level of both the community and the state, melding aspects of indigenism and various nationalisms may enable leaders to develop a framework of understanding and an ability to persuade and justify that can be applied to all cases. In the past, commonalities were built upon, power shared, differences respected. This confederate ideal, so prevalent in history, is the best example of a political tradition among indigenous peoples.

Leadership

What are the characteristics of a true Native leader? The indigenous assumption is that our traditions demand a higher standard of conduct—in fact, a completely different conception of the leader's role—than do the conventional corporate models that dominate business and politics in mainstream society. Simply put, for us, it is not enough to know how to gain, hold, and use power.

In the corporate model that forms the basis of so-called leadership or managerial training, the focus is on the acquisition and exercise of power both within a particular organization and in relation to other organizations. The effective leader/manager in this context is the Machiavellian victor in a zero-sum power game. He is guided by four principles:

- Jealously guard your reputation and status.
- Constantly analyze resources and the opportunity structure.
- Make others aware of their dependence on you.
- Create a web of relationships to support your power.

Adherence to these principles may guarantee success within an organization based on the adversarial premises of Western-style politics. But it is at odds with the basic assumptions about the role of leaders in traditional indigenous cultures. Contrast the contemporary managerial model with the counsel offered to newly appointed chiefs in the Rotinohshonni's *Kaienerekowa*. In this tradition, a royaner (literally "he is of the good" in the Kanien'keha language) is bound to fulfil certain requirements, which constitute the principles of Rotinohshonni leadership. The contrast between these principles and those described above is clear:

- "develop skin seven spans thick, which means that your mind will be strong and it will not let pass through a pointed object meant to puncture you while you work ..."
- "protect your family and nation ..."
- "be even-handed with all of the people ..."
- "think of others before thinking of yourself ..."

In the Rotinohshonni tradition, the women of each family raise a man to leadership and hold him accountable to these principles. If he does not uphold and defend the *Kaienerekowa*, or if the women determine that his character or behaviour does not conform to the leadership principles, he is removed from the position. As in other traditional cultures, this moral definition of leadership focuses on a person's adherence to the values of patience, courage, fairness, and generosity. This focus differs radically from the power-wielding model, which encourages the fundamentally immoral pursuit of self-interest and the acquisition of resources to secure a strategic advantage over others.

The goal of the indigenous model resembles what Burns in *Leadership* calls a "self-actualized" person: someone with the ability to lead by being led. In Burns's concept of transformative leadership, the ideal leader is able

to listen and be guided by others without being threatened by them, to depend on others but not be overly dependent, to judge other persons with both affection and discrimination, to possess enough autonomy to be creative without rejecting the external influences that make for growth and relevance.

It is the combination of certain skills with a grounding in sympathy and respect for the people that marks Burns's theoretical model, and that I think makes that model compatible with the ideal leader within indigenous cultures. A leader is a person of responsibility and respect as opposed to one of ambition and greed: an adviser rather than an executive.

Russell Barsh's study of traditional Native American political systems suggests that those people who occupy positions of leadership and are held in high esteem within indigenous communities share four general traits:

- They draw on their own personal resources as sources of power. They do not give other people's money away to gain support. They are very productive, they are generous, and their values are not materialist.

- They set the example. They assume the responsibility of going first and taking the greatest risk for the good of the community.
- They are modest and funny. They minimize personality conflict and use humour to deflect anger.
- They are role models. They take responsibility for teaching children, and they realize the educative and empowering role of government in the community.

Boldt and Long have used a martial analogy to illustrate their conception of indigenous leadership in relation to the community: In their view, an indigenous leader stands in relation to the people as a military drummer does to troops in formation. The drummer in a parade beats out the cadence to which the troops step, all of them relying on the authority of the march to structure their actions.

I prefer another analogy. I like to think of indigenous leadership in terms of the relationship between the drummers, singers, and dancers at a pow-wow. The drummers and singers give voice to the heartbeat of the earth, and the dancers move to the sound, giving life to their personal visions and to those of their people. The drum prompts and paces. Drummers, singers, and dancers act together to manifest tradition through the songs. All three groups are essential and related, the role of each group being to respect and represent the spirit of the creation in its own way, according to its own special abilities.

Responsibility

One of the fundamental characteristics in the traditional culture of Native leadership is the demand for mutual respect between leaders and the community. The importance of communication and consent in traditional government means that leaders are responsible for maintaining an unbroken chain of answerability and inclusion in decision-making.

For example, in the traditional Rotinohshonni system, men were chiefs and women selected them. Thus, the Condolence ritual focuses on "accountability to the women" as a fundamental requirement of government. In modern times, this sense of responsibility or accountability can be understood in terms of a simple (although crucial) requirement for universal inclusion and the maintenance of strong links between those charged with the responsibility of decision-making and those who will have to live with the consequences of their decisions. Accountability in the indigenous sense needs to be understood not just as a set of processes but as a relationship. In a very basic way, accountability can be thought of in terms of the answer to the question, "Who do you answer to?"

It is in the nature of traditional indigenous political systems that power is not centralized, that compliance with authority is not coerced but voluntary, and that decision-making requires consensus. (In practice, these principles mean that contention is almost a natural state in indigenous politics!) Because traditional systems are predicated on the ideal of harmony and the promotion of an egalitarian consensus through persuasion and debate, leaders must work through the diverse opinions and ideas that exist in any community. Because there is both an inherent respect for the autonomy of the individual and a demand for general agreement, leadership is an exercise in patient persuasion. Thus, active and fractious disagreement is a sign of health in a traditional system. It means the people are engaging their leaders and challenging them to prove the righteousness of their position. It means they are making them accountable. In an indigenous conception of accountability, then, the question, "Who do you answer to?" seems to have literal meaning.

Consider the words of an elder from the Fort Yuma Indian Reservation in California: "We Quechans try to get somebody to do better by tearing him down—criticizing him. You whites, you try to get somebody to do better by making him feel good, by praising him." This points to a view of accountability as not only a process of formal reportage, but a relationship between society and government. The purely technical sense of accountability—accurate bookkeeping and procedural transparency—is only a starting point for understanding what indigenous people demand of their government leaders.

Accountability is only one of the responsibilities of a leader. In his extensive work on American Indian community governance, the sociologist, Stephen Cornell, has demonstrated that it is in the nature of traditional indigenous systems to put a stronger emphasis on accountability than Western systems do. In all systems, accountability procedures basically reflect the cultural values of the people. In Western systems, with their delegated authority, representative government, and detached bureaucratic structures, there is a distance between leader and led that makes accountability a largely impersonal matter of procedure.

By contrast, in indigenous systems, leader and led inhabit the same political—and physical—space. In this context, the legitimacy of leaders and of governments is determined in part by the degree to which they adhere to accountability procedures, but to an even greater degree by the success leaders have in cultivating and maintaining relationships. It is through these relationships in particular that leaders gain the approval of the people and ensure that their actions are in the best interests of the community. The indigenous concept of accountability demands an intimate knowledge of the particular culture of the community and consistent close contact with the people. It is not enough to balance the books. A leader must constantly work to make sure the people know that he is answering to them and respects the appropriate protocol and procedures within the context of that culture.

In indigenous traditions, consensus decision-making is a group process in which the common will is determined through patient listening to all points of view. Leadership takes the form of guidance and persuasion within the larger respectful debate. In cases where individual interests must be balanced against those of the community, there should be a considered evaluation of the individual's needs (as opposed to wants). These needs should be balanced with those of the community, and the entire debate must be carried out on the firm ground of agreed-upon values and principles. If any one of these elements is missing, consensus decision-making cannot happen. Processes that purport to be consensual become mere exercises in power-wielding, manipulation, and enticement simply to gain the assent of the majority.

One of the biggest areas of neglect in terms of responsibility concerns women. For centuries, the patriarchy imposed by Western religion and political systems excluded women from decision-making. Today, this is no longer necessarily the case: In most communities, women do participate actively in politics. Yet their ability to achieve the kind of change they want is still limited, and the indigenous values of respect and balance in gender relations go largely unheeded.

In a recent Canadian study, Jo-Anne Fiske notes that

> contemporary aboriginal women have relatively high political status vis-à-vis men within their own communities. That is to say, women are not disadvantaged in comparison to men in regard to access to elected office, appointment to administrative positions, employment, and economic advantages within domestic units. On the other hand, these same studies also disclose the constraints women frequently confront: domestic violence, abuse related to alcohol dependency, the stress of parenting without male partners, and a lack of intimate, stable relationships.

These observations point to two factors limiting women's political participation, both of which are direct consequences of colonialism: One factor
is the psychological damage done to indigenous men, which often leads to
social dysfunction, if not outright violence; the necessity of defending themselves and taking full responsibility for their children can make it difficult
for women to take on any additional roles. The second factor is the imposed
Western political–economic system itself, which promotes goals and values that do nothing to meet indigenous people's basic needs for health,
safety, and security. The state's criteria of progress for women are satisfied
by their increased participation in the band council and free enterprise systems; but externally derived status and material success cannot solve the
severe social and psychological problems that Native communities face.

Native women in general are demanding that Native men, in the words
of Kanien'kehaka lawyer Patricia Monture, "respect our anger and work with
us through it." Most women recognize that their children's future depends
on restoring balance and health in the community, and especially returning
to respect for the special role and power of women. But they are equally committed to maintaining the integrity and security of their nations. The imposition of colonial solutions to internal problems does just as much to
undermine the long-term existence of indigenous people as does the continuing abuse of women and children by men. Another reason to reject external remedies is simply that people in white society can never fully appreciate
the intensity of the violence that Native women face or the variety of forms
it may take. As Monture writes,

> The anger that I carry as an Indian woman does not grow only in the
> abuse that women of First Nations have survived and continue to sur-
> vive on a daily basis. The anger also grows from what I have learned
> about Canadian law. Canadian law is not my aboriginal solution for
> many reasons. Discriminating in meaning or action in Canadian law
> does not reflect my experiences. I cannot be certain that a Canadian
> court will be able to successfully conceptualize a situation of discrim-
> ination within discrimination.

This fight-within-a-fight theme is a constant refrain among Native women
who remain part of Native communities. There are many different views of
the problem from the outside, but on the inside, the sentiment expressed
by Paula Gunn Allen is common:

American Indian women must often fight the United States government, the tribal governments, women, and men of their tribe or their
urban community who are virulently misogynist or who are threatened by attempts to change the images foisted on us over the centuries
by whites…. We must strive to maintain tribal status; we must make
certain that the tribes continue to be legally recognized entities, sovereign nations within the larger United States, and we must wage this
struggle in many ways….

This is not to say that Native women equate their men with the colonizers—
they recognize the harm done to the psyche of the Native male. They also hold
him responsible for dealing with it, but they know where the roots of the historic and present injustice lead. As Monture puts it, the state "is the invisible
male perpetrator who unlike Aboriginal men does not have a victim face."

Overcoming both the abuse of our nations by the state and the abuse to
which Native women are subjected depends on our recognizing that the
two are related. We cannot have strong nations without strong women, and
the solution is not to adopt external values concerning gender relations or
to impose male-defined roles for women (in what is still, after all, a colonial context). Monture points to the solution: "My ability to reclaim my
position in the world as a Rotinohshonni woman is preconditioned on the
ability of our men to remember the traditions that we have lost." There are
twin responsibilities for men and women. Men must acknowledge, respect,
and work to help eliminate the heavy burden that women carry. Women
must commit themselves to making their nation liveable from within the
culture. Neglect of either one of these responsibilities will lead to the eventual destruction of our peoples.

Righteousness

You shall be a good person, and, you shall be kind to all of the people, not differentiating among them, the people who are wealthy, and the poor ones, and the good natured ones, and the evil ones who sin readily; all of them you shall treat kindly, and you shall not differentiate among them. As to your own fireside, never consider only yourself, you must always remember them, the old people, and the younger people, and the children, and those still in the earth, yet unborn, and always you will take into account everyone's well-being, that of the ongoing families, so that they may continue to survive, your grandchildren.

—from the *Kaienerekowa*

One of the challenges we face when we commit ourselves to resurrecting an indigenous form of government based on traditional values is that the colonial system has some powerful incentives for non-action built into it. It is easier and safer to accept the status quo than it is to put forward a challenge. In comparison with the immediate gratification (in the form of jobs, resources, and authority) that the state offers those who co-operate and serve its agenda, the rewards for moving down the indigenous path seem insubstantial and far off in the future. This is a true dilemma for Native leadership: whether to seek internal peace by meeting the needs of the community and restoring it to strength and health or to promote stability in relations with others by satisfying the demands and expectations of mainstream society. In this sense, Canada and the United States are harsh places for Native people. Every day, communities must make choices between satisfying the basic imperatives of their own cultures and submitting to the assimilative pressures exerted by state institutions and policies. As individuals, Native leaders must choose between working to earn the respect of their own and other indigenous people and gaining esteem and status in the eyes of state agents and mainstream society—with all the differential rewards that choice implies.

The necessity of such choices is a result of the continuing colonial power structure and the state's unremitting desire to exploit indigenous lands. There is a terrible immediacy to the consequences of our decisions on both the collective and the individual level: Every minor concession made to keep the Indian agent happy is measured internally as another piece of land lost, another violent night, another child neglected, another life wasted. It is because these costs are so heavy that we must act to revitalize our traditional values—however much such action may offend the agent. The alternative is, in stark terms, the surrender of our nations. Many leaders who recognize the necessity of confronting colonialism are prevented from acting on that recognition because of their situation in an unjust system. They know what's right; they have long known what's wrong as well and what needs to be done. But they choose to suppress their knowledge and accept the dispossession and disempowerment that are part of being colonized. Wilfully ignoring what is ultimately the only resolution—to forsake good relations with the state—they join the conspiracy of silence that has perpetuated the historical injustice done to their people.

More than a hundred years ago, people of honour spoke out against the law. The historian J.B. Mackenzie wrote in 1896,

> I firmly believe the Indian craves ardently his thorough emancipation from subjection—a right that should be conceded him by the Central authority, urged only though it were by that silent, yet potent and weighty, appeal, the unswerving devotion of his forefathers—their support at junctures grave, disturbing, staunchly as unfailingly extended to—Britain's Crown.

Why are we still arguing about our "thorough emancipation" as we move deeper into the twenty-first century? Mackenzie's passage reflects a recognition of what we would today describe as indigenous nationhood and a right of self-determination rooted in treaty relationships! Surely by now we should have progressed beyond having to justify our emancipation and begun actually creating a new relationship. Yet we are still arguing our case, largely because most white people are ignorant of history (it was his understanding of history that enabled Mackenzie to perceive the injustice). But there is another reason why the debate continues: Because Native leaders themselves have wavered on their commitment to the goal of freedom from colonial domination. In Native politics, there are two approaches to the future: One that seeks to resurrect a form of indigenous nationhood (a traditional objective), and another that attempts to achieve partial recognition of a right of self-government within the legal and structural confines of the state (an assimilative goal). It is this divergence in the political positions of various indigenous organizations that allows the state to manipulate the so-called decolonization process toward its own objectives.

The historical and moral rightness of indigenous nationhood—in legal terms, the existence of the indigenous right to self-determination—is gaining acceptance outside indigenous communities. Historically conscious and well-educated people realize that the foundations of the traditional indigenous position are sound. It is ironic that, increasingly, Native politicians (many of whom have been co-opted and are to a large degree alienated from their own cultures and communities) are taking a softer stance on their people's rights than are progressives in mainstream society.

There are two issues to contend with in redressing the historical injustice. The first is the substance of the indigenous position: the principle of self-determination. The second is the remedy for the injustice: action. These are separate issues, and they require separate consideration. Co-opted leaders mistakenly equate the need to be accommodating on the remedy with a licence to compromise the principle. In fact, though, it is crucial to defend the principle, because recognition of the actual historical injustice and respect for the continuing existence of indigenous peoples as nations are the only bases on which substantial remedial action can be prescribed and justified (both politically and legally).

International law has made colonialism illegal. Because of the domination of settler states in the international system, however, this legal principle is applied only in the context of state-to-state relations: the forms of internal colonialism practised in Canada, the United States, Mexico, Australia, New Zealand, and other countries with substantial indigenous populations are excluded. If applied fairly (as in other parts of the world that Europeans eventually vacated), international law would prescribe remedial action for these situations: The decolonization process would not be subject to laws developed in the colonial context or constrained by contemporary legal doctrines or political justifications specifically intended to accomplish colonial objectives relative to indigenous peoples. That is, of course, unless indigenous people allow the settler state to limit the remedial action and to continue denying the full exercise of indigenous nationhood, by compromising their own position. Solutions to colonialism must be developed co-operatively and with respect for the principle of self-determination. To consent to a lesser standard that gives primacy to colonial law, or accepts political or economic constraints, is simply to capitulate to the skewed logic of colonialism.

I once heard an elder say, "I am an Indian, I have an Indian heart, and I have reason to fight." Sadly, it seems many contemporary Native politicians have lost their Indian heart and will to fight on. In contrast to the strong position developing in support of indigenous rights in international law and United Nations forums and to growing support among the general population, many Native leaders have compromised their nations' principled positions in favour of solutions developed within a colonial mentality. For example, in 1986, the Sechelt Indian band on British Columbia's lower mainland accepted structural integration and legal subjection to Canadian law. The band's former chief attempted to cast the transition to a quasi-municipal status as an act of self-determination. Stan Dixon's many public statements betray his blindness to his own co-optation, not to mention deep confusion and shocking naïveté. Reminiscing about the agreement, he wrote,

> After watching my friend ... raise our Sechelt flag, along with the British Columbia and Canadian flags; I felt a deep emotion and realized how much I loved Canada and my people. At that moment, I cried.... It signified what Sechelt is all about, a distinct people with a culture and a past. But for 130 years in between, we were wards of the Federal Government. And today, for the public perception we regained our distinction and Sechelt was granted local autonomy through Bill C-93.

Dixon's compromise is evident in the fact that his community's autonomy depends on the Canadian state. The irony is that although his community's governing authority, as of 1986, was set in law at the municipal level, Sechelt became responsible for all of the programs and services whose delivery would otherwise be the responsibility of the province of British Columbia had they not signed their self-government agreement. And because their agreement provided no funding for these programs and services, many First Nations who remain under the Indian Act, with less self-governing authority than Sechelt, are far ahead of the community when it comes to economic self-sufficiency and social development. The merging of identities and the rationalization of a subordinate political status, so important to the colonization process, are also clear. Just as clear are the consequences that inevitably flow from adopting such a posture. Following the Nisga'a nation's 1998 treaty signing, in 1999, the Sechelt became the second British Columbia group to sign an agreement that—for only $40 million and small parcels of fee-simple land in the Sechelt case—surrenders their traditional territory and submits to Canada's claimed sovereignty over indigenous people. In 2000, the ratification went to the community, where the Agreement-in-Principle was subsequently voted down. The people, as usual, had more sense than the leaders they elected. Sechelt has not been at the negotiating table since. Since then, Dixon was re-elected in 2005, only to be locked out of the band office and forced to resign by the people due to more backroom deals and his taking the side of the RCMP in an abuse-of-police-power incident in July 2007. Since then, in 2007 and 2008, there have been two other First Nations groups with entrepreneurs for chiefs that have fallen prey to corporate–government political coercion and surrendered their claims to traditional territories and invalidated their inherent rights in exchange for packages of monetary compensation and promises of business partnerships with non-indigenous companies: the Tsawwassen First Nation outside of Vancouver and the Maa-nulth First Nations on Vancouver Island, both of which, unlike the Sechelt example, were ratified by the community and passed into law by the Canadian federal and provincial levels of government.

This sort of active collaboration with colonial power cannot be supported within the framework of a traditional culture. The structure of colonialism (and, to a certain extent, the lack of education and awareness among indigenous people) allows co-opted politicians to cloud the air with misconceptions and avoid true accountability for their compromises.

To contrast the co-opted perspective with a view firmly rooted in traditional indigenous philosophy, consider the perspective that emerges in the following conversation. Atsenhaienton is a Kanien'kehaka, and a member of the bear clan. He has over ten years' experience working in United Nations processes on indigenous issues, has been a leading spokesman for the Kanien'kehaka people at the international level, and remains a respected voice on community issues and traditional government among the Rotinohshonni (the Iroquois Confederacy).

In our conversation, at his home in Kahnawake, we discussed the meaning of tradition and traditional governance, and politics in the broader Rotinohshonni context. Atsenhaienton spoke with clarity and depth about some of the key issues facing traditional-minded indigenous people.

Could you talk to me about traditionalism, and what it is to be a traditional person and a leader?

Let's start with the problems first—the problems we're having within the traditional movement—and then we could talk about some of the solutions. One of the main problems is the damage done to tradition by the Indian Act, because of the non-Native influence on our culture.

Do you believe in this concept of a "colonial mentality," of an internally colonized people?

Yes. You can call it "internalized oppression" or "internal racism." That's how I view the membership question here in this community: as an Indian Act way, a white way of thinking. To say that an Indian woman who marries a white man doesn't have any rights—that's not based on tradition, and yet it's so ingrained that even elders are talking like this now. That's not what our tradition is about at all, but that's what's been done.

I think there's a lot of that as well in the way people look at the *Kaienerekowa*. They look at the Great Law as a law book. They interpret each little phrase, each little word, and apply it.

So you don't know if it's so good to take our narrative tradition and treat it like a legal document?

No, no. The whole term "Great Law" is a mistake. That's not what it says in our language. In our language it says "the big warmth" or "the big harmony," or something along those lines.

One of our elders told me it meant "the great good way."

Yeah. But it's not a law: It's guidelines to help people get to harmony and coexistence. That's what it is. And yet now everybody interprets the written version and thinks that they're a $50 Confederacy lawyer! They look at the Great Law and interpret it the way a constitutional lawyer would. That's not the way it was intended to be treated. This is part of the damage—when people talk about traditional government, they are off in the wrong direction. This whole idea that "You're outside the circle," "You're outside of The Law," "Wampum so and so says this and you are out ..."

Without naming names of course!

Without any names, of course [laughter]. But a lot of people do that, eh? And even those who don't adhere to the "number system" interpretation of the Great Law may go off toward the other extreme—they take the Handsome Lake Code [a nativist revival doctrine in the Rotinohshonni tradition] and apply it so severely that it restricts the application of the *Kaienerekowa*. And they say that you have to follow *Kaienerekowa* and the Handsome Lake Code to be a part of the Iroquois Confederacy, which is really intolerant. It's against the tenets of the Great Law, the whole message of harmony.

I see the Kaienerekowa as a set of principles reflecting a set of values that were there before any type of structure. I think these values are what's essential, not the structure that evolved to perpetuate them.

I guess we get into the story of the Peacemaker here. Was there really a Peacemaker? You have to say that there was. People always talk about how as a people we were warlike, and reacted emotionally, and how we were told by the Peacemaker that we had to put emotions aside and use reason and a good mind to coexist. But there's another important part of the story: the clan system. He brought the clan system to us, where all the wolves and the bears and the turtles were of the same family. The bears in the Mohawks were brothers of the Oneida bears; there was a linkage. This is what broke down hostility and discouraged war: You would have to war against your brothers and sisters. Once all members of the same clan were brothers and sisters across the nations, it made it difficult to wage war against one another. People forget that is one of the reasons for the clan system. I think that the clan system breaks down nationalism; it's the nationalism that causes the conflict—Mohawk versus Oneida, or Onondaga. If we all sat in our clans and discussed the issues, we would get away from the nationalism that divides us. Peace would be achievable, and leadership would take on a different focus. We would talk about the issues rather than posture as a nation.

Could you talk about leadership in this sense?

I think there are some extreme views on the role of leaders that may have been applicable in the 1400s or 1500s. But in the modern era, with telecommunications, telephones, and faxes, the Confederacy has to adjust to a more participatory form of government than it had before.

So you believe that "adjusting" tradition is necessary?

It is truly necessary. I think that some of the problems we're having today in the Confederacy were felt before. When they talked about "adding rafters" [amending the constitution], they talked about other kinds of meetings, about the people having a right to meet with the band council, and the right to send messages back to Council meetings and to the chiefs. That shows that there was a change when it was felt that the chiefs were getting too far away from the people, too dictatorial. They had to be brought back. Those rafters were added to ensure that once the chiefs were put in place, they wouldn't be there forever. The people still had a voice.

You can see this today on the problem of taxation, for instance, with the Confederacy negotiators agreeing with the State of New York to keep the talks in camera, to not negotiate through the press, and to keep everything confidential. This alienated the chiefs from the people. The chiefs try to paint this as a "greedy businessmen versus the chiefs" thing, but it's not that at all. It's a "regular guy in the street who doesn't know what the hell's going on" thing.

To me, this brings up the question of whether or not our leaders, traditional or otherwise, actually do embody the values we claim to uphold within our society.

I think that it's the younger people within the Confederacy who have a clearer idea of the true intent of the *Kaienerekowa*. They know more about participatory government than the old guard does, as a tight inner circle of chiefs and clan mothers. Someday, the younger people will take over and that will change ...

And our understanding of tradition will change and evolve?

Yes, and I think for the better, because they know they have to find a better way. The new generation sees what's not working and how they can make it work. And they will, because they also see the problems with the Indian Act, the elected systems and the elected band councils and tribal council being pulled into the mainstream politics.

Do you see that yourself?

Sure I do. The situation in Akwesasne [another Kanien'kehaka community, up the St Lawrence River near Cornwall, Ontario] with their two tribal councils is an example of how traditional people get sucked into it. They're disenchanted with the traditional government, they don't like the tribal council trustee system, so they create their own tribal council—the "people's tribal council" or "the people's government"—and it's an aberration. It's not the way to go. They're losing sight of the values of traditional government. They're trying to keep both the values of the traditional government and the structures of the new government, of a tribal council system, and there's a clash. It's difficult to quote the Two-Row Wampum and still use the tribal council structure.

How do you see them getting beyond that? What would be the first step?

They have to sit down together and talk. Again, you have to look at the basic fundamentals of the *Kaienerekowa*, which means that you have to leave your emotions outside the door when you meet, and you have to use the reasoning of a good mind. The whole story of "Haiawatha" and the condolence—if the bitter man who lost all his daughters like that can set aside his hatred and revenge …

That's what always sticks in my mind: Aienwathe losing his daughters as the ultimate test of commitment to what he believed in and what he was doing.

And that's what Akwesasne has to go through, because there were those two killings and it's become a blood feud. You have to take that blood feud and put it aside. Over here in Kahnawake, we're trying. We've had two meetings between a few others and myself and people from the Mohawk Council of Chiefs and the Mohawk Trail longhouse. We've had a couple of informal sessions, just … to talk. No restrictions, you know, everybody's polite—maybe too polite! But at least we've started talking. On a couple of issues, we've agreed to disagree but to keep on meeting.

This traditional values system that we keep talking about, is this something that you would say is desirable? Or is it essential for the future if we are to survive? Do we need to focus on that as the foundation of our governance?

I think it's essential. How can we call ourselves Mohawks without it? It's part of our culture. Mind you, culture evolves, and I'm not saying that the *Kaienerekowa* is set in stone or that we can't change it. I reject that, because culture does evolve. But there are certain fundamental principles: using reason and a good mind, not using sharp words, etc.... Those are basic things that we should hang on to. But some of the other structures have to evolve to fit our modern society. I think this really is essential, because, otherwise, we're down the road to being assimilated. If we lose our traditional values, then we're just brown-skinned Canadians.

You talked about Akwesasne not being able to reconcile the Kaienerekowa *with the tribal council system, and, in a broader context across Canada, I think that problem is even more common. But isn't that what we're trying to do here in Kahnawake? In most cases, what we are trying to do as Native people is to take the band council and make it into something more accountable, more participatory, all those good things we talk about as being our tradition. That's in effect what the band council here is trying to do.*

It is. First of all, the people that are inside the band council are Mohawks. Some people feel that you're not a Mohawk if you're an elected council member—that's an extremist position. I reject the whole idea. I think there are some exceptions, but, for the most part, the people who run for band council are sincere people who are trying to make the community work. At the same time, the band council has changed and improved. But that's because of tradition. If we didn't have a traditional element in this community, we wouldn't have gone in that direction. We would be much more like some of the other communities further east or further west. It has been the traditional values and the traditional opposition that has made the band council evolve in this way. And really, those band councillors are threatened by tradition. This idea that comes out when they run for election that they're "working themselves out of a job" is a lot of crap!

Can I quote you on that one?

Oh yeah [laughter]. In the long run, it shows that they're really hanging on to their positions. They are threatened by any kind of action or any movement by the traditional people to organize or to take over anything. Whether it's the conflict between the Peacekeepers and the Warriors in the

1980s [band council police and traditionalist militants] or little things like doing traditional ceremonial openings to events, there's always that conflict with the band council. Because they have taken over, and because they have money, they have been able to gain the upper hand in any new development in the community. Because they have the money, the government recognizes that fact and feeds them even more. Actually, tradition was at its height in the late 1980s. After 1990, the traditional movement was sapped in terms of its energy and financial resources and so the band council is more comfortable now; it's been able to take the Canadian Indian Act and the "self–government" policy and go beyond it. They have pushed it, and I give them credit for that, but, again, I'll repeat that they would not have gone that way without us.

Leaving and looking at Kahnawake from the outside has made that a lot clearer for me. When I started working for the council, in the mid-1980s, it seemed as if there was some "slack" in the system and in the Indian Act: We could legitimately claim to be acting traditional and making progress along that way and to be making gains relative to what we say are our traditional goals. But now it seems as if all that slack has tightened up. There's no more room to manoeuvre and claim to be traditional. In one sense, we are being structured by the agreements we're negotiating. We try to do one thing, and even though we're sincere in the effort, we're almost being forced down a different path. We still may accomplish something for our people. But even with the best intentions, the structure of the situation may mean that we end up serving other people's interests.

I think the band council has been lucky that the [federal or provincial] government hasn't pushed. But the real damage is in the potential; the potential to damage this community is still there, it's just dormant. I don't know what will spark it, but something will happen in the future. Then we're really going to regret signing things like the Police Agreement. Right now, it's functioning on the surface.

On a broader level, the conflict between the traditional movement—which is taking hold, at least conceptually, in a lot of communities—and the established structures exists just about everywhere and for everyone. How do you see the other communities relative to the Kahnawake experience? Are they dealing with the same types of issues? Are they handling them better, or are they making mistakes?

I think the situation in Iroquois communities is unique because you have both the elected Indian Act system and the traditional governments. I know there are some places in British Columbia that have both as well, but the systems are close together there: You have traditional chiefs in elected positions, etc.… That is unacceptable in Iroquoian thinking. You also see some traditional–elected splits among the Mi'kmaq, and of course among the Hopi and Navajo people. What it always comes down to when you have these traditional–elected splits is that the [federal or provincial] government supports the money and the elected councils. You always know which side the government is going to take. Look at the American Indian Movement in Pine Ridge in the 1970s. Look at what happened there and how extreme it got. You see that over and over again.

That's been your experience here, too?

For sure it has. I think there was an attempt by the federal government to take the traditional people seriously. I think John Ciaccia [the former Quebec provincial minister of Indian Affairs] tried. We were having discussions about bingo, and we even almost came to some kind of understanding about cigarettes. There were even meetings with Revenue Quebec. But, then, he was reprimanded, got his wrist slapped, and when the 1990 crisis broke out, that was it—he was fired soon after. Of course, we don't know if they were ever sincere—but anyway, the discussions with traditional people just stopped. That kind of thinking was out the window.

One perspective that is coming forward now, especially from women and youth, is that all this talk and movement on self-government and politics is putting the cart before the horse. They say that a lot of Native communities are really sick, socially, physically, and psychologically, and that we need to deal with that sickness before we can progress on politics. What's your sense about the depth of the problem?

I can't talk about other communities, but in our own, it's true. One of the most overused words these days is *healing*. I don't like using it at all. But it is true that some healing has to take place before you can ever exercise self-determination. You have to have strong families before you can have strong communities, before you can have a strong nation. That's how I look at it. I do think we have a lot of strong families here in Kahnawake, and some strong communities elsewhere, too, but there is still some repair work to be done. For us, and for communities like Akwesasne that do have strong families, the jump to nationhood is not that far. Other communities may have a harder time.

Women and young people also say that you can't build a government around leaders who are abusing their wives and are disrespectful of everybody except themselves. I agree. It's almost as if you have to work on that problem before you start tackling the larger issues of nationhood and relations with other governments.

I shudder when I hear about communities like Davis Inlet [an Innu community in Labrador plagued by abuse and teen suicide]. But we have to remember that this is damage that was done to them—they didn't do this to themselves. They are victims, and Canada has to take a lot of responsibility for those situations.

Because of your roots in the traditional perspective, when I say the word "nationhood," it means something different to you than it does to a band councillor.

It does. The band council never talked about sovereignty; they never used the word "nation" twenty years ago. These are terms that they learned from traditional people. It actually came out of the constitutional debates in the late 1970s and 1980–82. When our Iroquoian traditional people were asked to go and speak in Yellowknife or Whitehorse, they started using those words. When the Assembly of First Nations was formed out of the National Indian Brotherhood, the term "nation" came mainly from the traditional Iroquoian people who had a lot of influence at that time.

What about the word "sovereignty"?

It would have been the same way, eh? You never heard of sovereignty before that. "Sovereignty" is a word I use a lot; traditional people use it a lot. You never hear the word "independence"—we don't use that term. It's easy to talk about sovereignty because I look at it as a state of mind. It means you think like a nation, like a sovereign people, or a sovereign person. We use all those elements of nationhood—treaty-making, population, government. The non-Native yardsticks that are used to measure nationhood—I use them a lot. As Mohawks, we have the same elements as other people; the only thing missing is our land, which they are occupying.

That's interesting, because one of the things I'm doing in this book is critiquing the word "sovereignty." Historically, I agree with your analysis of where it comes from, the contributions of the traditional perspective and all that. But I'm also considering the stage we're at now. Keeping in mind what sovereignty means intrinsically, where it comes from, and what it means as a power relationship between the government and the people, my idea right now is that it's useful for us today only as an external-ized concept. As you said, relative to Canada and the United States, we can use it to assert ourselves. But, internally, I don't think it's the appropriate frame for gover-nance. It's an imported idea. It implies certain things about how you govern and how you use power, and maybe internally it's not even relevant. When we talk internal governance, we have to use our own words, our own concepts. I look at the Navajo, and some of the other nations in Canada, and I see sovereignty used as an internal concept of governance. I see real problems when those Indian governments start act-ing just like white governments toward their own people, when they are supposed to be acting on traditional principles.

You're right—in the European system, the Crown is sovereign. In our sys-tem, the people are sovereign. Their concept of sovereignty is very differ-ent from ours historically.

So the word you're using is not necessarily the replication of their concept. It's mainly a word that's recognizable to them.

That's right.

You don't mean the full academic understanding of sovereignty ...

No, nor their historical development of the concept.

What are the key components in your understanding of it? What is the essence of sovereignty as a governmental principle? What does it mean to you to possess it?

To me, it's the Mohawk people using our terminology to express our self-determination—how we will exist, how we will relate to each other and to other people. We will make those decisions, and we will make decisions that affect our culture, our language, and how we teach our children. It's about decisions on survival; everything's based on survival.

In my last book, I used a Kanien'keha word that Joe [Norton] gave me—tewata-towie, which means "we take care of ourselves." Does that come close to what you mean?

Yeah, that makes sense.

I know when we're together, you and I talk mostly about the Iroquois, but you also have a lot of experience on the international stage. What commonalities or linkages do you see between our people's struggles and those of indigenous peoples in other parts of the world?

They are so similar! You just have to change the names, and it's the same thing: Everybody is fighting colonialism in one form or another. As Iroquoian people, we identify very strongly with the South Americans—we talk about self-determination and sovereignty, and the South Americans have that same concept. There are close ties between the Iroquois and the Central and South Americans based on our concepts of the people, our relationship to the land, and all of that. It's the same thing with the Aborigines in Australia. And, now, we're beginning to see how the same thing happens in Asia. The Asian groups are very active internationally now—people from India, Burma, the Philippines, and now even the Russians. We never knew indigenous people were so global, but we find that we have the same common problems and the same kind of world view in most cases. That's why, in the drafting of the UN Draft Declaration on the Rights of Indigenous Peoples, it was easy for indigenous people to come to agreement on what our rights are. It's easy for us to agree. The hard part is to get governments to see the declaration as necessary and not so threatening. We do have problems sometimes, among indigenous people, agreeing on a strategy to achieve that.

What about indigenous people who may differ fundamentally? Are there any groups in Canada or internationally that stand out as very different from others on these issues of governance and land and relationships?

We haven't run into that. Maybe it's because the people are so tolerant. We tolerate people having a different structure, a different way of doing things, because it's their own business. I think we recognize each other's right to self-determination. Sometimes, even internally within our own caucuses, we forget about that and we have to be reminded. Sometimes, we have a meeting and a non-indigenous person will show up, and we resent that, but we have to be reminded that indigenous people delegated him to speak because they felt he suited their purposes. So we have to respect the right of self-determination of that indigenous nation.

Anthropologists may look at indigenous people and see commonalties based on similarities in the organization of our societies, for example, or the way we distribute wealth or make decisions. But it sounds as if in your mind there is something more fundamental about being indigenous.

What's fundamental about being indigenous, and is common among us, is the relationship to the land—indigenous people have a long association with the land we are occupying. Some people, of course, have been "transmigrated" or forced to migrate to other areas, but they still have a strong attachment to the land. Also, we don't have a definition for being indigenous: We believe in group self-definition. Peoples can identify for themselves that they are, and other indigenous groups will recognize who is indigenous. That's how we do it. You yourself are an indigenous person, and other people recognize you as being indigenous; that's what makes you indigenous.

So, among those who may claim to be indigenous, who in your mind is not?

The Afrikaners, the Boers, who have come to Geneva and tried to claim that they are indigenous.

What about white ranchers in Alberta or Montana?

No. I don't consider them indigenous.

On what basis do you deny them? They have a "connection to the land," and they've "been there for generations" ...

Yeah, but the people they've supplanted to have their ranches, those are the indigenous people.

So there's a component of aboriginality to it, you have to be the first people?

That's right.

Are there any other common issues you see as important for indigenous people?

I'd like to focus on the issue of self-determination. There are three funda-mental problems that indigenous people are having with the UN and the other world. One is the right to self-determination, which is denied us based on a fundamental discrimination in the UN and the world against indigenous peoples. Another is that we have a right to land and resources. And the third point is collective rights—indigenous people exercise their rights collectively, and when other people talk about human rights as the rights of individuals, we feel threatened, because it's collective rights that are important for the survival of indigenous peoples. Those are the three areas where we have a conflict with nation-states.

Do you see any potential for progress?

Sure. The more educated governments become, the more we communicate and discuss, the less they feel threatened by us. One of the big problems they have with us is that *self-determination* to them means independence. They think we all want to become independent countries and further fractionalize the entire world. But they are finding that probably 95 percent of indigenous peoples have no intention of setting up separate states—all they want is respect. They want to control the lands they are in, and the resources, so that they can go on living within the nation-state that surrounds them and make sure they have a relationship that ensures their survival.

Would you put our people in that category?

I think … no.

So we're that other 5 percent then, eh?

We're that 5 percent [laughter] in the sense that it's culturally within the makeup of our people—because of our constitution, our state of mind, our world view—that we look at ourselves as an independent people. It's also because of the Two-Row Wampum model of relationships between independ-ent peoples, which existed before European contact as a common way of deal-ing with other indigenous peoples. We believe that we have a right to be independent; in the realpolitik sense, I do believe that we can coexist with the

Canadian and American governments without violating our own constitution. They have to understand that we don't intend to destroy Canada or the United States, but that we have a right to determine for ourselves our relationships.

"Independence" is not a word that we use. I remember being annoyed when you and I were interviewed by the *Washington Post* a few years ago: I talked about sovereignty, sovereignty, sovereignty the whole time, and then when the article came out, the caption read, "Advocates independence for the Mohawk Nation."

Anyway, independence is wrong. In our situation, it's a Two-Row Wampum concept. I think that we can be an independent people without using the word "independence." We can agree with Canada not to raise our own army if they promise not to use an army against us, and we can agree not to try to acquire nuclear weapons because it's not in our mutual best interests, etc. Most indigenous peoples can't develop the economy to be independent—all they want is to share the resources so that they can survive. In our case, we have to find a way to apply the Two-Row in a modern situation.

So that's the immediate challenge, to balance the contemporary reality with respect for our traditions?

Yes. There's a lot of wisdom in our tradition. We can be self-determining and live by the Two-Row and coexist in the next century.

Money

In recent years, one of the motivating forces behind Native politics has been the belief that increasing the material wealth of Native people will solve all the problems of colonization. The inherent contradiction between this approach and traditional philosophies aside, this notion has led to the emergence of governments oriented not toward making peace but toward making money (or, more fashionably, "accessing resources"). But development is not a panacea. In fact, without a sound traditional basis, it becomes a real danger. This is true not just for indigenous peoples. Mainstream society itself must also come to terms with the fact that money-minded materialism is not a good thing. John Ralston Saul, a clear-sighted social critic, has recognized the folly of relying on the market as a source of societal values. He sees through the corporate manipulation to the greed that drives contemporary politics and "free market" ideology:

I love the market. I like trade, money markets, global economic patterns, all of it.... But I'm not fool enough to mistake these necessary and important narrow mechanisms for a broad, solid, conscious force that can lead society. The history of the marketplace has been consistently written by its actions. To ignore history is to withdraw into severe unconsciousness. The important conundrum for us is to understand how we have come to so forget our own history that we are acting in a suicidal manner, believing that economics can lead—where in the past it has always failed to do so.

Unfortunately, many Native politicians share a political vision that mirrors the worst tendencies of mainstream society. In a capitalist economy, financial resources are obviously a precondition for community autonomy. But it is one thing to see money as a competitive lever and a measure of collective strength; it is quite another to see self-government as an exercise in accessing financial resources, or the accumulation of wealth as an end in itself. An ideology of accumulation, even if it's collective rather than individual, plays right into the consumptive commercial mentality shaped by the state corporatism that has so damaged both the earth and human relationships around the globe. From an indigenous perspective, appropriate economic development entails taking advantage of opportunities to build self-sufficiency in order to preserve the essence of indigenous cultures and accomplish the goals that emerge from the culture. This is quite different from tying a community to an exploitative economy promoting objectives that contravene traditional values.

What drives Native leaders to turn away from their communities and embrace the worst aspects of mainstream society? The process of co–optation outlined earlier explains in general terms how Native politicians can become alienated from their communities. But there is a more basic factor that must be considered if communities are to avoid assimilation. The desire for ego gratification is a key feature of contemporary politics. Most people who have risen to positions of authority in the colonial system do not have the internal references for their choices and actions that come naturally to a person who respects traditional values. Without substantial formal checks, these politicians will base their actions on the values they have assimilated from their colonizers/colleagues in mainstream society. As a result, the accumulation and conspicuous display of monetary wealth is becoming increasingly common. Considered a sign of assimilation by traditional-minded people, this sort of acquisitiveness is allowed to continue because of the way colonial structures prevent politicians from being truly accountable to their people. The danger is that the authority vested in the co-opted politicians is being used to turn communities in the same direction.

The egotistical desire for fame and fortune needs to be distinguished from the desire for what we might call glory, which is shared by the community and is achieved through hard work or skill in non-political activities. According to the ethnologist Nancy Lurie, in the Native context, political fame is often condemned because it is associated with a greedy desire for a status that will distinguish the individual in some permanent, privileged way from the rest of the community. "Greed" in this context signifies a lack of respect for others and for the values of the people; it is an unhealthy and unbalanced individuality. As Lurie describes it,

> Greed is evil, a kind of worst of bad things. It combines selfishness, avarice, acquisitiveness, neglect and disrespect for the welfare of others, usurping power or authority, a show of unwarranted self-importance, bossiness, mean-mindedness, dishonesty. Greed is almost a kind of wicked presence.

Within this culture, success is measured in terms of the dollar value of a particular option or the profitability of a given enterprise, rather than the overall health and well-being of the people and the continuing strength of the nation as indicated by its preservation of traditional values. The latter should be the criteria by which development is measured. Native people are sometimes afraid to use words such as "vanity" and "greed" in reference to their politicians; such words are so insulting that the price of confronting the co-optation outweighs the benefits. Yet the truth must be told about the motivations of some politicians and their alienation from community perspectives.

Another truth that must be told is that money in itself does nothing to solve the problems faced by indigenous people. Only by building economic relationships and trade with other peoples can we really strengthen and sustain our communities. Truly valuable development consists in the learning, the skills, the business acumen, and the empowerment that flow from taking control over our lands and using them for the collective benefit in ways that are consistent with indigenous values. Moving from wardship to partnership with the state and industry is progress toward self-determination; this is a matter of perspective, resolve, and skill. Ignoring the principle of self-determination and blindly moving from total wardship to a new form of dependency—for example, based on supplying raw materials to foreign industry—is in fact a step down, because it requires that indigenous people actively participate in their own exploitation.

The 1995 Report of the Alaska Native Review Commission illustrates this dynamic. Describing the destructive impact of the imposition of a corporate form of government in Alaska, it shows how deeply opposed the profit-motivated model of government, based on resource extraction, is to the traditional values of the indigenous people.

The 1971 Alaska Native Claims Settlement Act (ANCSA) made no substantial reference to indigenous values and perspectives. It was oriented solely toward guaranteeing white access to the resources on and under the land, and imposing a regime of economic assimilation on the indigenous population. Designed and promoted by an assimilationist senator from Washington State, ANCSA was implemented after it gained the support and collaboration of the major Native organizations in Alaska. There were no consultations, no hearings, and no votes on the Act at the village level.

The Alaska Native Claims Settlement Act extinguished the indigenous people's Aboriginal title and rights over 90 percent of their territories (confirmation of the extinguishment was pronounced by the United States Supreme Court in February 1998, in the landmark decision Alaska v. Native Village of Venetie Tribal Government) and gave them a total compensation package valued at three dollars per acre ($962.5 million) over an eleven-year period. The indigenous people retained 10 percent (44 million acres) of their land. The US government now owns (with the additional passage of the Alaska National Interest Lands Act, 1980) 60 percent (197 million acres) of previously unsurrendered territory; while the state of Alaska owns 30 percent (124 million acres). In the area of governance, the Act established 12 regional- and more than 200 village-level corporations, along with one based in Seattle. These so-called governments strictly follow the corporate model: community members are shareholders, and the primary responsibility of the government is to make profits to provide the shareholders with returns on the investments made on their behalf as part of the initial framework.

In 2005, the United States Senate passed a budget bill with a provision that approved opening the ANWR (Alaska National Wildlife Refuge) to oil drilling. Previous attempts to pass the drilling approval were blocked by filibustering Democrats, but Senate rules forbid filibustering on budget bills. But on 21 December 2005, the Senate temporarily blocked drilling in the wildlife refuge when the Republican majority failed to secure a 60 percent majority needed to prevent a procedural move. It effectively killed the attempt to approve drilling in the region for the time being.

This experience is a sickening example of the results of the co-optation of elite Native leaders and the forced assimilation of indigenous people into an exploitative system that fundamentally disrespects their culture and values. Indeed, the Alaska Natives themselves have begun to confront what they now realize was an open attack on their existence as indigenous peoples: a land grab and a blatant effort to make them conform to a white model of societal, government, and economic organization. As the review commission put it, "Alaska Natives now realize that ANCSA has failed them and that its goals are at cross purposes with their own." While recognizing the same fact, we might add that some Alaska Native politicians were and are complicit in this usurpation of their people's identity and nationhood.

Today, Alaska Natives are attempting to strengthen their own traditional economies and restore their tribal governments. Like many other indigenous peoples, they have recognized that it is impossible to preserve the essence of their cultures and identity as long as their internal economy is exploitative and profit-motivated. They have also come to see that both corporate and elective systems of representation are incompatible with indigenous political cultures. The Commission recognizes that what the Native people are rejecting is not modernity or the United States government, but forced compliance with an exploitative system and the imposition of an inappropriate form of government. Simply put, "It is their profound desire to be themselves, to be true to their own values, that has led to the present confrontation." The head of the Review Commission, Canadian judge Thomas Berger, recognized the commonalities between the Alaska Natives and all indigenous people who must deal with ongoing efforts by outsiders to gain access to their lands and impose state sovereignty on their nations:

Some persons say that Alaska Natives are unlike American Indians: their goals are different and they wish to integrate. That is not what Alaska Natives have been telling me. Their goals are fundamentally the same as those of American Indians as well as those related peoples throughout the Canadian and Greenland Arctic and sub-Arctic and indigenous peoples the world over.

At one point there was hope that Western states would prove capable of honouring indigenous nationhood and respecting the right of non–white peoples to determine their own future. But only slight progress has been made: The set-tler states are willing to accept the continuing physical existence of indigenous people—but only on the condition that they serve the corporate interests that dominate white society. In effect, indigenous people are respected by the state only to the degree that they adopt mainstream values, attitudes, and behaviours.

Money holds out the promise of a better life for indigenous people, but in the end it delivers them to the state as consumer/citizens differing only in skin colour and folklore from all the rest. Individual Native people who choose money over all but the most superficial aspects of their culture may prosper. But communities that take that path extinguish more than just their title to the land: They extinguish themselves as nations. The Creator gave indigenous people specific instructions to preserve their distinctive cultures and way of life. To the extent that accumulating financial resources helps them to do that it is a good thing. But when the only way to make money is by buying into the values system of exploitative capitalism, it requires a sacrifice—of the essence of the indigenous being—that cannot be justified.

The challenge for leaders is to create the conditions for self-sufficiency and at the same time to preserve the core community values that are fundamen-tally opposed to those underpinning the dominant mode of economic devel-opment in the larger society. This is no easy task. The structure of mainstream society is such that people who adhere to traditional values are not likely to have access to the resources and co-operation needed to achieve self-suffi-ciency. The only way around this problem is to think through the structure and the situation and find a way to achieve self-sufficiency on our own terms, not those imposed by outsiders as a condition for their co-operation.

In this intellectual and political context, leaders are forced to make hard choices. Of course, politics is always a matter of compromise, and it would be naive to imagine that indigenous leaders will not engage in some trade-offs for practical gain, especially when it is so important to address the material deprivation of Native communities. But clearly there are situations where the pursuit of money is simply wrong, because it means surrender-ing some of the nation's strength in other areas (land, identity, or freedom, for example). For indigenous people forced to live in a capitalist economy who are politically oppressed by colonial governments driven by big-money politics, it can be considered only a sin to disconnect economic develop-ment from the larger social and political project of self-determination. We must always look at the larger context. We must always consider the broader political and social implications of the choices we make in our drive to accumulate wealth, whether individually or collectively, and to co-operate with other governments to ensure our communities' economic development. Without a commitment to the development of economic self-sufficiency in a framework of respect for traditional values, money can do nothing to promote decolonization and reassertion of our nationhood. The political and economic realities in which we live ensure that the unprincipled pursuit of money, outside a traditional framework, can only further entrench our colonization by embedding us deeper in colonial structures.

Modern Treaties: A Path to Assimilation?

Related to the money issue, the contemporary treaty process as it is currently under way in Canada, most notably in British Columbia, is a prime example of co-optation. Together, state officials and indigenous representatives have developed a seemingly progressive framework for resolving the main obstacles to rebuilding indigenous communities and establishing relationships with other peoples based on justice and honour. In fact, behind the progressive facade, the BC treaty process represents an advanced form of control, manipulation, and assimilation.

The BC treaty process illustrates all the problems that indigenous peoples face in their struggle to overcome colonialism: racism and ignorance in the mainstream, apathy in Native communities, co-optation of Native leadership, and aggressive manipulation of the process by the state. The basic assumptions embedded in the process and the negotiating positions put forward in relation to indigenous peoples point to the state's innate prejudice against justice for indigenous peoples.

All land claims in Canada, including those at issue in the BC treaty process, arise from the mistaken premise that Canada owns the land it is situated on. In fact, where indigenous people have not surrendered ownership, legal title to "Crown" land does not exist—it is a fiction of Canadian (colonial) law. To assert the validity of Crown title to land that the indigenous population has not surrendered by treaty is to accept the racist assumptions of earlier centuries, when European interests were automatically given priority over the rights of supposedly "uncivilized" indigenous peoples. Those who do not accept the idea that indigenous people own all of their traditional territory unless it was surrendered by treaty are either ignorant of the historical reality or racists who ignore that reality in order to impose a hierarchy of rights based on "conquest."

In truth, it is white society that has staked a claim against history, morality, and the rights of indigenous peoples. But indigenous peoples have been
obliged to go along with the historically false idea that they must make a claim
against the state to gain ownership of lands that they have always possessed.
One reason the state has been able to impose its racist, anti-historical view is
simple cultural arrogance. The state still negotiates from a position of strength
based on its false claim to morality, justice, and authority.

Arrogance is evident even in the doctrine of Aboriginal title as it has
been developed in Canadian jurisprudence since the much-heralded 1998
decision in Delgamuukw v. The Queen, in which the Supreme Court pronounced the first substantive definition of *Aboriginal title* in Canadian law.
The Delgamuukw decision was the first in a string of decisions in Aboriginal
title cases, the most notable subsequent ones being the Haida Nation and
the Taku River Tlingit cases. These decisions were generally seen as progressive expansions of the notion of indigenous rights in their ruling that
Aboriginal title—defined as "the right to exclusive use and occupation of
land"—is "inalienable" except to the Crown (that is, such rights cannot be
extinguished except by the federal government), and indigenous peoples
have a constitutionally protected right to be consulted on, and compen-
sated for, title infringements that affect their access to or use of the lands
for purposes integral to their cultural survival.

The question is, what does that mean to people whose traditional territories have for the most part already been alienated from them by law, settled
by others, or handed over to corporate interests for resource development?

The court has determined that, to have their title recognized, indigenous peoples must prove to the federal government their exclusive and consistent occupation of the territory ever since European sovereignty was first
asserted. However, in the court's reasoning, *title* does not mean "ownership," much less governing authority. Indigenous peoples are, in fact,
severely constrained by Canadian law in the exercise of their delegated
rights within the territories to which they hold title. Basically, Aboriginal
title and rights protect only those activities and aspects of the indigenous
culture that Canadians have determined are pre-European in nature. In the
Canadian government's interpretation:

> A group may not use Aboriginal title lands for purposes that are irrec-
> oncilable with the nature of the group's attachment to the land. For
> example, if a First Nation has traditionally used a piece of land for

hunting, the group may not strip mine it, thus destroying its value for hunting.

Of course, this example is ridiculous—it is white people, not Natives, who are notorious for strip-mining. However, it points to limitations on the meaning of Aboriginal title that are unsettling. It clearly indicates that the high court and government of Canada have not relinquished their falsely assumed right to control indigenous people. The one concession to justice in the doctrine of Aboriginal title flowing from the Delgamuukw decision is that it does prevent individuals, corporations, municipalities, and provinces from themselves infringing on the most important aspects of an indigenous group's culture within that group's traditional territories (as has so often been done in the past, with blatant disregard for the law and morality)—and the recent decision in the Tsilqot'in Nation's title case emphatically reinforced this principle.

Even though it puts individual white people, corporations, and the provincial governments that serve them out of the extinguishment business, in essence, the Delgamuukw framework simply refines the logic of dispossession that has underpinned Canadian policy for generations. The absolute proof is contained in the court's clarification of the nature of Aboriginal title in relation to the Crown's prerogative, and the stipulation that Canada itself may "infringe upon Aboriginal title for valid legislative objectives, including, but not limited to, settling foreign populations and instituting economic development projects." The principle that only the federal government may usurp indigenous rights may look like progress in the specific context of British Columbia, where the provincial government had falsely assumed local power. However, the federal-only prerogative, recognized in the Royal Proclamation of 1763, in treaties elsewhere in Canada, and even in the Indian Act, has done nothing to prevent the alienation of huge areas of land from indigenous nations. Federal collusion with corporate interests to use indigenous lands and rivers for industrial development, hydro dams, transportation routes, and raw resource extraction continues to represent just as great a danger as gradual, small-scale encroachments by individuals for settlement and agricultural purposes. The post-Delgamuukw conception of Aboriginal title is fundamentally meaningless to indigenous peoples because it gives them no real protection. In fact, it perpetuates the faulty logic according to which indigenous rights can be put aside when they conflict with white settlement and economic development—the same played-out excuses for legalized theft on which all colonial states are founded.

In the post-Delgamuukw era, Canada's federal government has recommitted itself to policies and programs aimed at legitimizing its unjustly imposed control over indigenous lands and peoples. The stated objective of federal policy is to achieve "certainty about rights of ownership and use of land and resources" by exchanging "constitutionally protected but undefined common law Aboriginal rights for constitutionally, clearly defined treaty rights and benefits." The concern for certainty is undoubtedly valid, since all agreements between nations are based on trust. What certainty does any accord, agreement, or treaty provide without commitments of respect and honour on each side? The document itself, whether paper or wampum, is merely a symbol of those commitments and a reminder of the agreed-upon principles. So, certainty is important. But who is it that should be troubled by the lack of certainty in this process? The truth is that neither the Canadian nor the United States government has ever kept its word with Indians. Not a single treaty or agreement signed by white society has been honoured by its government. These statements stand unqualified. "Certainty" in these cases has nothing to do with trust and respect. What it really means is entrenchment of legal constraints and enshrinement of dependency. Achieving true, respectful certainty would go a long way toward rectifying the injustices done to indigenous people; but the actual process of negotiation is taking place within a different intellectual framework and is aimed at a different goal. What is Canada really saying? Its policy on the conduct of negotiations with indigenous peoples is clearly outlined:

> Canada will not lose sight of the need to achieve certainty with respect to land and resource rights for Aboriginal people and other Canadians in order to preserve and encourage economic development possibilities for all Canadians. Any policy on certainty will need to be consistent with the legal and political evolution of Aboriginal and treaty rights....

Preserving "economic development possibilities for all Canadians" has nothing to do with rectifying the injustice of colonization. It is a concession to industries that have illegally established themselves on Native land. It is a cynical manipulation that effectively makes the achievement of Native objectives impossible, by forcing efforts to achieve justice to accommodate the selfish interests of uninformed racists and the business community.

Furthermore, to ensure the limitation of indigenous rights, Canada insists on consistency with Canadian law—with all its faulty precedents and premises. Certainty for the group that controls the "legal and political evolution" of the other group's rights is certainly for the first group only.

In effect, the Canadian government arrogantly asserts ownership rights over the identity of indigenous nations. Well into the twenty-first century, Canada's final solution to the Indian Problem is to force indigenous peoples who have inhabited the land for millennia to do what no other people in the world are obliged to do: to formalize a definition of themselves for all time and agree to a set of criteria for determining membership that will not be subject to evolution or change as the group responds to the shifting realities of the political and economic environment.

In addition, the federal policy includes the following statements:

> Canada will also seek to ensure that settlement lands are subject to federal and provincial laws of general application....

What do *self-government* and *self-determination* mean if all federal and provincial laws apply on indigenous lands? The assumption here is that Canada has until now possessed rightful jurisdiction over indigenous peoples and lands, and that vacating said jurisdiction is a matter of delegating power to Native governments. Surely, though, if the lands are within the traditional territory of an indigenous nation, then it is the laws of that nation—not Canada—that should form the basis of authority within that territory.

> Canada will seek to ensure that settlements provide for innocent and limited public access, without charge, to selected or retained lands, by government, its contractors, the Canadian Forces and for commercial and third party use; and, that access rights pertaining to transportation routes in and through settlement lands and rights-of-way for necessary public purposes be provided for.

Canada will negotiate recognizing what it calls an "Aboriginal interest" in traditional indigenous territories, but, in return, white society must be conceded the privileges of general public access and free public recreation use, as well as continued access and use by government, business, industry, the military, and maintenance of all roads and expropriated passages throughout those traditional territories. This is most certainly not recognition of an interest based on aboriginality and unsurrendered Aboriginal title. This is a concept gutted of real meaning—making sense only in terms of a residual (read leftover) "interest" once all non-Native interests have been satisfied. As well, Canada explicitly states that the "arrangements" that flow from the treaty negotiations "will not involve the exercise of Aboriginal or treaty rights in established national parks." Thus, redress for historic injustice will be considered only in those areas that are not sufficiently beautiful, important, or accessible to be of interest to white society. Similarly, the government makes it clear that it has no intention of returning sacred objects or aspects of indigenous peoples' material culture stolen, seized, or pilfered over the years and ensconced in public collections: "Canada will seek to safeguard the integrity of collections of cultural artifacts for the enjoyment of all Canadians."

Most blatantly, Canada states that it will seek to ensure that "holders of subsurface rights have access to settlement lands"; that it "will retain final authority over the management of all fisheries"; and that it "will seek to minimize disruption, where possible, of all existing fisheries." In other words, it's business as usual: Mining and commercial fishing corporations can continue to pillage indigenous resources and destroy the Native peoples' environment.

Finally, the government of Canada will "seek to retain those expropriation powers required to fulfill its obligations as a national government." To ensure its ability to take what it needs from indigenous lands in the future (so much for "finality"), Canada will claim the right to expropriate (to take without consent) unsurrendered Aboriginal territories. How does it justify this shameless disregard for indigenous peoples' inherent rights as nations? On the grounds of fulfilling its "obligations."

This justification—putting a positive spin on a position that for Native people is clearly negative—is typical of the Canadian government's approach to the negotiation process. Throughout its policy statement, the government presents its anti-indigenous objectives in terms of positive efforts to protect Canadian "interests":

1. **Ensuring that processes are fair and democratic.** In its cultural arrogance, Canada forgets that indigenous peoples have practised democracy since time immemorial. By insisting on its own standards of fairness and democracy, it imposes a culturally specific conception of political participation on indigenous nations, and degrades the quality of Native people's rights by insisting that they remain subject to Canadian values.

Furthermore, the insistence on "fair and democratic" processes is a coded guarantee to the Canadian people that they will have the final say as to whether indigenous rights are recognized. In the context of British Columbia at least, this gives the organized racists who dominate local politics a virtual veto on progress.

2. **Ensuring affordability of settlements.** Claiming that it represents "all Canadians in the negotiations" (with the apparent exception of the citizens it claims among indigenous peoples), the Canadian government constrains the degree to which historic injustices will be redressed by setting the issue in the framework of contemporary fiscal crises. What indigenous people want is to get their land back; cash settlement in lieu of land is a compromise of that primary objective made in the context of the negotiations. It is the state that proposes to pay indigenous people cash instead—and then it limits the redress by claiming that the resolution must be affordable!

3. **Promoting self-reliant First Nations.** In this classic example of manipulative doublespeak, the Canadian government says that it will abdicate its fiduciary responsibilities with respect to Native peoples and insist that they integrate into the state system. In the words of the policy, "As First Nations take on more responsibility for managing their own affairs, it is expected that the federal role will be reduced proportionately." In theory, this is a good thing. In practice, however, what it means is that Canada insists that Native governments become tax agents of the state and that the historic principle of tax immunity for status Indians be surrendered.

In the Canadian system, 93 percent of the land within the territorial borders of British Columbia is under the legal control of the provincial government. The province has assumed responsibility for negotiating with indigenous peoples those aspects of treaties that pertain to land tenure and use. And its only response to the string of court decisions elaborating the doctrine of Aboriginal title has been to refine its consultation process for title infringements and, as in one case with the Musqueam First Nation, to sign a compensation agreement for its failure to accommodate the First Nation's existing title. On top of the federal positions outlined above, therefore, the province imposes further limitations to justice in the treaty process:

> Overall, the total land held by First Nations after treaty settlements are completed in British Columbia will be less than five per cent of

the province's land base. That five per cent set aside for Treaty Settlement Lands will include already existing Indian Reserves.

In January 1997, at a conference in Victoria following the release of the final report of the Royal Commission on Aboriginal Peoples, the provincial minister of Aboriginal Affairs, John Cashore, denied this policy in direct response to a point-blank question from a Native person. He lied. According to the province's policy, no more than 5 percent (minus the lands already held as reserves) would be considered for settlement of historic injustices.

> About five per cent of land in B.C. is privately owned, or land owned in fee simple and registered under the Land Titles Act. Privately owned property is exempt from any land claims settlements and the province will not expropriate or interfere with private property to conclude a treaty ... aboriginal rights can co-exist with other interests and may apply on private property. These aboriginal rights can conflict with the owner's desired use. Treaties will secure private property rights....

In other words, to provide additional support for the federal government's efforts to impose its own policies, the province has extended its policy to areas beyond its jurisdiction. Essentially, the federal and provincial governments have coordinated their approaches to the negotiations, ensuring that certain basic premises are defended by two of the three parties to the negotiation. This is clearly evident in the province's Principles for Negotiating Treaties:

- Private property is not on the table.
- Jurisdictional certainty between First Nations and municipalities must be clearly spelled out.
- Continued access to hunting, fishing and recreational opportunities will be guaranteed.
- The Canadian Constitution and Charter of Rights and Freedoms will continue to apply equally to all British Columbians.
- Agreements must be affordable to all British Columbians.
- The federal government's primary constitutional and financial responsibility for treaties must be maintained.

- Fair compensation for unavoidable disruption of commercial interests will be assured.
- Province-wide standards of resource management and environmental protection will continue to apply.

In addition to limiting the potential for settlement by putting an arbitrary cap on the total amount of settlement lands, the province's position denies the right of indigenous people to reacquire possession of their lands currently held by settlers. As well, the province has stated that tenures such as commercial leases and licences to extract resources from indigenous lands "will not be expropriated as a result of treaty negotiations." An outsider might well ask, "What is left for the Natives?" This question was answered clearly in two subsequent agreements negotiated in British Columbia: Not much is left for Natives, save for empty promises of goodwill and unprofitable business partnerships. In terms of actual land and compensations, the 2007 Tsawwassen agreement, for example, provided the First Nation with fee simple title to about 427 hectares, or 1055 acres, of provincial Crown territory in the land package in the final agreement—the current Tsawwassen reserve will also become "treaty" land. The federal government will provide a cash transfer of $10.1 million. Other cash components of up to $4.1 million are included in the agreement for fisheries, forestry, and economic development purposes.

To further limit the parameters of treaty negotiations, both the federal and provincial governments have instituted "advisory councils" of non-indigenous people and commercial interests. Thus, on top of the limitations imposed by the basic positions outlined above, the federal and provincial governments work with the settlers and organized commercial interests who currently occupy and use the lands under negotiation to develop the mandates their negotiators use to deal with indigenous people.

The list of non-indigenous interests that work with the federal and provincial governments to develop mandates and, in the case of local governments, sit on provincial negotiating teams is comprehensive:

- non-indigenous regional advisory committees (advise the federal and provincial negotiating teams): community, industry, business, labour, environment, tourism, and recreation
- non-indigenous treaty advisory committees (select members to sit on provincial negotiating team): local, regional, and municipal governments

- non-indigenous provincial regional caucuses (advise specific provincial ministries): employees of the provincial government
- non-indigenous treaty negotiations advisory committee (advise federal and provincial governments on policy and mandates): province-wide group of 31 members of business, industry, labour, local government, and environmental and outdoor recreation organizations

Further representation for non-indigenous people and interests is provided by the provincial government's policy of accepting input from the public on any issue related to the overall process by way of a toll-free telephone line.

In both form and content, the BC treaty process points to the urgent need for all indigenous peoples to challenge the policies and positions the state has designed to eliminate their nations. It also demonstrates the extent to which Native leaders have been co-opted into serving as agents of the state's agenda. Aside from the example of individual entrepreneur-chiefs leading their communities into ill-advised surrenders of rights and land, there is a larger structure of Native co-operation in BC that works to ensure compliance with the treaty process agenda within Native communities. The First Nations Summit is the largest representative of Native chiefs in the province, and its members "support and endorse negotiation currently under way" within an organization whose stated mandate is "to advance discussions with governments in order to position First Nations to conduct their own direct negotiations with the Government of Canada and the Government of British Columbia."

The state has a common approach to resolving the inconsistencies between history and the law that continue to haunt us. Like the Native people of Alaska in the 1970s, indigenous people in British Columbia are being led toward a non-indigenous future by their elected chiefs, although, to this point, only two groups have ratified by referendum the modern "treaties" negotiated for them by their leaders. State-sponsored processes such as the one currently under way in British Columbia can never offer an honourable resolution so long as they refuse to demonstrate respect for the nationhood of our peoples. As it is, the process is a mere facade, and cynical manipulation is only perpetuating the problems that the negotiations are supposed to resolve.

Around the world, indigenous peoples must fight for their survival. Not only must they adapt their societies to the changes (technological and social) that affect all people, but at the same time, they must defend themselves against both the efforts of the state to undermine their existence and the choices of indigenous representatives who claim to speak for their people yet agree to resolutions based on the state's premises and policies.

Its methods may have become more subtle and devious, but the state's goal is still clear: to assimilate Native people.

For the Youth: Toward a New Native Leadership

The complexity of the problems outlined here is immense, and it should be no surprise if people feel overwhelmed and confused as to the next step, apart from the broad objectives of healing, reforming government, and reviving a traditional indigenous value system. Clearly, though, Native communities must focus on creating a new generation of leaders who are grounded in traditional values and capable of undoing the damage done to their nations by white society and two generations of complicit Native politicians.

In a way, this is an obvious point: We all know that young people are the future of our nations. For too many of our politicians, however, this is only a platitude. Politicians may pay lip service to it, but, in practice, they ignore young people's concerns. Because of this, young people are becoming increasingly alienated, and our communities are in real danger of losing the next generation of leaders. Some youth self-destruct, through suicide or substance abuse. Others, disillusioned by the hypocrisy of older people, especially politicians, simply turn their backs on their communities and drift toward the mainstream society, where racism still prevents their participation as full human beings.

These problems are not confined to North America. Research on the situation of indigenous youth in the Solomon Islands, for example, has found similar evidence of cultural and social disruption. Young people there, who are bored with, and tired of, traditional life and obligations, move to the city and form a class cut off from the benefits of both societies. Not finding meaning or relevance in traditional obligations, they are forming a new culture with values and mores suited to their existence as alienated people. Because they do not have a stake in preserving either society, dissipation and self-destruction follow.

Native leaders must recognize a similar potential in North American indigenous communities. Traditional value systems attach great importance to honouring the interdependence of the generations, but this importance has for the most part been lost in the colonial systems that have supplanted them. Stable societies are secure in the transmission of their culture from one generation to the next because the young people are shaped by respected elders. The culture defines the rights and obligations—forms the moral universe—of all people. That circle of respect and responsibility has been broken in indigenous communities. Young indigenous people are developing a set of values very different from those of their parents—most of whom have only a tenuous hold on tradition themselves.

From any perspective, indigenous or mainstream, it is dangerous to ghettoize "youth" concerns as a separate set of issues (although it is a popular strategy among governments because of young people's inherent immaturity; lack of material resources; and fluid, transient identity). The truth is that there is no separating the problems facing young people from those of the society as a whole. To take indigenous traditions seriously means to have a vision for the future; and the current situation of indigenous youth provides a crystal-clear picture of the general state of our communities.

Native politicians need to be reminded that youth are real human beings, and that, as a group, they represent needs and wants, good and bad characteristics, and a collective way of thinking that will soon come to define the social and political landscape in Native communities. Their issues are significant today and will become more so as the dominance of people raised in a different time and shaped by different circumstances fades. Communities must respect their youth, and not close their eyes to the future by denying the validity of their concerns. Communities cannot do what is right for the next generation without involving them and gaining their consent—where the link between young people and leaders is broken, a future negotiated solely by politicians and elders will last only as long as those people stay in control. Then who will lead our communities?

If indigenous peoples are to have any future at all, every person counts. But those young people who self-destruct are not the only ones lost to the society. So, too, are the apathetic—those who have become so alienated that they simply don't care. And among those who do care, many actively fight the establishment that controls their lives because it does not listen to their concerns. As the 1996 report of the Royal Commission on Aboriginal Peoples in Canada emphasized, it is essential to begin respecting and empowering young people by involving them in decisions affecting their future.

In April 1997, activist young people opposed to the conducting of treaty negotiations without youth representation occupied the Vancouver offices of the British Columbia Treaty Commission. The protesters belonged to the

Vancouver-based Native Youth Movement (NYM). One of their representatives told reporters that "none of our chiefs have ever consulted us."
Another described in a radio interview the frustration that indigenous youth
felt at being left out of the process and seeing the legitimacy of their political perspective denied by their own community leaders:

NYM: The point we're trying to make is that Aboriginal youth haven't been
consulted on the process. The whole process is fraudulent, and we oppose
it 100 percent. All the peers, all the people we've met so far, have totally
told us that they 100 percent oppose it.

*CBC Radio: So many Native communities in BC, though, have bought into the
process. Why are you so strongly opposed to it?*

NYM: It's not internationally recognized, for one thing. A lot of jurisdiction, like roads and access and stuff like that, falls under the province and
so you kind of wonder. Sure you're supposed to be doing nation to nation,
so why would the province be involved? It's a real joke, and it's a joke to
our integrity as a people, you know?

*CBC: I'm wondering, realistically, how much success do you think you'll actually
have in altering the process here?*

NYM: I think we'll have a good opportunity, because for so long everybody
has been just silently opposing this process. If you talk to any of the Native
organizations, individual people will tell you that they're opposed to the
process, but nobody has made a real stand. So I feel that maybe this will
start the momentum of opposition to the treaty. All the silent people will
start coming out....

CBC: Why do you think this is so important to the youth especially?

NYM: Native youth are the lowest people on the scale here. We're affected
by all the things that the chiefs are negotiating about. We're affected most by
poverty, suicide, HIV, and all the other social problems that are attributed to
being First Nations. And our needs aren't being met in any of these processes.

Frustration, combined with the unfulfilled universal need for community and belonging, is leading to delegitimization of governing structures.

Many people believe that the problem can be traced directly to the abandonment of traditional initiation rituals and the loss of specifically assigned social and ceremonial roles for individuals within the community. In the vacuum created by the loss of those rituals, alternatives emerge that are not rooted in indigenous culture. Adoption of these alternatives will eventually lead to the destruction of indigenous nations just as surely as the loss of land and the continuing denial of indigenous governmental authority. The problem needs to be seen in that perspective.

Native youth are warriors in a very traditional sense: They are the ones who will be expected to carry out the community's decisions. If things were operating in a traditional mode, they would have had input into those decisions and participated freely in shaping their future. But in the colonial mode, they remain doubly bound, to their situation and to a future not of their own making. These warriors need purpose and guidance. They will find them. The question is where and from whom?

Shortly before he died in 2005, I was honoured to have the opportunity to speak publicly with Vine Deloria, Jr, on these questions, their meaning in our academic work, and their impact on the activist and political work we have done over the years. Our dialogue took place in front of an audience of mostly Native college students in Albuquerque, New Mexico. The exchange offered some reflection on the questions of our purpose as Natives today as well as some pragmatic guidance for the next generation of indigenous scholars and activists. The following is an excerpt from that conversation, which was introduced to the audience by the event's organizer, the Cherokee scholar, Jeff Corntassel.

Jeff Corntassel: We are here on the territory of the Tuha people, and also the Sandia and Isleta Pueblo people, so I want to start off by acknowledging that. I welcome you here today where we're honoured to have Vine Deloria, Jr, and Taiaiake Alfred speaking together. The title that we've given the panel is "From Playboy to Postmodern"—which has been subject to a lot of mystery and ridicule—"Past and Future Paths of Indigenous Activism." We got a little creative, maybe a little crazy, with the title. I've been asked a number of times today, "Which one is the playboy and which one is the postmodern?" [laughter] I leave them to decide that.... But seriously, we wanted to pay tribute to the fact that one of Vine's first published works was in *Playboy* magazine, and then nod to the fact that activism today has, sort of, a postmodern stance.

Taiaiake Alfred: Well, Vine conferred with me before the session, and I guess it must be that we think alike in some ways—we're both Marines—because we agreed right away that it's best to have the young guy start off and make a fool of himself and then have the elder come in and clean up the mess. [laughter] So, I'll be going first! I want to start off first by letting everybody know what an honour it is to be up here with Vine today. Obviously, Vine is a person who has influenced us all, and maybe some of you don't know, though, just how supportive he is behind the scenes for younger Native scholars. I was talking earlier in the day with some of you, and we shared stories of the letters that have come forward, the mentoring emails, and the voices of support when it comes time for tenure, promotion, and books, and all of that—it's just invaluable. So I wanted to thank you for that, Vine, for everything you've done for me and for all of us over the years.

The first time that I had come into a political awareness as an indigenous person was when I read Vine's book *Custer Died for Your Sins* as a young boy. I went to a Jesuit high school in Montreal, where they encouraged us in the critical thinking path, and they allowed us read what we wanted to read. Anything except the Bible, actually. [laughter] Hey ... Jesuits! So, I picked *Custer Died for Your Sins*, and it really opened up my eyes. I was struck by its insolence, not in an insulting way, because I took its attitude as a point of pride. It was just dismissive of all of the bullshit that had been fed to us over the years, and that now I recognize was part of my own think-ing about myself. You know, everything that had been foisted on us through religion, through the culture, through the oppression that we felt, through the systems of government that we had to live with, and not being able to name it. Not being able to name it; not being able to grab it by the throat and squeeze it and kill it. That was the feeling I had even as a young person when I grew up in the 1960s and '70s. This was probably around 1977 or something like that. And the lights came on. The lights come on and then you start to do your own investigations; and it's really that point I've identified as the start of my own path, intellectually and politically.

Now, of course, my own political life has been shaped growing up in Kahnawake in a Mohawk community. As a Mohawk of Kahnawake, at that time, you lived in the midst of an intense political struggle between your community and all of your neighbours, and you were forced into this situation because ours was a radicalized community at that time. It caused us to construct identities and a sense of being indigenous which I believe is reflected in the work I do. But at the same time, we have changed and adapted because of the different threats we've encountered and the successes we've had in confronting the power of the colonial mentalities and mythologies that controlled us in earlier eras. Collectively, we started to ask deeper questions about how colonialism has embedded itself, how it has polluted our vision of the world, and then do the hard work inside of us to clean up that pollution and begin to again reassert ourselves as indigenous people, as Onkwehonwe. And this is, of course, the work that all of us are doing, and that Vine especially has done over his whole career, which is to try to respect indigenous knowledge for what it is and to understand our traditional philosophies and world views. By doing this, we are regenerating ourselves, our cultures, and our nations. By "regenerating," I mean taking something old and making it new again. We are not saying, "Let's go back to the way it was two hundred years ago." But let's take the power of what was, let's take what is good in our tradition, let's take what's useful, let's take what's powerful, and let's make it something we can use to go forward.

What I've taken from Vine's writings all these years is the commitment to maintain oneself and the mentality of a Native person. And to engage; to continue to engage colonial power in the spirit of a struggle for survival. This is what I see as the warrior ethic, and it's something that is lacking among our people. Collectively, in terms of our movement today, that warrior ethic is missing. We have become complacent; our politics is a politics of complacency and co-operation, and, to me, it just seems like it's too early to give up the fight. You know, when I read *Custer* at 13 or 14 years of age, I wanted to fight; I wanted to, like, burn Jesuits! Start the fire, you know, let's go, let's do it again! [laughter] I didn't want to sit down at a negotiating table with some white guy and work out the surrender of my land for some money. That's not what it was about. So I have this frustration in the work that I do, and my attitude generally is that it's not that negotiation is inherently wrong or [that] getting along with white people is wrong, or anything like that. It's just that we're settling too easy. We're settling for less than what we deserve as human beings.

Certainly, we're settling for even less than what the treaties, and what ethical principles and politics, would demand in North American society. So it's still time to fight, the war is still on, and how do we do that smartly? How do we be warriors today? Not where we're going to charge machine guns carrying knives, or anything like that. How do we charge the adversary in a way that ensures success? It's about how do we regenerate a warrior ethic in politics, in scholarship, and in our personal lives today. I'll leave it at that for now.

Vine Deloria, Jr: What do you want me to talk about?

Taiaiake: What's different today than in the 1960s or '70s? What's different about the younger generations of Native scholars and activists?

Vine: Really?

Taiaiake: Sure, we'd love to hear you talk about that.

Vine: Some time ago, I got a frantic email from the University of Washington saying, "Shepard Krech is coming to our university. Would you come up here and give a lecture refuting his book *The Ecological Indian*?" So I sent them back an email. I said, "What the hell kinda thing is this? That's an idiotic book, and you can take care of a guy like that." They said, "No, no, we need someone to do it for us!" I said, "Your damn generation, if we moved time back to 1876, you would sit in the tepees and debate *indigenous*, and *hegemony*, and *colonialism*, while old guys like me went out and took care of Custer!"

Taiaiake: That's exactly what I wanted you to say. [laughter]

Vine: I said, "I'm not gonna do it. You organize, and you raise hell with him." And it's easy to do. My god, I never saw so many errors in one book in my life. So they did, and they complained. Some of them actually read the book instead of talking. And they stopped the guy from getting an appointment as museum director at the university. And I thought, my god, do we have to explain this to each and every member of the younger generation, or what? It's absurd. For some reason, that generation—and I think it's a lot of you here in the audience today, but basically people about six years older than you that I'm really talking about, six to ten …

Taiaiake: [gestures to himself]

Vine: They seem to believe that the way things are now is the way they've always been. You have a hell of a time talking with them. I was invited to one place in California, talking about sovereignty, and I said, "I'm so damn tired of talking about that. Why doesn't somebody exercise it for a change instead of talking about it?" And this young man said, "Your generation was interested in that also?" I said, "Well, from probably 1622—the founding of Jamestown—it's been a popular subject." [laughter] I'll tell you what I think happens, though, and some historian might look into it: I'm probably dead wrong, but I think it would hold for the twentieth century. And that is, you start a reform movement, and you start making progress, and you're not just fighting the government, you're fighting an inner majority in the country that could support you or turn against you. You're fighting a whole series of outside institutions; they're outside government, they're outside the tribe—churches, universities, anthropologists, do-gooders, chambers of commerce, you name it. You can't just fight the government; you gotta hit all these others and back them all up. So if you look at the twentieth century, you find occasional spurts of Indian activism, or Indians approaching any number of these groups with a new reform idea that no one has thought of, and they start to make some progress. It ends up with political change; you end up with the Indian Claims Commission, or Indian Reorganization Act, self-government, the so-called War on Poverty—all these things. But once you make that progress in the political area, people go to sleep and they don't realize that all they did was knock off a person who is representative of an attitude that was anti-Indian. And you replace that person, and you're back at the same plight, all the time. And we've seen that over and over again. So all through the 1960s, we made grade progress, and then in the 1970s, that choke comes back. The Indians who are running tribes and institutions in the 1970s begin to think that because it's easy to talk to the [US] president and some of these people, that they can solve all these problems. They let things go to hell on the periphery. There have been more anti-Indian books and articles written in the last fifteen years than in the previous ... 1876 to the present. Look at all this stuff: Indians are not ecologists, Indians are not this, they're not that, and whatever ... Kennewick Man is George Bush's grandfather ... [laughter]

I want to say, "Look, you're trying to keep the institutions away from you, and sometimes they're going to be peopled by good people, and sometimes by evil people—like [they are] today—and so you can't ever let your guard down." If you win a battle, you've only won in that one sector; you want to look around and see how that affects other people.

When I was directing National Congress of American Indians, almost all the chairmen were a generation older than I was. I was in my thirties, a lot of them were late fifties and sixties. They had a genius for analyzing what situation you were in and then recommending what you should do about it. And they were right, they were always right. You've gotta learn timing, you've gotta analyze who the enemy is, you gotta learn how to approach people with power and get them to do the things you want done for reasons they can accept. You'll find yourself almost always alone, anyway, and you will find all these tempting tidbits, and "You do this and you're gonna be our Indian," or whatever, and if you don't get caught up in it, it's a giant step forward for you, because you can always turn on them later, once you've consolidated your base. [laughter] I'm happy to say I did that with the Museum of the American Indian. I was appointed aboard with a five-to-four vote, with four abstaining because they didn't know what I was going to do. Now, every meeting I'd say, "Well, we gotta add some Indians to the board." They'd say, "Oh yes, we're going to add Indians!" Meantime, all these rich, white art collectors are getting on the board. So I bided my time for three whole years, and then they were gonna open the Customs House Exhibit, and they were gonna have a board meeting that day. So I went to the exhibit and I told the chairman of the board, "Well, today's the day we're gonna add four new Indian board members." He says, "Oh, well, that's not on the agenda." I said, "Do you realize the *New York Times* is in this building? And if it isn't on the agenda and we don't get it passed, I'm going have a long session with them?" "You can't do this to me!" he says. And I told him, "You knew what I was like when you let me on the board! You knew I was going to do this at some point, and today's the day!" After that, they had four good Indian trustees, and they ended up taking over the board eventually. But, at first, you gotta swallow your pride, you gotta soften your intellect, you've got to let them pat you on the head, and when it's time and when you've consolidated your position, strike!

Taiaiake: What you just said about listening and watching and learning from the ones that have come before us is just so important. It's been a big part of my experience too. When I started out in politics, I would just sit there for hours listening to the older guys who were our community leaders talk about how they did things. They got into some serious discussions and laid out their detailed analyses of power dynamics in Ottawa or New York, and with this company or that company. We don't get that kind of perspective from our leaders any more because people are separated from the necessity—in their mind—of doing battle as an indigenous nation against another nation, Canada or the United States. These days, they believe they can just access entitlements that are there for our people under the law, and they don't feel like they have to act strategically, they don't have to be diplomats and go and do these types of things to represent the people. The thing that was coming to mind as you were talking, Vine, because it's such a prominent feature of Native politics, is the idea of co-optation. It's so easy to get the Native leaders away from that nation-to-nation mode. There're two reasons for this, I think. One is that, in the generations of leaders up to and including yours, there was a strong cultural foundation among the people who were representing us. For them, to engage with white society and to be working in the halls of power, this was done from a solid foundation of knowledge of language and culture, and membership, and history, and heritage, and so forth. They'd go and they'd recognize that they were going to lose some of that in the battle, there were going to be some compromises made, but with such a strong foundation it was something they could rationalize. Then, you look at what happened over the years to where the cultural foundation that our people are operating from is very small. It's more like a pedestal, not a foundation now.

I would say that knowledge of history is probably the most important thing that we are lacking today. It's the thing that, for me, motivates me, inspires me. Language and all that feeds into it, and they're important, but just the sense of history and who we are as a people, that's just not there any more for most of our leaders. So when you go and engage with white power now, the stakes are so much higher. If you go as a person with a small cultural foundation as opposed to a larger one, you're liable to be swept up by white power and begin to believe the lies that they're telling you, eh?

Vine: Yeah. The guys I was talking about, they were well aware as teenagers of the Wounded Knee Massacre—take someone who was a 17-, 18-, or 19-year-old at the time of the Wounded Knee Massacre, and add 40 years, they're 57 years old. Now, they're asked to adopt the Indian Reorganization Act.

What are they going to do? You know, they were the same distance genera-tionally from the Wounded Knee Massacre as I am from World War II, and I remember all kinds of things from World War II. At the NCAI Convention in 1961, there were two of Chief Joseph's warriors there, who were still alive in their nineties. With that kind of connection to history, you can really get to know it, and you learn that the feelings of the people were not surrendered by any means. Those were fresh memories for those people. But look at the NCAI now … there's not much shooting or anything else going on. You've got some people with memories of the 1950s and '60s, but as a whole, the younger generation simply doesn't know us.

Two years ago, I got a call from the Newbury Library. They had this Indian summit session going on. They had voted that they should not use the works of Charles Eastman or Luther Standing Bear because they were co-opted by white society. And I said, "You don't understand anything about history. These people were among the handful of Indians who emerged in the eyes of white society as being human beings, who could write a book, or could have a law office, or a doctorate, who could practice medicine." And so that's the first emergence of a whole new kind of Indian society which was willing to duke it out with the older society. I said, "Jesus, look at the lives of these guys. Luther Standing Bear, in the end of his books, he just kicks the Bureau of Indian Affairs all over the place. Eastman went back and lived on a lake in Minnesota, and just said to hell with the whole thing. And you little snot asses are sitting there in the Newbury Library, issuing judgments on guys that their whole lives were … You're goddamn lucky I'm in Rapid City and not in Chicago! There'd be bodies all over the place." [laughter] That just drove me crazy … There were four-strand barbed wire fences around those Sioux reservations as late as 1926, and there were troops that were going to fight the Sioux up in the Black Hills. They had three regiments ready to go into those reservations and kill people, and this was in 1926! So any Indian that tried to manipulate that system and suc-ceeded is co-opted? I detest that snotty attitude and these people saying, "Well, this is old, it's post-trauma, or premodern …" [laughter]

Taiaiake: When I was starting out in the 1980s, Andrew Delisle, Sr, a promi-nent political guy from my nation said to me, "I know people are critical of what we're doing now." By then, he was seen as a conservative or whatever. "But," he said, "remember, when we started our move for self-government not that long ago, in the 1960s, we couldn't have a meeting of three Indians without the police or the Indian agent there. It was illegal. We'd get thrown in jail. That's what we had to deal with only twenty years ago. What he said has always stuck with me. Young people need to build on what's been done and not look back and dismiss the efforts of the previous generations because their views don't fit with our views. Let's learn from the past rather than cast judgment on it. But, I think that what we have now is a generation of leaders who actually don't even want to know the history. There's a sense of arrogance that they've "made it," and they dismiss anybody who wants to go back and learn from and revitalize the kinds of struggles that have helped us survive as being a throwback.

Do you want to take some questions?

Vine: Yeah!

Taiaiake: Let's do some questions, comments, whatever …

Questioner 1: Our leaders have been co-opted and are sitting in this place where they don't know how to, and won't, move forward. They find ways to keep themselves in the positions they occupy utilizing culture and our traditions as weapons to keep them in their positions of power. It's like, "This is how things are done because this is how they're done. This is how the elders did it." I come from a strict hereditary chieftain system, and I see it used over and over again this way by our chiefs. If you question their leadership or challenge their leadership, you're also attacking tradition. How do you move from there, as somebody who sees that change needs to happen, that something needs to be done? How do you do it facing that?

Taiaiake: Indians don't always think critically about tradition. This is where the intellectuals come in. Because of the erosion of knowledge and culture and heritage in our communities, we are as thinkers, teachers, writers, artists—even if we don't want to be—in a position to hold the leaders accountable. I've personally interpreted this as one of my roles, which is to look at the traditions in a critical way, not trying to take them down, but to test them and to make sure they're still strong. And what doesn't work doesn't work. Look at the privilege that we have living in a university environment and having a means of income, and an ability to sustain ourselves

outside of the band or reservation economy. It's a privilege and a responsibility to be able to say to those in power, "Here's where you're wrong."
Somebody on the reserve will know the truth, too, but they're in no position to challenge it because of the family, social, and economic dynamics
in the community being used as a weapon against them.

Vine: Always remember that when the people lead, the leaders will follow. So
just start rumours or whatever ... [laughter] But seriously, once, we were dealing with a situation where a tribe was facing termination. The government
said, "We're going to buy the whole reservation for $40 million and that will
be it for you." And then some damn kind of mineral was discovered on the
reservation. A bunch of us went up to the anti-termination rally and said,
"Why are you selling a reservation for $40 million when it's worth $2 billion?"
So they started fighting with each other. "Why are we doing this?" "Let's hold
out for more money!" They ended up throwing the terminators off the tribal
council, squashed them. So a good rumour is worth something! [laughter]

Questioner 2: As you were talking about the "regeneration of indigenousness," and "new warriors," Taiaiake, I was trying to think of one thing that
has been consistent through the whole period here. The only thing that has
been consistent is change itself. What is different today? Clearly, the one
big thing is that we have Indian lawyers and Indian consultants as opposed
to a dependence on white lawyers and consultants in the past. Are they a
contributing positive thing, or what?

Taiaiake: Well, there's the Indian lawyer sitting right here beside me!
[laughter]

Vine: Well, we used to have attorneys representing tribes years before the
tribes knew they had attorneys representing them. [laughter] When things
started to move, we started to see local attorneys getting involved. But the
ones in Washington pretty much called the shots. Now, your Indian attorneys working for tribes call the shots too, and they're like any other group of
professionals. Until they get about twenty years' experience, and a little
humility, they're gonna go running off into the bushes and do dumb things.
Things that I would, in my old age, consider dumb. [laughter] Speaking as
a law graduate, law school teaches you to be stupid. You come out of there
convinced that litigation's the only way to do things. And you gotta go back

to the non-educated people and have them describe the problem to you, and then you see ... litigation. There's legislation, there's arbitration, there's exchange, there's all kinds of things, different ways to solve a problem. You don't have to run into court all the time. That really should be your last resort, and too often it's the first resort. But that comes from inexperience. I'm not saying these Indian lawyers are evil. In fact, they're having a meeting over there at another hotel in town right now. They're all dressed in conservative blue suits, with blue vests, and little gold chains. They look like nuns when they walk by. [laughter] Someday, they'll be formidable attorneys.

Vine: [holding up a pack of cigarettes] You know how I get when I've been without a cigarette!

Taiaiake: One more question, he says, one more ...

Questioner 3: Who's the playboy, and who's the postmodern?

Taiaiake: All I'm saying is that I'm the one with a ring on his finger! [laughter]

Native communities need to remind themselves that substantial change happens only when those in control change, and this can happen only when the sources of power (or access to them) shift. How do we bring this about? One way to achieve substantial change is through a legal mandate; this is the object of the negotiated decolonization processes that have been established thus far. The other way is to inject new social or political capital into the system. The first approach has failed or is failing, but the second holds great promise: effecting change through the injection of the human capital built through higher education.

The way to overcome the bonds, external and internal, that continue to hold indigenous people down is to awaken people's minds to their situation. In mainstream society, it is the ignorance, prejudice, and fear of the general population that allows the state to maintain its colonial dominion over indigenous peoples. In Native communities, it is the people's lack of understanding of political reality and blindness to the roots of their pain that keep them passively suffering. In both cases, there are serious inconsistencies between the current reality and the principles that form the basis of the people's identity, indigenous and non-indigenous alike. And in both cases, education holds the best promise for positive change, because it creates awareness of the inconsistencies between the world as it is and as it should be.

This notion is predicated on the existence of basic values and higher principles within both cultures that are capable of promoting peaceful harmonious relationships. There is no inherent conflict between basic indigenous and non-indigenous values. Rather, it is the historical practice of politics (and the institutionalization of these patterns of governance) that contravenes the basic values of liberal-democratic and traditional indigenous philosophies alike. Manipulative mechanisms of control work against the best instincts of both Western and Aboriginal value systems. Education holds the key because, in creating a general historical sensitivity and a critical awareness of reality, it activates a basic human urge to move reality closer to the ideal—to close the gap that, until now, the state has worked to obscure by denying history, lying about its true intentions vis-à-vis indigenous people, and co-opting those who might challenge its power.

What is needed in countries such as Canada and the United States is the kind of education that would force the general population to engage with realities other than their own, increasing their capacity to empathize with others—to see other points of view and to understand other people's motivations and desires. Admittedly, it is not likely that the entire North American primary and secondary education system will become so open-minded anytime soon. However, indigenous people have succeeded in altering non-indigenous people's perceptions through dialogue in institutions of higher learning. As a result, we are beginning to see empathy for the indigenous experience and a political space for change on which Native leaders must capitalize.

To do so, leaders must promote Native education both in the conventional Western sense and in terms of re-rooting young people within their traditional cultures. In time, such education will produce a new generation of healthy and highly skilled leaders who will be able to interact with the changing mainstream society from a position of strength rooted in cultural confidence. These leaders will practice a new style of Native politics that will reject the colonial assumptions and mentalities that have allowed state domination to continue. It will recognize and counter the state's efforts to co-opt, divide, and conquer communities. It will be founded on the essential wisdom of tradition. It will blend respect for the ancestors' wisdom with a commitment to live up to their example.

The sources and guiding beacons of indigenous governance remain the traditional teachings. While specific techniques are unique to each nation, there is a basic commonality in their essential message of respect. Beyond this, the teachings that could form the basis of the new style of Native politics continue to live and are accessible to those who seek them out. Our world has changed, and the skills we need are no longer the ones that allowed our ancestors to live free and happy in the bush. Instead, we need the skills to operate in the information age. To live as we do in the post-industrial First World, we must be able to take wisdom from our own traditions and apply it to contemporary challenges in innovative ways, to develop self-reliance and autonomy. This means knowing our traditions, of course, but also knowing as much as we can about the larger world we are living in today.

Some people may question the viability of an approach to empowerment based on education and tradition; given the social, cultural, and political disruption within Native communities, and the sacrifices that must be made to acquire a well-rounded education, maybe this isn't a realistic solution. I would answer that "realistic" is usually a code word for "easy." There is no easy way out of the situation we are in. The world is becoming more complex, more specialized, and more technical every day. In this new environment, the only real power is knowledge. Education is the way to knowledge, the weapon our warriors need for the remainder of the twenty-first century. To confront the state without an education today would be like going into battle against the cavalry with bow and arrows. Besides, at a time when the Native reality plainly "sucks," an approach that isn't realistic, that doesn't reflect the present reality, may be the best one we could take.

There is a related question worth asking: Is a social transformation, individual and collective, necessary to achieve the goals associated with political traditionalism? The experience of those communities that have successfully asserted themselves against the state has shown the need for coherence and consistency in the practice of politics within the community and in the posture taken toward other communities. This is not to say that people should go back to wearing buckskin or reject all the modern world in a material or cultural sense. But it does mean that there has to be a principled reconstruction of the values system and institutions that govern social and political lives within the community. How we relate to one another, how we make decisions, what we believe in—these are the elements that need to be recreated to reflect the wisdom contained in traditional teachings. So yes, a transformation is necessary, but one that manifests itself in changing attitudes, not looks or lifestyles. Orientation to traditional values is the key.

The only reason it is possible to advocate this position is that its indigenous premise is strong. Both in rhetoric and in substance, there are commonalities in the traditional wisdom expressed in the philosophies of most Native American peoples. The perspectives of the diverse people I have consulted and quoted in this book share fundamental similarities with the Rotinohshonni philosophy that it is structured around. This suggests that a solid traditional basis does exist for reconstructing Native community politics. The traditional wisdom of the Anishnaabeg people, for example, mirrors the Rotinohshonni teachings in its promotion of respectful coexistence among the diverse elements of creation:

- "To be wise is to cherish knowledge ..." (Humans must reflect, acknowledge, seek guidance, know and practise wisdom.)
- "To know love is to know peace ..." (Care, kindness, hope, harmony, and co-operation are fundamental values.)
- "Respect is honouring all of creation ..."
- "Bravery is to face challenges with honesty and integrity ..."
- "Humility is to know yourself as a sacred part of creation ..." (Other beings should be approached with modesty and sensitivity, and our goal should be to listen and learn from them.)
- "The truth is to know all these things."

An elder from the West Coast told me,

Traditionalism is the way you live your life. It means having a clean body and mind. Traditionalism isn't only ceremonies and art, but government as well. Many people don't realize the distinction between ceremonial traditionalism and government in a traditional way. Governing people according to the values and principles of tradition is what's really important.

How does the philosophical consistency among indigenous peoples translate into the base for a new style of Native politics? All intellectual movements are inspired and to a certain extent defined by certain texts (consider Machiavelli's realism, Weber's bureaucracy, Marx's socialism). Among indigenous peoples, the basic "texts" are the traditional teachings that form the narrative backbone of each culture. These are the sources of wisdom. But guidance is needed in interpreting and implementing the messages they

convey. Our communities lack the solid, well-defined cultural roles for elders and traditional teachers that would aid in the transmission of knowledge
and meaning. Thus, contemporary scholars, writers, and artists must take
on the responsibility of translating the meaning of traditions and providing
the guidance required to make those traditions part of the contemporary
reality. The formation of a new indigenous intelligentsia that understands
the essence and commonality of the traditional teachings is crucial to reforming politics and society.

The guiding light in efforts to use our common ground as a basis for
leadership, government, and politics is the thought of Vine Deloria, Jr. Both
in stressing the importance of consciousness-raising and enhancing self-
esteem through the affirmation of tradition, and in suggesting how patterns
of governance might be changed, Deloria's work paved the way for a
younger generation of thinkers to take the movement further. Deloria's
approach was uniquely suited to the contemporary context because, as was
illustrated in our dialogue above, he cautioned against the sort of simplis-
tic thinking that puts tradition on a pedestal and refuses to recognize the
changes that have taken place in response to colonization. Opposing uses
of tradition that are not in a certain sense pragmatic, he knows that simple
reimmersion in tradition is useless without conscious reflection on how traditional teachings can be applied to the contemporary crisis.

Deloria contrasts traditionalist leadership with what he calls "agency
Indians" (those who frame their identity and politics in the colonial structure)
and notes the great advantage of a traditionalist style. What makes traditional
people so powerful, both as human beings and as political forces in Native
communities? Traditionalists are powerful because they embody the core values that define the nation. First, they have a high concentration of Indian
blood, and their social and political lineage in the community is strong; thus,
they are free of alternative identities and allegiances, and they are not marginal
to the community in any way. Second, they know and practise the traditional
culture, which means they have access to the spiritual resources and personal
power that come from living according to the teachings. Third, they speak
their own language—a sign that they have not been assimilated into mainstream society. Fourth, and last, they know and respect oral history; traditionalists recognize oral history as the key to the knowledge that is at the root of
the most powerful historical and political defences of nationhood.

Our communities need the strength and integrity inherent in traditionalist leaders. But we also need to develop the practical, technical capacity

to govern our communities effectively. As Deloria pointed out in his work, we need to blend the inherent power of tradition with the skills required to manage the institutions of a modern society.

Four Basic Objectives

Building on Deloria's views, I would say that we need to alter the patterns of governance in our communities and achieve four basic objectives:

1. **Structural reform.** Native governments must be made legitimate within their communities. The only way to accomplish this is by rejecting electoral politics and restructuring Native governments to accommodate traditional decision-making, consultation (with all members of the community, including the elders, youth, and women), and dispute-resolution processes. At the same time, the community's reliance on white advisers should be minimized by enhancing the administrative capacity of Native governments to self-manage. This will require a sustained effort to educate and train community members.

2. **Reintegration of Native languages.** Native languages embody indigenous peoples' identity and are the most important element in their culture. They must be revived and protected as both symbols and sources of nationhood. This can be accomplished only by making the Native language the community's official language—the one in which leaders speak, the processes of government are conducted, and the official versions of all documentation are written. In addition, communities must make teaching the Native language, to both adults and children, a top priority.

3. **Economic self-sufficiency.** Meaningful progress toward self-determination can never be made until Native communities are free of economic dependency. Self-sufficiency is impossible without a resource base and adequate lands to build an economy. To achieve it, Native communities must expand their land bases and gain control of the economic activities that take place on their territories, so that they can benefit from them. In addition, communities must focus on business and technical education; only by developing our human resources can we reduce individuals' dependency on government and increase their ability to contribute to the general development of the community.

4. **Nation-to-nation relations with the state.** A political space must be created for the exercise of self-determination. Native communities must

reject the claimed authority of the state, assert their right to govern their own territories and people, and act on that right as much as their capacity to do so allows. Communities must be prepared to move between defending their territories and nationhood at times when the state entrenches itself in a position of denial and negotiating innovative ways for the state to recognize the principle when their activism creates space for movement toward justice.

For a long time, Native politics has been portrayed as a competition between traditionalist leaders who live the culture and agency or band council leaders who work within the state system. Today, our survival depends on the emergence of new Native leaders who embody traditionalism as a personal identity and at the same time have the knowledge and skills required to bring traditional objectives forward as the basic agenda of the political and social institutions within which they work.

Another way of understanding what might be termed a traditional style of Native politics is to contrast it with the two dominant forms that Deloria's agency Indian can take: the *realist* and the *bureaucrat*. Indigenous peoples asserting their nationhood today face reactionary state policies and entrenched institutions of control determined to limit their progress toward self-determination. As important as it is to understand shifting social movements, legal manoeuvres, and evolving structural arrangements within the state, the most essential point to grasp is that the politics of decolonization is largely determined by the fact that the state is founded on a *realistic* approach to power and a *bureaucratic* approach to governance.

To a realist, power resides in force. This approach to power is employed from a position of dominance only—Canada would never deal with the United States the way it does with indigenous peoples—and serves to entrench and justify a distribution of power favouring the state. It operates in a universe of legal fiction where calculations of interest rule.

It is anti-historical, disrespectful, and immoral because it cannot admit the existence of localized knowledge or different forms of power without undermining (in the realist's view) the very existence of the state. This is the dominant style of politics as practised by servants of the state at the political level (politicians and negotiators).

The realist style breeds a special type of political actor for whom calculations of power as control take on an almost spiritual meaning. Native people are constantly obliged to deal with representatives of the state who operate in the realist style and adhere to three basic principles: (1) human affairs are always contingent; (2) the ends justify the means; and (3) deception is necessary. For the realist, there is no need for values to support and guide human relationships: decisions are contingent, made according to calculations of self-interest. In the end, the goal of achieving a dominant position relative to others justifies the strategies and tactics used to get there. The need to hide true intentions is a fact of political life. And the separation of political choices from all moral or emotional constraints is essential. Such realism will be familiar to anyone who has dealt with Indian Affairs officials, federal or provincial treaty negotiators, corporate lawyers, or co-opted Native politicians.

The realist believes that his ideas are universal laws, and that his approach to power and politics is the only one. He does not see that he is operating within a specific historical and intellectual framework. Granted, he can impose it on others because he shares in the power the state derives from its ownership of the implements of coercive force and the wealth of colonized nations. But this perspective is, in fact, a localized form of knowledge in itself, one that has become dominant only because the realists have silenced other discourses of power in the course of the establishment and maintenance of colonial regimes. There is no intellectual, moral, or logical superiority to white ways of knowing. In fact, the intellectual implosion of any justification for colonialism (together with the increasing economic failures in the states built on realist premises) underlines the limitations of realism as a long-term approach to human affairs.

The challenge is to recognize the limitations of the realist style and persuade the people who are still bound to that style to see beyond it—to reject the intellectual framework that perpetuates injustice and denies even the dominant person a peaceful and fulfilling existence (despite material wealth and the trappings of power, no happiness can come from constantly having to defend an unjust empire from unruly subjects).

Indigenous people confront the power imbalances justified by realism every time they deal with the various bureaucracies that are their points of contact with the state. The bureaucrats who inhabit these structures represent the state's passive resistance to change (even when its realist premises begin to weaken). The bureaucratic style of politics is, like the realist style, primarily concerned with maintaining the status quo. In the context of decolonization, it is the state's safeguard against the weakening intellectual justification for its dominance over indigenous peoples.

The bureaucratic style sees the "office" as the primary form of authority: Anti-historic and immoral in the extreme, it is concerned only with maintaining control according to abstract regulations and fulfilling its mandate within the legal system to which it owes its existence. The bureaucratic form has six essential features: (1) dependence on formal procedures; (2) hierarchy; (3) tension between protocol and real life; (4) endless deferral; (5) subordination of speech to writing; and (6) substitution of the bureaucratic persona for real personality and accountability. For the bureaucrat, rules are tokens of power; order is maintained through an elaborate system of assigned jurisdictions, appointments, and offices, with the "top" of a pyramidal structure defining the "ideal" in terms of both power and right. Psychological insecurity is a constant feature because life can never be as perfectly regulated as the bureaucratic system. There is strict reliance on the authority of written documentation because words and people cannot be trusted; and the anonymous facade of the office becomes a shield that protects its holder from having to interact with people on the strength of her own character and skills as leader, while the imperatives of office serve as convenient substitutes for thinking and morality.

Native people are intimately familiar with both realistic and bureaucratic behaviours and attitudes. But they do not always realize that these are consequences of the choice to integrate oneself within the colonial framework. In fact, they often see the disruptive and disrespectful actions of Native politicians and bureaucrats as reflections of a social or psychological disorder.

Together, both the realistic and bureaucratic styles illustrate what an indigenous style of leadership should not look like. In the broadest terms, a style of leadership and politics consonant with traditional indigenous values would draw its imperatives and operate within parameters established by the vast reservoir of traditional teachings partially reflected and woven throughout this text. Describing a Native style of leadership is not so much a matter of positing rules, features, and criteria (as was so easy to do with the realist and bureaucratic styles). It is more a matter of advocating an approach to politics combining innovation and flexibility with a core commitment to uphold the basic values of respect, tolerance, harmony, and autonomy. It is at the same time rooted and adaptive; and it is inherently capable of promoting harmonious coexistence because it is set in a real context and not bound to an abstract or obsolete power structure. It is strong and confident, because it does not compromise the basic values and principles of indigenous philosophies.

In this new style of Native politics, individuals are not subjugated to a collective sense of right and wrong: The tension between the individual and the collective is a dynamic of rights-based arguments rooted in the Western liberal tradition. The concept of "rights," especially in the common Western sense, leads nowhere for indigenous peoples because it alienates the individual from the group. By contrast, the tension between individual and collective rights is a mainstay of discussions about justice in Western societies, which conceive of rights only in the context of a sovereign political authority because the law that defines and protects them depends on the existence of a single sovereign. There can indeed be acknowledgment of diversity, and even concessions to real difference, but to gain access to this tolerance it is necessary to be part of the community ruled by the sovereign state.

Indigenous leaders who engage in arguments framed by a Western liberal paradigm cannot hope to protect the integrity of their nations. To enlist the intellectual force of rights-based arguments is to concede nationhood in the truest sense. "Aboriginal rights" are in fact the benefits accrued by indigenous peoples who have agreed to abandon their autonomy in order to enter the legal and political framework of the state. After a while, indigenous freedoms become circumscribed and indigenous rights get defined not with respect to what exists in the minds and cultures of the Native people, but in relation to the demands, interests, and opinions of the millions of other people who are also members of that single-sovereign community, to which our leaders will have pledged allegiance.

The indigenous conception, and the politics that flows from it, maintains in a real way the distinctions between various political communities and contains an imperative of respect that makes homogenization unnecessary. Native people respect others to the degree that they demonstrate respect. There is no need, as in the Western tradition, to create political or legal uniformity to guarantee respect. There is no imperial, totalizing, or assimilative impulse. And that is the key difference: Both philosophical systems can achieve peace, but, in return, the European demands assimilation to a belief or a country, while the Native demands nothing but respect.

Internally, instead of creating formal boundaries and rules to protect individuals from each other and from the group, a truly indigenous political system relies on the motif of balance. For the Native, there is no tension in the relationship between the individual and the collective. Indigenous thought is based on the notion that people, communities, and the other elements of creation coexist as equals. The interests and wants of humans, whether as individuals or as collectives, do not have a special priority in deciding the justice of a situation.

Finally, the value of an indigenous tradition and a new style of Native politics is not limited to indigenous peoples. Nor does the indigenous critique of colonialism and the political ethos of the dominant Western tradition imply a racial superiority. One of the central messages in this book is that some Native leaders themselves have become proponents of the statist style. If the dichotomy at the heart of my argument is not necessarily indigenous versus white, what is it? To some extent it can be seen as tradition versus modernity, but this is only because modernity has become so unjustly skewed in favour of the possessive materialism and destructive exploitation of corporate capitalism: Tradition is respect and modernity is disrespect. Consider the Tujia people of central China and their struggle to preserve their homeland against the Three Gorges Dam flooding of the Yangtze River by the modern, internationally capitalized Chinese state. This can be perceived in simple racial or ethnic terms as a struggle by indigenous tribal people against the hegemony of Han Chinese. But it is not inherently a racial or ethnic struggle so much as it is an ideological or philosophical one that has racial implications because of the distribution of power in the modern world. At its root, it is a philosophical and values-based difference, which manifests itself in political–economic terms, and has racial/nationalist implications. Colonization and imperialism cannot be separated from the philosophical problem, but they can be overcome by philosophical and rational persuasion.

Promotion of traditional perspectives on power, justice, and relationships is essential to the survival of indigenous peoples. To defend our nationhood against co-optation, it is essential to redirect our energies and resources toward education for our young people and the (re)development of a new *indigenous intelligentsia* rooted in tradition and committed to preserving their nations and creating the conditions for harmonious coexistence with others.

Our youth must begin to acquire the knowledge and skills that are the true weapons of the information age. Bringing a final end to colonialism will demand the complete destruction of its intellectual and moral premises. In their place, we must establish a set of justifications for indigenous self-government that will resonate with the best alternative traditions within the dominant society as well. This can happen only if we collectively develop the ability to argue the justice of our position in a universal logic and language. We must add our voices to the narrative that is history, translate our understandings of history and justice, and bring the power of our wisdom to bear on the relationships we have with others. We cannot do this from a position of intellectual weakness.

Eloquent speakers, profound thinkers, and creative leaders abounded in traditional indigenous societies. The recovery of these traditions and the reestablishment of respect for knowledge in all its forms are what I mean in calling for the (re)development of an indigenous intelligentsia. One of the major consequences of colonialism was the loss of our ability to think for ourselves; thus, many of our leaders and communities rely on others to think for them (for a price). The cost of delegating intelligence is enormous in terms of the misrepresentation or misappropriation of indigenous knowledge and perspectives (not to mention the exorbitant fees paid to mercenary consultants). People who can shape ideas, translate, and create language will be essential to the process of decolonization, once we have created an informed and critical polity by increasing the general level of education in our communities. Structural and psychological decolonization is an intellectual process as well as a political, social, and spiritual one. We would not consider allowing a white person to represent our people, to initiate and effect healing, or to teach us lessons about our spirituality. Similarly, the revitalization of our ideas and institutions should not be contracted out to others.

At first, the notion of an indigenous intelligentsia may seem counterintuitive, conjuring up visions of the privileged, educated elites in Western societies. But, in the context of a unified or holistic approach to decolonization, writers, philosophers, teachers, and artists are essential if we are to confront the state at a deep level. Those who advocate such segmentation of social roles and specialization of knowledge may be accused of elitism, but the idea of an intelligentsia made up of teachers and wisdom-keepers is actually very traditional.

Traditionally, indigenous societies had strict qualifications, arduous rituals, and ceremonial initiations for those who would serve in such roles. To propose an indigenous intelligentsia should by no means be seen as an attempt to supplant the traditional elders and healers within those communities who still possess these rich gifts. To respect the role the intelligentsia would play in relation to the others who hold knowledge and guide their people, some thought must be given to the question of qualification.

The respected indigenous scholar Elizabeth Cook-Lynn has written on the role of indigenous intellectuals, focusing on the importance of remaining rooted in a real community and living traditional culture. She sees it as the responsibility of the intellectual to play an active political role in the transmission of knowledge, as a means of promoting justice. To fulfil this role one must know and respect traditional knowledge and the communities where it lives. This concept is clearly opposed to the individualist, non-accountable "escapism" of pure theory and strictly academic endeavour common in universities. Cook-Lynn's perspective on the dangers inherent in the misrepresentation of indigenous nations' perspectives by non-rooted, marginal (in her words, "mixed-blood") appropriators in contemporary fiction and literary criticism applies as well to those legal, political, and social thinkers who gain acceptance and fame in the mainstream media and academic circles by promoting an assimilationist agenda:

> A great deal of the work done in the mixed-blood literary movement is personal, invented, appropriated and irrelevant to First Nation status in the United States. If that work becomes too far removed from what is really going on in Indian enclaves, there will be no way to engage in responsible intellectual strategies in an era when structures of external cultural power are more oppressive than ever.

Cook-Lynn's uncompromising views point to the true character of indigenous intellectualism and activism. The contentiousness, autonomy, and reverence for traditional teachings and nationalism that are the core traits of an indigenous perspective have not been conveyed by the so-called cultural mediators and people with no roots in indigenous communities, intellectual or otherwise. The time has come for people who are from someplace Indian to take back the discourse on Indians. There is nothing wrong with valuing traditional knowledge. A real Indian intellectual is proud of our traditions and is willing to take a risk in defending our principles. Contrary to the impression conveyed by many non-rooted intellectuals, our traditions are not being constantly reinvented, redefined, or individually experienced by people whose real wish is to integrate with the mainstream. The traditions are powerful, real, and relevant. As intellectuals, we have a responsibility to generate and sustain a social and political discourse that is respectful of the wisdom embedded within our traditions. We must find answers from within those traditions, and present them in ways that preserve the integrity of our languages and communicative styles. Most importantly, as writers and thinkers, we should be answerable to our nations and communities.

These themes—respect, honour, pride, courage—are the same themes that run throughout this book as both values and goals. I have argued for renewed communities, renewed activism, and a renewed leadership ethos to bring an end to a harmful way of life imposed on us by history and to restore balance, respect, and harmony to our lives. My guiding vision is of a retraditionalized politics, and the re-establishment of our nations and relationships on the basis of the sacred teachings given to us by our ancestors.

It is not enough to imagine a better and more just future. Without a commitment to action, we will continue to suffer. What corrupt ruler has ever turned over a new leaf? What oppressive regime has ever smiled benevolently and handed back power to the oppressed? When has justice prevailed without sacrifice? And when has change taken place without friction? We cannot expect a better future in the absence of a commitment to take action, to attack and destroy the heart of colonialism.

There is no hope—or sense—in attacking the state with physical force, or in seeking peace by unpeaceful means. The goals that flow from our traditions demand an approach based on undermining the intellectual and moral foundations of colonialism and exposing the internal contradictions of states and societies that promise justice and practise oppression. Non-indigenous people need to be brought to the realization that their notion of power and its extension over indigenous peoples is wrong by any moral standard. This approach holds the greatest promise for the freedom of indigenous people.

I have outlined an approach to decolonization that focuses on the reform of indigenous communities as a first stage in a general reform of society's understanding and use of power. The strategic and tactical choices to be made will, over time, vary within each community. Internally, indigenous communities must recover the notions of power that led to the formation of respectful regimes of mutual coexistence. Along with new leaders, a new leadership ethos grounded in tradition must be put in place, one that promotes accountability to the people through the revival of traditional decision-making processes. We must become educated both in the ways of our ancestors and in the new knowledge and skills required to carry our communities forward. And, most urgently, we must begin to recreate a place of honour and respect within our societies for young people.

In our relations with others, we need to engage society as a whole in an argument about justice that will bring about real changes in political practice. We need to convince others to join us in challenging the state's oppression of indigenous peoples. This will require a broad-based intellectual and political movement away from prevailing beliefs and structures. All actions in this effort—not just our own but those of everyone who supports us—must be inspired and guided by four principles: (1) undermine the intellectual premises of colonialism; (2) act on the moral imperative for change; (3) do not co-operate with colonialism; and (4) lastly, resist further injustice. We can achieve decolonization through hard work and sacrifice based on these principles, in concert with the restoration of an indigenous political culture within our communities.

These words are a manifesto, a challenge, and a call for action. Don't preserve tradition, live it! Let us develop a good mind and do what is necessary to heal the damage done to us and bring back to life the culture of peace, power, and righteousness that is the indigenous way.

Haih, he is my grandfather, haih
you should listen,
when they seek it,
they who are your grandchildren,
that which now has grown old,
that which you all established,
the great peace.
Haih, he is my grandfather, haih
truly, may it happen
that one listens again.

—from the *Kaienerekowa*

Notes

8   On the Rotinohshonni world view and its key concepts: M. Dennis, *Cultivating a Landscape of Peace* (1993), 20–22, 91; D. Bedford and T. Workman, "The Great Law of Peace: Alternative Inter-National (al) Practices and the Iroquoian Confederacy," *Alternatives* 22 (1), 87–112; A.A. Shimony, *Conservatism among the Iroquois at the Six Nations Reserve* (1994). And on the notion of freedom as the central concept: A.F.C. Wallace, "Dreams and Wishes of the Soul: A Type of Psychoanalytic Theory among the Seventeenth Century Iroquois," *American Anthropologist* 60 (April 1958), 246.

11   Conventionally, academic debate on the definition and meaning of tradition focuses on determining whether or not indigenous peoples are authentically representing "traditional" beliefs and practices as observed, recorded, and described (read "defined") by anthropologists from outside the culture—the object being for the anthropologists and government officials located within colonizing institutions to define indigenous peoples off their land and out of existence by creating an unrealistic (certainly unliveable) concept of tradition as a base reference against which to check the authenticity of contemporary indigenous peoples. In recent years, this project has been challenged within academe, and many anthropologists now take the alternative (though still unacceptable) view that indigenous cultures are authentic in any representation by a person or an institution having a connection to an indigenous nation. While the academic debate rages, indigenous people still must face the fact that the state uses both perspectives against them in the courts and in politics—the static scholars to justify state incursions into indigenous lands ("they are not the real Aboriginal people") and the evolutionaries to justify state incursions into indigenous cultures ("they have no right to deny anyone's aboriginality"). Nevertheless, the concept of traditionalism is very clearly defined among real indigenous people. Tradition is the stories, teachings, rituals, ceremonies, and languages that have been inherited from previous generations. Without specific reference to a particular form or structure, something is authentically indigenous and traditional if it draws on what is indigenous to the culture to honour the values and principles of the inheritance. If it fails in its primary reference to inherited ways, beliefs, and values, it is not traditional or authentically indigenous. The present essay can be seen as an exercise in traditionalism, reflecting what Gregory Dowd, in his study of the often misunderstood "pan-Indian" politico-religious movements of the eighteenth century, described as a form of nativism:

> Nativists did not retreat wildly into a pristine tradition that never was, hopelessly attempting to escape a world changed by colonial powers. Rather, they identified with other native inhabitants of the continent, they self-consciously proclaimed that selected traditions and new (sometimes even imported) modes of behavior held keys to earthly and spiritual salvation, and they rejected the increasing colonial influence in native government, culture, and economy in favor of native independence. What is more, there are good reasons to employ the term nativism for the movement ... because

it sought native-directed solutions, based primarily upon a cosmology, composed by Native Americans, to the problem of European, and more particularly, Anglo-American, ambition (*A Spirited Resistance* [1992], xxii). For further discussion, see Alfred, *Heeding the Voices of Our Ancestors* (1995); L. Donald, "Liberty, Equality, Fraternity: Was the Indian Really Egalitarian?" in J.A. Clifton, ed., *The Invented Indian* (1990), 145–68; M.D. Levin, ed., *Ethnicity and Aboriginality* (1993); and C.H. Scott, "Customs, Tradition, and the Politics of Culture: Aboriginal Self-Government in Canada," in N. Dyck and J.B. Waldram, eds., *Anthropology, Public Policy and Native Peoples in Canada* (1993), 311–33.

12   On the study of leadership: J.G. Burns, *Leadership* (1978); L.J. Edinger, "Approaches to the Comparative Analysis of Political Leadership," *The Review of Politics* (1989), 509–23; B. Kellerman, ed., *Political Leadership* (1986); and J. O'Toole, *Leading Change* (1995).

17   The late John Mohawk on the Rotinohshonni oratorical tradition: from a speech delivered at the University of Buffalo in April 1985 and quoted in G.E. Sioui, *For an Amerindian Autohistory* (1992), 47–48.

22   On methodology, hermeneutics (the art of interpreting texts) and its relevance to the resolution of political conflict, and emerging methods of interpreting narrative texts for purposes of political analysis: T. Ball, ed., *Idioms of Inquiry* (1987), 96–109, and E. Roe, *Narrative Policy Analysis* (1994), 155–62. On the approach and method of cross-national comparisons of political culture, as well as the inter-connectivity and mutual influence of institutions and cultural values: M. Dogan and D. Pelassy, *How to Compare Nations* (1984), 58–66. And on qualitative research standards and the general criteria for soundness in qualitative social science (trans-ferability, external validity, dependability, and confirmability): C. Marshall and G.B. Rossman, *Designing Qualitative Research* (1989), 144–53.

26   On Native nationalism: Alfred, *Heeding the Voices*.

27   On the Indian Problem: S. Cornell, *The Return of the Native* (1988), 33–50.

28   On traditional Native values: R.L. Barsh, "The Nature and Spirit of North American Political Systems," *American Indian Quarterly* (Spring 1986); D.L. Fixico, "The Struggle for Our Homes: Indian and White Values and Tribal Lands," in J. Weaver, ed., *Defending Mother Earth* (1996), 30–40; J.A. Long, "Political Revitalization in Canadian Native Indian Societies," *Canadian Journal of Political Science* 23 (4), 751–73; and A. Mills and R. Slobodin, eds., *Amerindian Rebirth* (1994).

30   On the characteristics of indigenous political systems relevant to power: M.S. Dockstater, "Towards an Understanding of Aboriginal Self-Government" (1993), 32–4.

43   Oka: see note to page 129 in this section.

43   In 1985, Canada amended the Indian Act to restore status to those who had been "enfranchised" (who had given up their status in order to receive the benefits of Canadian society) and to eliminate its discrimination against Indian women who married non-Indians, permitting them to pass on their Indian status to their chil-dren. The series of amendments that effected the change also included the partial devolution of control over membership to Indian bands, resulting in what has become known as a two-tiered membership system with a distinction made between Indian status on the federal level and band membership on the local level. The new

system created a situation where the federal government defined and imposed membership criteria for those communities that did not design and implement a local code in accordance with the Indian Act. In effect, where the new Indian Act theoretically allowed for band-controlled definitions of membership criteria, only those local membership codes that were acceptable to the minister and that conformed to Canadian laws were ratified and formalized by the Department of Indian Affairs.

44   "Anglo-Americans and Natives are fundamentally different ...': Fixico, 41.

45   On differing perspectives on land and the environment, historically and today: W. Cronon, *Changes in the Land* (1983); and C. Merchant, *Radical Ecology* (1992).

46 ·   "With their awareness ...": Sioui, 9.

46   On the importance of Aboriginal values in Kahnawake: Kahnawake Shakotiia' Takehnas Community Services, *Aboriginal Values and Social Services* (1994), 22–3. On the enduring importance of maintaining a connection to traditional indigenous values as a source of identity: D. Jensen and C. Brooks, eds., *In Celebration of Our Survival* (1991); J.M. Watanabe, *Maya Saints and Souls* (1992), 157–84.

47   "True, the white man brought great change....": F. Turner, ed., *The Portable North American Indian Reader* (1974), 569.

50   "The evil of modern states ...": Barsh, 186.

51   On greed and jealousy in indigenous societies: N.O. Lurie, "Money, Semantics, and Indian Leadership," *American Indian Quarterly* (Winter 1986), 47–63.

52   On the eighteenth-century revivalist movements: Dowd, *A Spirited Resistance*; and C. Vecsey, *Imagine Ourselves Richly* (1991).

55   "I'm not going to run interference for the white government....": *Globe and Mail*, 23 November 1996, D1; on Mercredi's "consensus": *Globe and Mail*, 11 July 1996, A8.

55   On the difference between Native and non-Native leadership: K.B. Chiste, "Aboriginal Women and Self-Government: Challenging Leviathan," *American Indian Culture and Research Journal* 18 (3), 19–43; N. Dyck, "Representation and Leadership of a Provincial Indian Association," in A. Tanner, ed., *The Politics of Indianness* (1983); *Globe and Mail*, 23 November 1996, D1; Ehattesaht Tribe, *Back to Basics* (1992); M.A. Louie, *Visionary Leadership from a Native American Perspective*; and L. Maracle, *I Am Woman* (1996).

56   "Brown and bureaucrat ...": Dyck, "Representation and Leadership," 288.

56   On Forbes's four categories of Native people: R.A. Warrior, *Tribal Secrets* (1995), 34–5.

57   On co-optation: H. Adams, *Prison of Grass* (1989), 123–62; Breton, *The Governance of Ethnic Communities*; and R. Tannenbaum and W.H. Schmidt, "How to Choose a Leadership Pattern," *Harvard Business Review* (May–June 1973), 162–73.

58   "Blinded by niceties and polite liberality ...": Maracle, *I Am Woman*, 12.

59   "Once a group of people have been assaulted ...": E. Duran and B. Duran, *Native American Postcolonial Psychology* (1995), 29. On the lingering effects of multi-generation alcohol and sexual abuse in Native communities: P.C. Mancall, *Deadly Medicine* (1995), 5–9; and R.C. Trexler, *Sex and Conquest* (1995), 173–80.

59   On the psychology of the colonized Native American male and the post-traumatic stress disorder model applied to contemporary Native people: Duran and Duran,

35–42. For a concrete description of the experience: C. Haig-Brown, *Resistance and Renewal* (1988). For a perspective on colonial state policies: A. Armitage, *Comparing the Policy of Aboriginal Assimilation* (1995).

61   "Politics of pity": thanks to my friend Audra Simpson for this phrase.

61   For data on the physical effects of colonization on Native communities: T.K. Young, *The Health of Native Americans* (1994); and J.B. Waldram et al., *Aboriginal Health in Canada* (1995).

61   On "retraditionalization": T.D. LaFromboise, A.M. Heyle, and E.J. Ozer, "Changing and Diverse Roles of Women in American Indian Cultures," *Sex Roles* 22 (7/8), 455–76. On the political role, status, and perspectives of Native women in general: P. Gunn Allen, *The Sacred Hoop* (1986); J. Katz, ed., *Messengers of the Wind* (1995); L.F. Klein and L.A. Ackerman, eds., *Women and Power in Native North America* (1995); and C. Niethammer, *Daughters of the Earth* (1977).

62   "American Indian women have achieved success …": LaFromboise et al., 469.

66   There are thinkers within the Western tradition who have challenged the dominant approach to power and put forward visions of justice, relationships, and leadership that offer strong bases for dialogue with indigenous peoples. The most notable of these people are the Canadian scientist and environmental philosopher David Suzuki, in his many writings and media communications, and the Czech writer and former republic president Vaclav Havel, particularly in his book *Summer Meditations* (1993).

68   Burns on moral leadership: *Leadership*, 42–6.

70   "The essence of leadership …": Burns, 43.

71   On the traditional notion of power in indigenous societies: R. Barsh, "The Nature and Spirit of North American Political Systems," *American Indian Quarterly* (Spring 1986), 181–98; G.E. Dowd, *A Spirited Resistance*, 1–22; S. Kan, *Symbolic Immortality* (1989); H. Robinson, *Nature/Power* (1992); B. Neidjie et al., *Australia's Kakadu Man*, 39; and H.K. Trask, *From a Native Daughter*.

71   Burns on power: *Leadership*, 13–18.

71   Foucault's two approaches to the analysis of power: M. Foucault, *Power/Knowledge* (1980), 91–2, and *The Politics of Truth* (1997), 29–52.

72   "If one wants to look for a non-disciplinary form of power …": Foucault, *Power/Knowledge*, 108.

73   Tlingit *Shagóon*: Kan, 68.

73   Harry Robinson on power: *Nature/Power*, 100. See also G. Blondin, *Yamamoria The Lawmaker* (1997), 43–70.

74   On the Havasupai concept of power: L. Hinton quoted in K.M. Donovan, *Coming to Voice* (1998), 48–9.

74   The Diné concept of power: J.R. Farella, *The Main Stalk* (1984), 64–8.

75   Diné battle song "Big Black Bear": Farella, 169.

75   "It is at this point, when one begins to believe …": Farella, 66.

76   Paiute song told by Simon Ortiz: P. Mathiessen, *Indian Country* (1979), 11.

77–78 Vine Deloria, Jr, on nationhood and sovereignty: Deloria and R.M. Lyttle, *The Nations Within* (1984), 8–15. "Self-government is not an Indian idea," 15.

80   "By adopting the European-Western ideology ...": M. Boldt and J.A. Long, "Tribal
        Traditions and European Political Ideologies: The Dilemma for Canada's Native
        Indians," *Canadian Journal of Political Science* 17 (1984), 548.

80   On the notion of sovereignty and the difference between sovereignty and nationhood:
        T. Anderson, *Sovereign Nations or Reservations?* (1990); J.G. Biersteker and C. Weber,
        eds., *State Sovereignty as a Social Construct* (1996); Boldt and Long, "Tribal Traditions,"
        537–53; and J.R. Wunder, ed., *Native American Sovereignty* (1996).

80–81   Mercredi on sovereignty ("I'm not going to allow ..."; "We are not talking about
        secession ..."): *Globe and Mail*, 11 July 1996, A8.

82   "The people already living on or near the area ...": F. Korsmo, "Claiming Memory
        in British Columbia: Aboriginal Rights and the State," *American Indian Culture and
        Research Journal* 20 (4), 72.

83   On sovereignty as a concept and its effect on knowledge and politics: J. Bartelson,
        A Genealogy of Sovereignty (1995), 3–7.

87   "One of the important discoveries of the twentieth century ...": J. Tully, *Strange
        Multiplicity* (1995), 56. On accommodating indigenous nationhood within the state
        paradigm, see also R.L. Barsh and J.Y. Henderson, *The Road* (1980); V. Deloria, Jr,
        and R.M. Lytle, *American Indians, American Justice* (1983); and C.F. Wilkinson,
        American Indians, Time, and the Law. For a post-colonial perspective on the state:
        F. Buell, *National Culture and the New Global System*, 217–62.

87   "The Great Law of Peace promotes unity ...": S.J. Anaya, *Indigenous Peoples in
        International Law* (1996), 79.

87   "the indefinite occupation ...": A. Kroker, *The Possessed Individual* (1992), 48.

87   "Judges should break with a knowledge of the law ...": A. Lajoie et al., *Le Statut
        juridique des peuples autochtones* (1996), 265 (translation provided by the authors).

95–96   Quotes from judgments in Twinn and Six Nations of the Grand River Band Council
        v. Henderson in L. Gilbert, *Entitlement to Indian Status and Membership Codes in
        Canada*, 208–11.

96   "The continuing and still virtually unlimited federal power ...": D.E. Wilkins,
        "Indian Treaty Rights: Sacred Entitlements or 'Temporary Privileges'?" *American
        Indian Culture and Research Journal* 20 (1), 121.

97   On the sources of power in strategic resources: R. Breton, *The Governance of Ethnic
        Communities* (1991), 64–65.

98   "Co-optation is a process ...": Breton, 77. On co-optation as a concept and its
        implications in indigenous communities, see also H.K. Trask, *From a Native
        Daughter* (1993), 140–41; and H. Adams, *A Tortured People* (1995), 143–75.

99–100 Breton's analysis of the co-optation process and how external agents use ethnic
        leaders: *Governance*, 74–8.

100   "Leaders and their organizations ...": Breton, 77.

102–103 Advice on politics and leadership: personal communication from Vine Deloria, Jr,
        Boulder, to Gerald Taiaiake Alfred, Kahnawake, 28 September 1995.

105   On the need to reclaim traditional values: E.J. Hedican, "On the Ethno-Politics of
        Canadian Native Leadership and Identity," *Ethnic Groups* 9 (1991), 1–15.

106   On characteristics of strong contemporary communities: J.W. Gardner, *On
        Leadership* (1990), 116–18.

107   "In periods of calm ...": D.J. Elazar, "From Statism to Federalism—A Paradigm Shift," *International Political Science Review* 17 (4), 428.

108   "The attempted transformation of the Indian ...": Turner, *The Portable North American Indian Reader*, 568.

112   On the political function of a "pan-Indian paradigm": S. Harvey, "Two Models to Sovereignty: A Comparative History of the Mashantucket Pequot Tribal Nation and the Navajo Nation," *American Indian Culture and Research Journal* 20 (1), 167–68.

113   A classic example of the corporate model of leadership: J. Hayes, "The Politically Competent Manager," *Journal of General Management* 10 (1), 24–33.

114–15   On the characteristics of a Native leader and transformative leadership: R. Barsh, "The Nature and Spirit of North American Political Systems," *American Indian Quarterly* (Spring 1986); Burns, *Leadership*, 112–17; and J.A. Gibson, *Concerning the League* (1992), 1.

115   Boldt and Long's martial analogy for leadership: "Tribal Traditions."

115   For a discussion of the concept of accountability and other core notions of traditional indigenous political systems: G. Alfred and F. Wilmer, "Indigenous Peoples, States, and Conflict," in Carment and James, *Wars in the Midst of Peace* (1997); Barsh, "The Nature and Spirit of North American Political Systems"; C. Price, "Lakotas and Euroamericans: Contrasted Concepts of 'Chieftainship' and Decision-Making Authority," *Ethnohistory* 41 (3), 447–63.

116   On political instability as a natural feature of indigenous politics, including the quotation from the Fort Yuma Quechan elder, see R. Bee, "The Predicament of the Native American Leader: A Second Look," *Human Organization* 49 (1), 56–63.

116   On accountability and legitimacy in Native cultures see S. Cornell, "Accountability, Legitimacy, and the Foundations of Native Self-Governance," Harvard Project on American Indian Economic Development (January 1993).

117   "contemporary aboriginal women ...": J. Fiske, "Political Status of Native Indian Women: Contradictory Implications of Canadian State Policy," *American Indian Culture and Research Journal* 19 (2), 1–30.

118   "The anger that I carry ...": P. Monture-Angus, *Thunder in My Soul* (1995), 147.

119   "American Indian women must often fight ...": Gunn Allen, 193.

121   The dilemma of Native leadership, discussed in terms of ideological tension: Boldt and Long, "Tribal Traditions," 537–53.

122   "I firmly believe the Indian craves ...": J.B. Mackenzie, *The Six-Nations Indians in Canada* (1896), 146.

123   On indigenous peoples and self-determination in international law: Anaya, *Indigenous Peoples in International Law*, 83.

124   "After watching my friend ...": *Kahtou* (newspaper; Sechelt, BC), August 1997, 2.

124   On the Sechelt offer in the BC treaty process: "Extinguishment Offered to Sechelt," *Windspeaker* 15 (6), 1. On Tsawwassen and Maa-Nulth, see their websites, www.tsawwassenfirstnation.com and www.maanulth.ca.

129   The Mohawk nation endured a great deal of civil unrest and violent political conflict, internal and external, during the 1980s and '90s. In Akwesasne and Kahnawake in particular, Mohawks battled with each other over competing notions of tradition. Two Mohawk men were killed by competing factions in

Akwesasne in 1990. In the same year, Kahnawake and Kanesatake Mohawks faced the Quebec police, the RCMP, and the Canadian military in a summer-long armed standoff (the so-called Oka Crisis).

131   In 1996, the Mohawk Council of Kahnawake entered into a tripartite agreement with the federal and provincial governments. The Police Agreement provided for mutual recognition of jurisdictional authority but left questions such as the supremacy of laws open to interpretation.

135   *Tewatatowie*, the Kanien'kehaka concept of sovereignty: Alfred, *Heeding the Voices*, 102.

137   It should be noted that on 13 September 2007, Canada was one of only four countries that voted against the adoption of the United Nations Declaration on the Rights of Indigenous Peoples, along with the United States, Australia, and New Zealand. The declaration ultimately was passed with 143 countries voting in favour, 4 opposing, and 11 abstaining.

139   "I love the market ...": J.R. Saul, *The Unconscious Civilization* (1995), 122.

139   On Native leaders betraying egalitarian principles: T. Morantz, "Northern Algonquian concepts of status and leadership reviewed: A case study of the eighteenth-century trading captain system," *Canadian Review of Sociology and Anthropology* 19 (4), 482–501.

140   On greed in Native society ("Greed is evil ..."): Lurie, "Money, Semantics, and Indian Leadership," *American Indian Quarterly* (Winter 1986).

141–42   References to the Alaska situation and quotes from Berger's report: T.R. Berger, *Village Journey* (1995), 19, 25, 157. Also see www.cbc.ca/news/background/oil/anwar.html.

144   On land claims in Canada: K. Coates, ed., *Aboriginal Land Claims in Canada* (1992); and Grand Council of the Crees, *Sovereign Injustice* (1995). On claims internationally: J. Burger, *Report from the Frontier* (1987); A. Gedicks, *The New Resource Wars* (1994); and Trask, *From a Native Daughter*. For indigenous perspectives on treaties and treaty-making: Treaty 7 Elders and Tribal Council, *The True Spirit and Intent of Treaty 7* (1996), 111–45; and R.A. Williams, Jr, *Linking Arms Together* (1997).

145–46   The Delgamuukw decision and its definition of Aboriginal title: Federal Treaty Negotiation Office (Canada), *Treaty News* (March 1998), 3–4.

146ff.   Canadian policy in negotiating treaties in British Columbia and quotes from the federal government's position statements: Federal Treaty Negotiation Office (Canada), *British Columbia Treaty Negotiations: The Federal Perspective*, November 1996. See also Report of the British Columbia Claims Task Force, www.bctreaty.net/files/pdf_documents/bc_claims_task_force_report.pdf, the Tsawwassen, Lheildi T'enneh, and Maa-Nulth Final Agreements www.gov.bc.ca/arr/treaty/default.html, and T. Alfred, "Deconstructing the British Columbia Treaty Process," *Balayi: Culture, Law and Colonialism*, Vol. 3 (2001) 37–66.

150   On the Musqueam First Nation agreement and on the First Nations Summit position and mandate: Musqueam Reconciliation Agreement (embargoed access, March 2008), www.musqueam.bc.ca/ubc%20golf%20course/Backgrounder-Nov.%209,%202007.pdf, and First Nations Summit, *Fundamental Principles*, www.fns.bc.ca/about/fp.htm.

150ff.   Provincial policy and quotations from British Columbia's position statements: Ministry of Aboriginal Affairs (BC), Communications Branch, publications, including *Treaty Update* (series); *Information About the Effect of Treaty Settlements on Crown Leases and Licenses* (October 1995); and *Information About Provincial Treaty Mandates* (October 1995).

154–57   On the situation of indigenous youth and government responses: T. Alfred, B. Pitawanakwat, and J. Price, "The Meaning of Political Participation for Indigenous Youth," Research Report, Canadian Policy Research Network (September 2007); G. Alfred, "A Review and Analysis of the Major Challenges and Concerns of Aboriginal Youth in Canada," in the Royal Commission on Aboriginal Peoples (Canada), *Research Studies* (Ottawa: Canada Communications Group, 1996); G. Alfred and N.S. Huggins, "Learning from the International Experience: A Comparative Review of State Policies for Indigenous Youth," ibid.; and L. Pal, "Aboriginal Youth Policy: An Inventory and Analysis of Federal, Provincial, and Territorial Programs," in ibid. On youth culture as a contemporary political issue: V. Amit-Talai and H. Wulff, *Youth Cultures* (1995), 224–25; and J.E. Coté and A.L. Allahar, *Generation on Hold* (1994), 157–63.

154   Alienated youth in the Solomon Islands: C. Jourdan, "Masta Liu," in Amit-Talai and Wulff, 202–22.

156   The Native Youth Movement in British Columbia and quotations from youth leaders: *The Province* (Vancouver) 18 April 1997: A04 and 22 April 1998: A8C; and CBC Radio, *Early Edition*, 8:55 AM, 18 April 1997.

157   On the effects of losing initiation rituals: Duran and Duran, *Native American Postcolonial Psychology*, 42–45; and K. Deer, "Mohawks of Kahnawake Community Study: A Narrative of a Future Beyond Disunity," in the Royal Commission on Aboriginal Peoples (Canada), *Research Studies* (Ottawa: Canada Communications Group, 1996).

157–67   The dialogue with Vine Deloria, Jr, is the partial transcript of a longer discussion between Deloria and me, which took place at the Western Social Sciences Association Annual Conference in Albuquerque, New Mexico, in April 2005.

170   On the interrelationships and common origins of indigenous American cultures: G. Brotherston, *Book of the Fourth World* (1992).

170   Anishnaabeg traditional teachings: L. White, "Medicine Wheel Teachings in Native Language Education," in S. O'Meara and D.A. West, eds., *From Our Eyes* (1996), 119–21. See also Bopp et al., *The Sacred Tree* (1985).

171   Vine Deloria, Jr, on tradition: Deloria and Lyttle, *The Nations Within*, 233–45; and Warrior, *Tribal Secrets*, 95.

173–77   On styles of politics: R. Harriman, *Political Style* (1995). See also M. Howlett and M. Ramesh, *Studying Public Policy* (1995), 187.

176–77   For hundreds of years, the Iroquois Confederacy has served as an inspiration for the design of confederal political configurations. In 1986, the US Senate acknowledged the Confederacy's contributions to the design of the US Constitution.

178–79   Elizabeth Cook-Lynn on the role of Indian intellectuals: "Intellectualism and the New Indian Story," in D. Mihesuah, ed., *Natives and Academics* (1998), 111–38; "A great deal of the work …": 130.

Bibliography

Adams, H. *Prison of Grass: Canada from a Native Point of View.* Saskatoon: Fifth House Publishers, 1989.

———. *A Tortured People: The Politics of Colonization.* Penticton, BC: Theytus Books, 1995.

Alfred, Gerald R. [Taiaiake]. *Heeding the Voices of Our Ancestors: Kahnawake Mohawk Politics and the Rise of Native Nationalism.* Toronto: Oxford University Press, 1995.

Alfred, Taiaiake. *Wasáse: Indigenous Pathways of Action and Freedom.* Peterborough, ON: Broadview Press, 2005.

Amit-Talai, V., and H. Wulff. *Youth Cultures: A Cross-Cultural Perspective.* London: Routledge, 1995.

Anaya, S.J. *Indigenous Peoples in International Law.* New York: Oxford University Press, 1996.

Anderson, B.R.O'G. *Language and Power: Exploring Political Cultures in Indonesia.* Ithaca, NY: Cornell University Press, 1990.

Anderson, K. *Chain Her by One Foot: The Subjugation of Native Women in Seventeenth-Century New France.* New York: Routledge, 1991.

Anderson, T. *Sovereign Nations or Reservations? An Economic History of American Indians.* San Francisco: Pacific Research Institute for Public Policy, 1995.

Armitage, A. *Comparing the Policy of Aboriginal Assimilation: Australia, Canada, and New Zealand.* Vancouver: University of British Columbia Press, 1995.

Armstrong, J. *Slash.* Penticton, BC: Theytus Books, 1992.

Armstrong, V.I., ed. *I Have Spoken: American History Through the Voices of the Indians.* Athens: Ohio University Press, 1971.

Asch, M., ed. *Aboriginal Treaty Rights in Canada: Essays on Law, Equality, and Respect for Difference.* Vancouver: University of British Columbia Press, 1997.

Ball, T., ed. *Idioms of Inquiry: Critique and Renewal in Political Science.* Albany: State University of New York Press, 1987.

Barsh, R.L., and J.Y. Henderson. *The Road: Indian Tribes and Political Liberty.* Berkeley: University of California Press, 1980.

Bartelson, J. *A Genealogy of Sovereignty.* Cambridge: Cambridge University Press, 1995.

Berger, T.R. *Village Journey: The Report of the Alaska Native Review Commission.* Vancouver: Douglas and McIntyre, 1995.

Biersteker, J., and C. Weber, eds. *State Sovereignty as a Social Construct.* Cambridge: Cambridge University Press, 1996.

Blackman, M.B. *During My Time: Florence Edenshaw Davidson, A Haida Woman*. Seattle: University of Washington Press, 1982.

Blondin, G. *Yamoria the Lawmaker: Stories of the Dene*. Edmonton: NeWest Publishers, 1997.

Boldt, M. *Surviving as Indians: The Challenges of Self-Government*. Toronto: University of Toronto Press, 1993.

Bopp, J., et al. *The Sacred Tree: Reflections on Native American Spirituality*. Lethbridge: Four Worlds Development Press, 1985.

Bordewich, F.M. *Killing the White Man's Indian: Reinventing Native Americans at the End of the Twentieth Century*. New York: Doubleday, 1996.

Breton, R. *The Governance of Ethnic Communities: Political Structures and Processes in Canada*. New York: Greenwood Press, 1991.

Brotherston, G. *Book of the Fourth World: Reading the Native Americas Through Their Literature*. Cambridge: Cambridge University Press, 1992.

Buell, F. *National Culture and the New Global System*. Baltimore, MD: Johns Hopkins University Press, 1994.

Burger, J. *Report from the Frontier: The State of the World's Indigenous Peoples*. London: Zed Books, 1987.

Burns, J.G. *Leadership*. New York: Harper and Row, 1978.

Carment, D., and P. James. *Wars in the Midst of Peace: The International Politics of Ethnic Conflict*. Pittsburgh: University of Pittsburgh Press, 1997.

Churchill, W., ed. *Marxism and Native Americans*. Boston: South End Press, 1983.

Clifton, J.A., ed. *The Invented Indian: Cultural Fictions and Government Policies*. New Brunswick: Transaction Publishers, 1990.

Clutesi, G. *Potlatch*. Sidney, BC: Gray's Publishing, 1969.

Coates, K., ed. *Aboriginal Land Claims in Canada: A Regional Perspective*. Toronto: Copp Clark, 1992.

Cornell, S. *The Return of the Native: American Indian Political Resurgence*. New York: Oxford University Press, 1988.

Coté, J.E., and A.L. Allahar. *Generation on Hold: Coming of Age in the Late Twentieth Century*. Toronto: Stoddart, 1994.

Cronon, W. *Changes in the Land: Indians, Colonists, and the Ecology of New England*. New York: Hill and Wang, 1983.

Deloria, V., Jr. *We Talk, You Listen*. New York: Macmillan, 1970.

————. *Custer Died for Your Sins: An Indian Manifesto*. Norman: University of Oklahoma Press, 1988.

————. *Red Earth, White Lies: Native Americans and the Myth of Scientific Fact*. New York: Scribner, 1995.

Deloria, V., Jr, and R.M. Lyttle. *American Indians, American Justice*. Austin: University of Texas Press, 1983.

————. *The Nations Within: The Past and Future of American Indian Sovereignty*. Austin: University of Texas Press, 1984.

Dennis, M. *Cultivating a Landscape of Peace: Iroquois-European Encounters in Seventeenth-Century America*. Ithaca, NY: Cornell University Press, 1993.

Denzin, N.K., and Y.S. Lincoln, eds. *Handbook of Qualitative Research*. London: Sage, 1994.

Dickason, O.P. *The Myth of the Savage: And the Beginnings of French Colonialism in the Americas*. Edmonton: University of Alberta Press, 1984.

Dockstater, M.S. "Towards an Understanding of Aboriginal Self-Government: A Proposed Theoretical Model and Illustrative Factual Analysis." J.D. thesis, York University, 1993.

Dogan, M., and D. Pelassy. *How to Compare Nations: Strategies in Comparative Politics*. Catham: Catham House Publishers, 1984.

Donovan, K.M. *Coming to Voice: Feminist Readings of Native American Literature*. Tucson: University of Arizona Press, 1998.

Dowd, G.E. *A Spirited Resistance: The North American Indian Struggle for Unity, 1745–1815*. Baltimore, MD: Johns Hopkins University Press, 1992.

Dudley, M.K., and K.K. Agard. *A Call for Hawaiian Sovereignty*. Waipahu: Na Kane O Ka Malo Press, 1990.

Duran, E., and B. Duran. *Native American Postcolonial Psychology*. Albany: State University of New York Press, 1995.

Dyck, N., and J.B. Waldram, eds. *Anthropology, Public Policy and Native Peoples in Canada*. Montreal: McGill-Queen's University Press, 1993.

Ehattesaht Tribe. *Back to Basics: The Land and Sea Claims and Self-Government*. Vancouver: Ehattesaht Tribe, 1992.

Engelstad, D., and J. Bird, eds. *Nation to Nation: Aboriginal Sovereignty and the Future of Canada*. Concord: Anansi Press, 1992.

Farella, J.R. *The Main Stalk: A Synthesis of Navajo Philosophy*. Tucson: University of Arizona Press, 1984.

Fleras, A., and J.L. Elliott. *The 'Nations Within': Aboriginal-State Relations in Canada, the United States, and New Zealand*. Toronto: Oxford University Press, 1992.

Foucault, M. *Power/Knowledge: Selected Interviews and Other Writings, 1972–1977*. C. Gordon, ed. and trans. New York: Pantheon Books, 1980.

————. *The Politics of Truth*. S. Lotringer, ed. New York: Semiotext(e), 1997.

Gardner, J.W. *On Leadership*. New York: Free Press, 1990.

Gedicks, A. *The New Resource Wars: Native and Environmental Struggles Against Multinational Corporations*. Montreal: Black Rose Books, 1994.

Gibson, J.A. *Concerning the League: The Iroquois League Tradition as Dictated in Onondaga*. H. Woodbury, trans. Winnipeg: Algonquian and Iroquoian Linguistics, 1992.

Giddens, A. *Modernity and Self-Identity: Self and Society in the Late Modern Age*. Stanford, CA: Stanford University Press, 1991.

Gilbert, L. *Entitlement to Indian Status and Membership Codes in Canada*. Toronto: Carswell, 1996.

Gill, S.D., and I.F. Sullivan. *Dictionary of Native American Mythology*. New York: Oxford University Press, 1992.

Grand Council of the Crees. *Sovereign Injustice: Forcible Inclusion of the James Bay Crees and Cree Territory into a Sovereign Québec*. Nemaska: Grand Council of the Crees, 1995.

Gunn Allen, P. *The Sacred Hoop: Recovering the Feminine in American Indian Traditions*. Boston: Beacon Press, 1986.

Haig-Brown, C. *Resistance and Renewal: Surviving the Indian Residential School*. Vancouver: Tillacum Library, 1988.

Havel, V. *Summer Meditations*. P. Wilson, trans. Toronto: Vintage, 1993.

Harriman, R. *Political Style: The Artistry of Power*. Chicago: University of Chicago Press, 1995.

Hirschman, A.O. *The Rhetoric of Reaction: Perversity, Futility, Jeopardy*. Cambridge, MA: Harvard University Press, 1991.

Howlett, M., and M. Ramesh. *Studying Public Policy: Policy Cycles and Policy Subsystems*. Toronto: Oxford University Press, 1995.

Jensen, D., and C. Brooks, eds. *In Celebration of Our Survival: The First Nations of British Columbia*. Vancouver: University of British Columbia Press, 1991.

Johnson, S., ed. *The Book of Elders: The Life Stories of Great American Indians*. New York: HarperCollins, 1994.

Jones, C., and S. Bosustow. *Queesto: Pacheenaht Chief by Birthright*. Penticton, BC: Theytus Books, 1981.

Josephy, A. *Red Power: The American Indians' Fight for Freedom*. Lincoln: University of Nebraska Press, 1971.

Kahnawake Shakotiia'Takehnhas Community Services (KSCS). *Aboriginal Values and Social Services: The Kahnawake Experience*. Kahnawake: Canadian Council on Social Development, 1994.

Kan, S. *Symbolic Immortality: The Tlingit Potlatch of the Nineteenth Century*. Washington, DC: Smithsonian Institution Press, 1989.

Katz, J., ed. *Messengers of the Wind: Native American Women Tell Their Life Stories.* New York: Ballantine, 1995.

Kellerman, B., ed. *Political Leadership: A Source Book.* Pittsburgh: University of Pittsburgh Press, 1986.

Kelsay, I.T. *Joseph Brant, 1743–1807: Man of Two Worlds.* Syracuse: Syracuse University Press, 1984.

Klein, L.F., and L.A. Ackerman, eds. *Women and Power in Native North America.* Norman: University of Oklahoma Press, 1995.

Knudtson, P., and D. Suzuki. *Wisdom of the Elders.* Toronto: Stoddart, 1993.

Kroker, A. *The Possessed Individual: Technology and the French Postmodern.* Montreal: New World Perspectives, 1992.

Kuehls, T. *Beyond Sovereign Territory: The Space of Ecopolitics.* Minneapolis: University of Minnesota Press, 1996.

Lajoie, A., J.M. Brisson, S. Normand, and A. Bissonette. *Le Statut juridique des peuples autochtones au Québec et le pluralisme.* Cowansville: Éditions Yvon Blais, 1996.

Levin, M.D., ed. *Ethnicity and Aboriginality: Case Studies in Ethnonationalism.* Toronto: University of Toronto Press, 1993.

Louie, M.A. "Visionary Leadership from a Native American Perspective: A Leadership Profile of the Coeur d'Alene Indian Tribe." Ph.D. Dissertation, Gonzaga University, 1996.

Lyons, O., et al. *Exiled in the Land of the Free: Democracy, Indian Nations, and the U.S. Constitution.* Santa Fe, NM: Clear Light Publishers, 1992.

McFarlane, P. *Brotherhood to Nationhood: George Manuel and the Making of the Modern Indian Movement.* Toronto: Between the Lines, 1993.

Mackenzie, J.B. *The Six-Nations Indians in Canada.* Toronto: Hunter, Rose Co., 1896.

Mancall, P.C. *Deadly Medicine: Indians and Alcohol in Early America.* Ithaca, NY: Cornell University Press, 1995.

Mankiller, W., and M. Wallis. *Mankiller: A Chief and Her People.* New York: St. Martin's Press, 1993.

Maracle, L. *Bobbi Lee, Indian Rebel.* Toronto: Women's Press, 1990.

———. *I Am Woman: A Native Perspective on Sociology and Feminism.* Vancouver: Press Gang Publishers, 1996.

Marshall, C., and G.B. Rossman. *Designing Qualitative Research.* London: Sage, 1989.

Mathiessen, P. *Indian Country.* New York: Penguin, 1979.

Merchant, C. *Radical Ecology: The Search for a Livable World.* New York: Routledge, 1992.

Mihesuah, D., ed. *Natives and Academics: Researching and Writing about American Indians*. Lincoln: University of Nebraska Press, 1998.

Miller, J.R. *Skyscrapers Hide the Heavens: A History of Indian-White Relations in Canada*. Toronto: University of Toronto Press, 1989.

Mills, A., and R. Slobodin, eds. *Amerindian Rebirth: Reincarnation Belief Among North American Indians and Inuit*. Toronto: University of Toronto Press, 1994.

Monture-Angus, P. *Thunder in My Soul: A Mohawk Woman Speaks*. Halifax: Fernwood, 1995.

Morrison, D., ed. *American Indian Studies: An Interdisciplinary Approach to Contemporary Issues*. New York: Peter Lang, 1997.

Murray, D. *Forked Tongues: Speech, Writing and Representation in North American Indian Texts*. Indianapolis: Indiana University Press, 1991.

Nabokov, P., ed. *Native American Testimony: A Chronicle of Indian-White Relations from Prophecy to Present, 1492–1992*. New York: Viking Penguin, 1991.

Neel, D. *Our Chiefs and Elders: Words and Photographs of Native Leaders*. Vancouver: University of British Columbia Press, 1992.

Neidjie, B., et al. *Australia's Kakadu Man*. Darwin: Resource Managers, 1986.

Niethammer, C. *Daughters of the Earth: The Lives and Legends of American Indian Women*. New York: Collier Books, 1977.

Nuu-chah-nulth Community Health Services. *The Sayings of Our First People*. Penticton, BC: Theytus Books, 1995.

O'Brien, S. *American Indian Tribal Governments*. Norman: University of Oklahoma Press, 1989.

O'Meara, S., and D.A. West, eds. *From Our Eyes: Learning From Indigenous Peoples*. Toronto: Garamond Press, 1996.

O'Toole, J. *Leading Change: Overcoming the Ideology of Comfort and the Tyranny of Custom*. San Francisco: Jossey-Bass, 1995.

Pal, L.A. *Public Policy Analysis: An Introduction*. Toronto: Nelson Canada, 1992.

Parker, A.C. *The Constitution of the Five Nations or the Iroquois Book of the Great Law*. Albany: University of the State of New York, 1916.

Political Studies Association. *Contemporary Crisis of the Nation State?* J. Dunn, ed. Oxford: Blackwell Publishers, 1995.

Ray, A.J. *I Have Lived Here Since the World Began: An Illustrated History of Canada's Native People*. Toronto: Lester Publishing, 1996.

Reynolds, H. *The Law of the Land*. Melbourne, AU: Penguin, 1992.

Robinson, H. *Nature/Power: In the Spirit of an Okanagan Storyteller*. W. Wickwire, comp. and ed. Vancouver: Douglas and McIntyre, 1992.

Roe, E. *Narrative Policy Analysis: Theory and Practice*. Durham, NC: Duke University Press, 1994.

Ross, R. *Returning to the Teachings: Exploring Aboriginal Justice*. Toronto: Penguin, 1996.

Rotman, L.I. *Parallel Paths: Fiduciary Doctrine and the Crown–Native Relationship in Canada*. Toronto: University of Toronto Press, 1996.

Royal Commission on Aboriginal Peoples (Canada). *Report*. 5 vols. Ottawa: Canada Communication Group, 1996.

Saul, J.R. *The Unconscious Civilization*. Toronto: Anansi, 1995.

Schulte-Tenckhoff, I. *La Question des peuples autochtones*. Paris: Bruylant-Bruxelles, 1997.

Sewid, J. *Guests Never Leave Hungry: The Autobiography of James Sewid, a Kwakiutl Indian*. J.P. Spradley, ed. Montreal: McGill-Queen's University Press, 1972.

Shimony, A.A. *Conservatism among the Iroquois at the Six Nations Reserve*. Syracuse, NY: Syracuse University Press, 1994.

Shoemaker, N. *Negotiators of Change: Historical Perspectives on Native American Women*. London: Routledge, 1995.

Sioui, G.E. *For an Amerindian Autohistory: An Essay on the Foundations of a Social Ethic*. Montreal: McGill-Queen's University Press, 1992.

Spinner, J. *The Boundaries of Citizenship: Race, Ethnicity, and Nationality in the Liberal State*. Baltimore, MD: Johns Hopkins University Press, 1994.

Sullivan, W. *The Secret of the Incas: Myth, Astronomy, and the War Against Time*. New York: Three Rivers Press, 1996.

Tanner, A., ed. *The Politics of Indianness: Case Studies of Native Ethnopolitics in Canada*. Social and Economic Papers, No. 12. Institute of Social and Economic Research, Memorial University of Newfoundland, 1983.

Tedlock, D., trans. *Popul Vuh: The Mayan Book of the Dawn of Life*. Revised ed. New York: Simon and Schuster, 1996.

Thomas, J., and T. Boyle. *Teachings from the Longhouse*. Toronto: Stoddart, 1994.

Trask, H-K. *From a Native Daughter: Colonialism and Sovereignty in Hawai'i*. Monroe: Common Courage Press, 1993.

Treaty 7 Elders, et al. *The True Spirit and Intent of Treaty 7*. Montreal: McGill-Queen's University Press, 1996.

Trexler, R.C. *Sex and Conquest: Gendered Violence, Political Order, and the European Conquest of the Americas*. Ithaca, NY: Cornell University Press, 1995.

Tully, J. *Strange Multiplicity: Constitutionalism in an Age of Diversity*. Cambridge: Cambridge University Press, 1995.

Turner, F., ed. *The Portable North American Indian Reader*. New York: Penguin, 1974.

Vanderwerth, W.C., ed. *Indian Oratory: Famous Speeches by Noted Indian Chieftains.* Norman: University of Oklahoma Press, 1971.

Vecsey, C. *Imagine Ourselves Richly: Mythic Narratives if North American Indians.* New York: HarperCollins, 1991.

———. ed. *Religion in Native North America.* Moscow: University of Idaho Press, 1990.

Waldram, J.B., D.A. Herring, and T.K. Young. *Aboriginal Health in Canada: Historical, Cultural, and Epidemiological Perspectives.* Toronto: University of Toronto Press, 1995.

Wall, S., and H. Arden. *Wisdomkeepers: Meetings with Native American Spiritual Elders.* Hillsboro: Beyond Words Publishing, 1990.

Warrior, R.A. *Tribal Secrets: Recovering American Indian Intellectual Traditions.* Minneapolis: University of Minnesota Press, 1995.

Watanabe, J.M. *Maya Saints and Souls in a Changing World.* Austin: University of Texas Press, 1992.

Wearne, P. *Return of the Indian: Conquest and Revival in the Americas.* London: Cassell, 1996.

Weaver, J., ed. *Defending Mother Earth: Native American Perspectives on Environmental Justice.* Maryknoll: Orbis Books, 1996.

Webster, P.S. *As Far As I Know: Reminiscences of an Ahousat Elder.* Campbell River, BC: Campbell River Museum and Archives, 1983.

Wilkinson, C.F. *American Indians, Time, and the Law: Native Societies in a Modern Constitutional Democracy.* New Haven: Yale University Press, 1987.

Williams, R.A., Jr. *Linking Arms Together: American Indian Treaty Visions of Law and Peace, 1600–1800.* New York: Oxford University Press, 1997.

Wilmer, F. *The Indigenous Voice in World Politics: Since Time Immemorial.* Newbury Park, CA: Sage, 1993.

Wunder, J.R., ed. *Native American Sovereignty.* New York: Garland, 1996.

Young, T.K. *The Health of Native Americans: Toward a Biocultural Epidemiology.* New York: Oxford University Press, 1994.

Index

Aboriginal, 23
Accountability, 92–93, 115–16, 130
Advisory councils, 152
Agency Indians, 171, 173
Akwesasne, 129, 130, 187n129
Alaska, 141, 153
Alfred, Gerald R. [Taiaiake], 3, 157–67
Algonkian, 23
Alienation, 12
American Indian, 23
American Indian Movement, 36, 93, 132
Ancestors, 4, 9
Anishnaabeg, 170
Aotearoa (New Zealand), 59
Apathy, 53
"Apple" leadership, 101
Assembly of First Nations (AFN), 55, 80, 94,
    112, 133
Assimilation, 8, 25
Atsenhaienton, 125

Band councils, 49, 55, 94, 99, 130–31
Banyacya, Thomas, 104
Barsh, Russell, 49, 50
Bartelson, Jens, 87
Berger, Thomas, 142
Bill C-93, 124
Bissonnette, Alain, 88
Blood, 79, 97
Boldt, Menno, 79, 115
Bousko, Osoko, 60
Breton, Raymond, 97, 98
British Columbia, 31, 124–25, 132, 144, 146,
    150–52
British Columbia Treaty Commission, 155–56
"Brown bureaucrats," 56
Bureaucratic leadership, 56
Bureaucrats, 173–75
Burns, James MacGregor, 68–69, 70, 114

Canada: Aboriginal rights and title in, 81–83,
    95, 107, 145; citizenship in, 43; constitution
    of, 55, 95, 96; court cases in, 95–96,
    124–25, 145, 146; government agenda in,
    147–50; ideal relationship with, 42–43;
    indigenous identity in, 19; land claims in,
    144, 146–50; Native status in, 95, 107,
    110–111, 183n43; provincial governments

in, 147–53; terminology in, 23; see also
    Indian Act
Capitalism, 3, 85, 138–44
Carpenter, Craig, 104
Cashore, John, 151
Casinos, 83
Centre for First Nations Governance, 10–11
Change from within, 57, 99
Cherokee, 93
Cheyenne, 91
Ciaccia, John, 132
Citizenship, 11, 43
Civilization, 46–47
Clans, 50
Coercion, 49–52, 80
Colonialism, 16, 58, 135; contemporary, 44; co-
    operation with, 97; history of, 83; influence
    of, 29; intellectual dishonesty and, 107–8;
    international, 10, 123, 135; mentalities of,
    94–97, 126; recovery from, 8, 30–31, 47,
    123; as source of community conflict, 51;
    traditional government v., 5; transference of
    knowledge and, 32; youth and, 154–55
Communication, 106
Communities, 14; cohesion in, 111–12;
    decision making in, 50; erosion of, 9;
    leadership in, 40–41; membership in,
    109–10; political divisions in, 51; traditional
    values in, 46–47; transformation of, 61;
    types of organization in, 49
Condolence ritual, 4, 8, 9; accountability in, 115;
    "Adding to the Rafters," 20, 31; "Beware the
    magic," 19, 44; parts of, 17–20; "Recognizing
    our pain and sorrow," 18, 58–59; "Rejoicing
    in our survival," 18, 57–58; "Responsibility to
    our ancestors," 18, 60–61
Conflict resolution, 50, 67, 77
Conscience, 49
Consensus, 106, 116, 117
Consumerism, 3, 12, 46, 85
Contention, 100
Control: of land, 10, 27–28; over self-
    government, 10–11, 94–96; Western
    ideology of, 8, 11, 13, 29, 45, 71–72, 83, 87
Cook-Lynn, Elizabeth, 178–79
Co-optation, 19, 54, 57, 72, 91, 97–103, 124;
    exploitation and, 141–42; materialism and,
    139–40; methods of, 99–100

Cornell, Stephen, 116
Corntassel, Jeff, 157–58
Corruption, 93
Cranmer, Agnes, 40, 41
Cranmer, Dan, 40
Cree, 61
Culture: changes in, 16; communities and, 14; differences in, 36–37; influence of, 29; loss of, 9; political values in, 28; shared, 106; *see also* Teachings
Custer Died For Your Sins (Deloria), 158

Davis Inlet, 133
Decision-making, 115–16; collective, 49; non-traditional, 55; traditional, 50
Decolonization, 26, 28, 94–95, 178
Delgamuukw v. The Queen, 145, 146, 147
Delisle, Sr, Andrew, 164
Deloria, Jr, Vine, 77–78, 90–91, 93, 102–3, 157–67, 171
Democracy, 69, 149
Dependency, 9, 50, 94, 99, 101, 140–41
Diné, 74
Dison, 125
Diversity, 13, 106
Dixon, Stan, 124
Diyin, 74
Domestic dependent nations, 77, 96
Duran, Eduardo, 59
Dyck, Noel, 56

Eastman, Charles, 164
Economics, 27–29, 66–67; materialist and exploitative, 85–86; self-sufficient, 172
Education, 32–33, 167–68
Ehattesaht, 61
Elders, 33, 60, 171
Elites, 54–57
Empowerment, 65, 106, 155
Environment, 29, 45, 67, 84–86
Equality, 13, 50, 51–52, 116
Europeans; *see* Western ideology
Executive authority, 11
Expropriation, 149

Family, 32, 132; in community, 49; condolence ritual and, 9–10; extended, 46, 50
Federalism, 77
First Nations Summit, 153
Fiske, Jo-Anne, 117–18
Fixico, Donald, 44
Folklore, 35
Fontaine, Phil, 13, 55
Forbes, Jack, 56–57

Fort Yuma Indian Reservation, 116
Foucault, Michel, 71–73
Fragmentation, 38
Freedom, 70–71, 176

Ghost Dance, 52
Globalization, 46
Governance: four objectives of, 172–73; indigenous, 47–51, 51; *see also* Leadership
Governance of Ethnic Communities, The (Breton), 97
Government: federalism, 77; force, manipulation and, 49–50, 52, 71–72, 80; Foucault on, 71–72; Native people in, 55–57; participatory and consensus-based, 106, 127; post-colonial, 10; provincial, 147–53; representative, 50; resistance against, 61; traditional, 5, 49, 52–53, 127–32; transforming and recovering, 52–53; types of power of, 71–72; Western-style, 25; *see also* British Columbia; Canada; State
Greed, 13, 51, 53, 114, 138, 140
Gunn Allen, Paula, 118–19

Haiawatha, 129
Handsome Lake, Code of, 52, 127
"Hang around the fort" leaders, 100–101
Havasupai, 74
Healing, 132; justice as, 67
Heeding the Voices of Our Ancestors (Alfred), 3, 22, 105
Hierarchy, 36, 80
Hinton, Leanne, 74
Humility, 41

Identity, spectrum of, 56–57
Indian, 23
Indian Act, 27, 36, 43, 49, 55, 107, 124, 132, 146, 183n43
Indian Affairs, Department of, 36, 55
Indian agents, 36, 122
Indian Reorganization Act, 27, 163
Indigenism, 112–13
Indigenous intelligentsia, 177–78
Individual autonomy, 49
Individualism, 3, 12, 44, 93, 176
Ing, Rosalyn, 61
Intellectualism, 7, 158, 165, 178–79
Interdependence, 13–14
Interest groups, 152–53
Internalization, 58–59, 126
Interviews: Atsenhaienton, 125–38; Deloria and Alfred (Taiaiake), 157–67; Kwa'kwa'ka'wakw' woman, 31–44; Laura Simpson, 89–93; Native Youth Movement, 156–57

Intuition, 33
Inuit, 27
Iroquois Confederacy, 127–28

Jacobs, Beverley, 55
Justice, 13, 45; colonialism and, 6–7;
    indigenous v. Western, 66–68, 85–87

Kahnawake, 14, 16, 22, 30, 36, 46, 105, 129,
    131–32, 159, 187n129
Kaienerekowa (The Great Law of Peace), 25, 65,
    87–88, 113–14, 121, 126–30, 181
Kanien'kehaka, 88, 89, 104, 105, 125
Kanien'kehaka kaswentha (two-row wampum),
    76, 126, 129, 137, 138, 147
Kaswentha, 77
Knowledge: intellectuals and, 179; as power,
    88; traditional, 32, 35
Korsmo, Fae, 82–83
Krech, Shepard, 160
Kroker, Arthur, 88

Labelling, 107–8
Land: colonialism and, 10; ownership and
    control of, 10, 27–28; removal from, 27;
    struggle over, 26
Land claims, 81–82, 83, 90, 121–22, 144, 150
Languages, 9, 87, 172
Leadership: "apple," 101; capitalism and,
    141–44; characteristics of, 92, 113–15; co-
    optation of, 99; examples of, 40–41; "hang
    around the fort," 100–101; importance of, 13,
    15, 47; moral, 68–69; "mystic warrior," 101;
    Native, 13–14, 55–56; persuasion and, 17,
    49, 117; power and, 113–15; recreating, 48;
    values of, 49, 61–62, 165–66; Western,
    55–56; women and, 117–19; youth and,
    154–57; see also Co-optation; Native
    politicians; Politics
Leadership (Burns), 68–69
Legal pluralism, 88
Legal system, 10; change through, 166–68; land
    and, 28, 145–46; myths about, 82–83, 107;
    Native lawyers in, 166–67; Native politics and,
    71; Native status in, 95–96, 107–10; pluralism
    in, 88; resources and, 28; sovereignty and, 78,
    82–83, 91; Western framework of, 45
Long, Tony, 79, 115
Longhouse, 31
Loss, 32, 37, 58, 65
Lurie, Nancy, 140

Maa-nulth First Nations, 125
Mackenzie, J.B., 122

Magic, 19–20, 44
Manipulation, 55, 69–71, 105, 144, 168
Maori, 59
Maracle, Lee, 58
Materialism, 36, 46, 68, 85, 138–44, 177
McCloud, Janet, 65–66
McDonald, Peter, 93
Medicine wheel, 34
Men, 41–42
Mercredi, Ovide, 55, 80, 81
Militancy, 42–43
Minority peoples, 78
Mohawk, John, 17
Mohawk Council of Chiefs, 129
Mohawks, 14, 30, 36–37, 42, 130, 159, 187n129
Mohawk Trail longhouse, 129
Money, 138–44
Monture, Patricia, 118, 119
Morality, 52, 66–67, 69–70, 123
Moral leadership, 68–69
Musqueam First Nation, 150
Mystic warrior leadership, 101

National Congress of American Indians (NCAI),
    93, 162
National Day of Action, 55
Nationalism, Native, 5, 14, 56–57, 77
Nationhood, 77–78, 89–91, 96, 133;
    characteristics of, 106; righteousness and,
    123; the state v., 80, 173–74
Native, 23
Native nationalism, 14
Native politicians, 28, 52, 79–80, 94, 123–24, 139
Native status, 95–96, 107–10
Native Women's Association of Canada
    (NWAC), 55
Native Youth Movement (NYM), 156
Navajo, 74, 93, 134
New Zealand, 59
Nisga'a treaty (1999), 124–25
Norton, Joe, 135
Nunavut, 27
Nuu-chah-nulth, 48

Oka, 43
Okanagan, 73
Once Were Warriors (film), 59
Onkwehonwe, 6, 12, 16, 30, 159
Oppression, 58–59, 71–72
Ortiz, Simon, 76

Paiute, 76
Peacemaker, 127
Peigan, 79

Persuasion, 17, 49, 117
Peyoteism, 52
Police Agreement, 131
Political elites, 54–57
Politicians, 69; Native, 28, 52, 79–80, 94, 123–24, 139; sovereignty and, 81
Politics: importance of, 28; Native elites in, 54–57; process of, 162–63; realist v. bureaucratic, 173–75; traditional teachings and, 12, 25–31; two approaches to, 122–23; see also Politicians
Post-colonialism, 10, 11, 27
Potlatch, 34, 36, 39
Poverty, 10, 12
Poverty funds, 93
Power: abuse of, 68–70; colonial mentalities and, 94–97; control, 88; co-optation and, 97–104; force and, 173; indigenous vision of, 11, 73–77; knowledge, 88; land and, 10; leadership and, 113–15; as manipulation, 55, 69–71, 71, 105, 144, 168; "naked," 71; persuasion and, 17; re-empowerment and, 70–79; responsibility and, 115–16; self-conscious traditionalism and, 104–13; sovereignty and, 79–94; Western idea of, 13; see also Coercion
Power-wielders, 68, 69, 70
Primacy of conscience, 49
Principles for Negotiating Treaties, 151–52
Punishments, 67

Quechans, 116

Racial minority, 56–57
Racism, 44, 62, 83, 107, 126, 154, 177
Realists, 173–75
Re-empowerment, 70–79
Reserves, 10, 11, 12
Residential schools, 13, 32, 37, 40
Resources, 110–11; in Alaska, 141–42; in Arctic, 27; exploitation of, 27–28, 84–86, 149; power and, 71
Respect, 5, 15–16, 18, 106, 147, 155, 169
Responsibility, 92, 114, 115–19, 179
Revolution, 77
Righteousness, 121–38; money and, 138–44; treaties and, 144–54; youth and, 154–58
Rights, 9, 176; Aboriginal, 176; fishing and hunting, 82, 83; identity, 95; state power and, 71–72; to vote, 36, 43
Robinson, Harry, 73–74
Romanticizing the past, 53
Rotinohshonni (Six Nations), 8, 9, 12, 15–17, 65, 87, 91, 105, 113–16, 119, 170

Royal Commission on Aboriginal Peoples, 43, 151, 155
Royal Proclamation of 1763, 146
Royaner, 4

Sanctions, 67
Saul, John Ralston, 138
Sechelt Indian band case (1986), 124–25
Secular nationalist, 56
Self-actualization, 114
Self-conscious traditionalism, 16, 90, 104–13
Self-determination, 11, 49–50; action and, 123; collective, 49–50; importance of, 137; land and, 28; nationhood and, 77–78; obstacles to, 9; sovereignty as, 134; struggle for, 8
Self-government, 5; mainstream control of, 10–11; minority status and, 77–78; movement for, 26; nationhood v., 77–78; problems with, 3; within state government, 10–11, 94–96; vision and fear about, 26–27
Self-identification, 108–10, 136
Seven generations, 20, 33, 34
Shagóon, 73
Simpson, Audra, 89–90, 93
Sioui, Georges, 45
Sioux, 91, 164
Six Nations case, 96
Smith, Moses, 48
Social work, 37–38
Solidarity, 111–12
Songs, 15, 20, 28, 34, 39
Sovereignty, 3, 26, 133–34; nationhood v., 77–78, 89–90, 90–91; Western concept of, 11, 134; see also Self-government
Space, 19
Spirituality, 34, 67
Squaw, 23
Standing Alone, Pete, 97
Standing Bear, Luther, 47, 108, 164
State: myths about, 82–83; nationhood and, 80, 173–74; Native communities and, 27–28; power and, 71–72; resources and, 86, 110–11; self-government and, 10–11, 94–96; see also Canada; Coercion; Government
Subsurface rights, 149
Sumáaga, 74
Superficiality, 34, 35, 51; in leadership, 41–42
Symbols, 51

Taiaiake Alfred, 3, 157–67
Taxation, 11, 43, 83, 128
Teachings, 92; commonality of, 168–69; escapism v., 61; justice and, 68; on leadership, 49, 61–62, 92, 113–15, 126,

129, 137, 138, 147, 165–66; on men and women, 40; on politics, 12, 25–31; on power, 73–77; on race, 44–45; on values, 69–70; *see also* Traditionalism
Technology, 45
Tekaniawítha, 16
Termination, 93, 166
Tewatatowie, 135
Thowhegwelth, Haida, 78–79
Tlingit, 73
Tradition, 182n11
Traditionalism: basic principles in, 35; criticism of, 35; empowerment and, 72–77; problems with, 5; recovery of, 177–78; self-conscious, 16, 90, 104–13; *see also* Teachings
Traditional nationalism, 56
Traditional values, 41; importance of, 53–54; in Kahnewake survey, 46; in Native leadership, 48; *see also* Teachings
Treaties, 141, 144–54; in British Columbia, 147–53; contemporary, 33, 34; honouring of, 147
Tribal councils, 99, 129
Tribal pragmatist, 56
Tsawwassen First Nation, 125, 152
Tsilqotìn Nation case, 146
Tujia, 177
Tulalip (Janet McCloud), 65–66
Tully, James, 87
Turtle Island, 12, 29
Twinn case (1995), 95
Two-row wampum, 76, 126, 129, 137, 138, 147

United Nations, 124, 125, 135, 137
United States: Indian Reorganization Act, 27; legal system in, 96; oil drilling in Alaska, 141–42; sovereignty in, 81; treaties in, 141–42

Values, 180; consumerism, 3, 12, 46, 85; individualism, 3, 12, 44, 93, 176; leadership, 69, 70; materialism, 36, 46, 68, 85, 138–44, 177; traditional, 70; *see also* Teachings
Vancouver Island, 48, 61, 125
Village Island, 40
Violence, 58–59; *see also* Coerçion

Wasáe: Indigenous Pathways of Action and Freedom (Alfred), 5, 7
West Coast culture, 36–37, 170–71
Western ideology: as fixed, 44; of government, 25, 49, 52, 71–72, 77, 80; integration into, 28; of justice, 66–68; Native critique of, 45; power and control in, 8, 11, 13, 29, 45, 71–72, 83, 87; of rights, 176; *see also* Values
White people; *see* Western ideology
Wilkins, David, 96
Women: aspirations of, 132–33; leadership of, 62; Native status of, 183n43; oppression of, 59; respect for, 38–40; responsibilities toward, 117–18; in Rotinohshonni leadership, 114
Wounded Knee Massacre, 163–64

Youth, 39, 128, 132–33; leadership and, 154–56; teaching of, 177–78